ideals®

Wok COOKBOOK

By Carol DeMasters

Ideals Publishing Corp.
Milwaukee, Wisconsin

Contents

Cover recipe: Shrimp and Vegetable Stir-Fry,
page 50

ISBN 0-8249-3017-7

Copyright © MCMLXXXIII by Carol DeMasters
All rights reserved.
Printed and bound in the United States of America.
Published by Ideals Publishing Corporation
11315 Watertown Plank Road
Milwaukee, Wisconsin 53226
Published simultaneously in Canada

Wok Basics

Cooking in a wok is not difficult; it is different. You will acquire a feel for split-second timing, a sense of sequence and a knowledge of the amount of heat that will produce the best results. As you stir and toss food in the wok, your eyes will be on the food but your mind will be anticipating the next step.

Stir-frying is the most-used method of wok cookery. It is fast and fun, and results in delicious-tasting food. Searing meat and vegetables at high heat seals in their flavors, nutrients and juices while at the same time preserving their textures. A wonderful form of self-expression, stir-frying in a wok is a lot like tossing a salad. With a spatula in one hand and a ladle in the other, you maintain a constant motion of tossing and turning food over high heat.

Wok cookery need not necessarily mean Chinese cooking, although it is best illustrated in that ancient cuisine. Several of the recipes for basic, familiar foods in this book are not Chinese in origin. A wok can also be used in place of a conventional skillet, saucepan or deep-fryer. It can be a steamer when fitted with a rack or bamboo basket.

Wok cookery is adaptable. After you've made several stir-fry recipes in this book,
you'll understand the technique, enabling you to combine your favorite foods in dishes which reflect your own personal style and taste preferences.

Using a wok, you will prepare nutritious, flavorful, crisp and colorful foods in a matter of minutes.

WOK COOKERY BASICS

Successful cooking in a wok depends on proper utensils and several cutting techniques and cooking methods.

UTENSILS

Chopsticks Wooden sticks that taper to points. They are used for stirring ingredients, beating eggs and testing oil temperature, in addition to being eating utensils. To determine if oil is hot enough for stir-frying, place one end of a chopstick into the oil. If the oil sizzles around the chopstick, it is hot enough to begin stir-frying.

Cleaver A broad, rectangular-bladed knife used for cutting, chopping, shredding, slicing and transferring food. A large chef's knife also may be used.

Ladle A metal utensil with a rounded scoop used for stir-frying foods to prevent them from burning.

Rack Made of wood or steel and used in a wok for steaming foods. The rack is placed over boiling water in a wok, and a plate or bowls of food may be set on it. The wok is covered so the food is steamed.

Ring Made of metal and placed on gas or electric burners to hold the wok steady during stir-frying. Place the ring with the smallest opening down on an electric burner. This will put the wok closer to the heat source. Reverse the ring on a gas burner. A ring also is a metal device which fits around the top circumference of a wok and is used as a place for tempura-fried foods to drain before serving.

Spatula A metal utensil used for stir-frying foods to prevent them from burning. It has a flatter scoop than the ladle.

Steamer Available in two forms. One is bamboo and can be set directly over boiling water in a wok and covered to steam or reheat foods. The other is an aluminum utensil that comes with manufacturer's directions for use in steaming and reheating foods.

Strainer A utensil with a shallow wire-net scoop and a bamboo or wooden handle. It is used to remove foods from hot oil or liquid in the wok.

Wok An all-purpose concave cooking pan with sloping sides that is thought to be one of the oldest cooking utensils. It cooks food evenly and quickly over very high heat. It is used for stir-frying, deep-frying, braising, stewing, blanching and steaming. Most woks are sold with a cover and ring. A 14-inch wok is standard, and most are made of steel, although they also can be stainless steel, copper, brass or aluminum. A rolled carbon steel wok must be seasoned so foods will not stick to it and so less oil can be used during stir-frying. To season a steel wok, first wash and dry it thoroughly. Put it over high heat and add ¼ cup cooking oil. Tilt the wok to coat its sides with oil. When the oil starts to smoke, remove the wok from the heat and let it cool. Wipe out the excess oil; repeat this process once more. Once seasoned, the wok should not be scrubbed with either an abrasive pad or cleanser. The best way to clean a wok is to soak it in warm water and use a sponge and mild detergent to remove any food particles. Dry the wok thoroughly and place it over high heat 30 seconds to prevent the formation of rust. Then lightly coat the inside of the wok with a small amount of cooking oil before storing it. Use and care of electric woks are best outlined by their manufacturer's directions.

Wok Basics

CUTTING TECHNIQUES

All ingredients for stir-frying in a wok should be cut in thin uniform-size pieces for attractive appearance and even, fast cooking. It is easier to cut meat in thin slices if it is partially frozen; then it will not slip under the pressure of a knife. Always slice across the grain to retain tenderness. Sharp knives are a must. Following are the cutting techniques used on most meats and vegetables:

1. **Slicing or Straight Cutting:** Hold the knife or cleaver straight up and down to cut to the desired thickness, usually from paper-thin to ½ inch thick.

2. **Shredding or Julienne Slicing:** Food is first sliced, then cut into uniform strips about the size of matchsticks. Shreds vary from ⅛ to ¼ inch thick and from 1½ to 2 inches long.

3. **Cubing:** Food is first sliced ½ inch thick, then again across the slices every ½ inch to produce ½-inch cubes.

4. **Chopping:** This is the coarsest cut and results in ½-inch pieces.

5. **Dicing:** Food is first sliced into thin slices, then into thin strips, then into small pieces varying from ¼ to ½ inch square.

6. **Mincing:** Food is chopped into rice-size pieces. It is much easier to mince vegetables if they are first chopped or diced.

7. **Diagonal Cutting:** Used mostly for vegetables. The knife or cleaver is held at a 45-degree angle for slicing. Practice with celery. Position the knife blade about ¾ inch from the end of the rib. Slant the knife blade away from you and slice the stalk with a sharp, angled cut. Discard this first irregular piece. Continue cutting at the same slant in small, regular intervals to produce thin, flat slices.

8. **Rolled or Oblique Cutting:** Used mostly for vegetables. The knife or cleaver is held at an angle to the food while the opposite hand rolls the food before the next cut is made, thus changing the angle of the cut. Practice with a carrot. Make a diagonal cut across the carrot; discard this first piece. Then, keeping the knife in the same position, roll the carrot over and cut through it diagonally again to form a piece with two slanted sides. Continue rolling and cutting in this manner.

COOKING METHODS

A wok is a versatile cooking utensil. All of the following cooking methods are possible in a wok.

Stir-Frying The most common cooking method in a wok, stir-frying is the vigorous stirring of food in a small amount of oil over high heat for a brief cooking time, usually just a few minutes. Before beginning, read the recipe through. Have all ingredients cut and/or measured as directed; place in small bowls arranged in the order in which they will be added to the wok. This can be done hours in advance. Have all utensils and serving pieces at easy access. Stir-frying should be done just before serving. Before beginning, reread the recipe. Stir-frying requires swift movements and split-second timing. Get used to the sound of sizzling, a sign of successful stir-frying. Heat the wok 30 seconds before adding the oil. Then drizzle soybean or peanut oil around the sides of the wok. Heat until hot. To test for hotness, flip a drop of water into the wok. If it sizzles and evaporates, the oil is hot enough. Then proceed as the recipe directs.

Deep-Frying Food cooks immersed in hot fat.

Blanching Food is parboiled in boiling water. When stir-frying, this is usually done to partially cook vegetables before they are completely cooked in the wok. They are immersed in boiling water, partially cooked and rinsed in cold water to stop the cooking and to set bright color.

Braising Food cooks in a small amount of liquid in a covered wok on low heat.

Steaming This method uses no oil. It can be done on a rack or in a bamboo basket in a wok. To steam food, place the rack above 2 to 3 inches of water in a wok. The rack and the food should not touch the water. Bring the water to a rapid boil, place the food on a shallow heatproof plate and place the plate on the rack. Cover the wok. If using a bamboo basket, place the food in it, cover the basket with the bamboo lid and place over boiling water. It is not necessary to cover the wok.

Simmering Food cooks at temperatures low enough to cause bubbles to appear and barely break the surface of the cooking liquid.

Appetizers

Chicken Nuggets in Spinach with Oriental Dip

Makes 30 pieces
Preparation Time: 45 minutes

  1 whole chicken breast, split, boned and skinned
1¾ cups chicken stock
  ¼ cup soy sauce
  1 tablespoon Worcestershire sauce
  1 bunch fresh spinach, washed, stems discarded
    Oriental Dip

Simmer chicken breasts in chicken stock, soy sauce and Worcestershire sauce in wok until tender, 15 to 20 minutes. Remove from liquid; cool. Discard liquid. Pour 1 quart boiling water over spinach in colander; drain; set aside to cool. When chicken is cool enough to handle, cut into 30 bite-size pieces. Place 1 chicken piece at stem end of 1 spinach leaf, top side facing counter. Roll over once, folding leaf in on both sides; continue rolling around chicken piece. Place seam-side-down on decorative platter. Place dip in small bowl in center of platter. Spear each chicken piece with toothpick.

Note: Wrapped chicken can be prepared ahead of time, wrapped in plastic wrap and refrigerated. Dip can also be made in advance.

Oriental Dip

  1 cup sour cream
  2 teaspoons toasted sesame seed
  ½ teaspoon ground ginger
  4 teaspoons soy sauce
  2 teaspoons Worcestershire sauce

Mix all ingredients in bowl; chill at least 4 hours.

Chinese-Flavored Beef

Makes approximately 40 pieces
Preparation Time: 15 minutes; 1 hour to cook

  2 tablespoons peanut oil
  4 green onions, cut in 1-inch pieces
  1 tablespoon peeled and minced fresh gingerroot
  1 pound boneless beef chuck, cut in 1-inch cubes
    Sauce Mixture

Heat oil in wok until hot. Add onions and gingerroot; stir-fry 1 minute. Add beef cubes; stir-fry 2 to 3 minutes or until browned. Add Sauce Mixture; reduce heat to simmer; cover; cook 30 minutes. Uncover; increase heat to high; cook until sauce thickens, about 30 minutes. Remove from wok; serve hot with picks for spearing meat.

Sauce Mixture

  ¼ cup sugar
  2 tablespoons soy sauce
  ⅓ cup dry sherry
  1 cup water
  ½ teaspoon dried red pepper flakes

Mix all ingredients until sugar dissolves.

Crab Won Tons

Makes 36
Preparation Time: 30 minutes

  1 8-ounce package cream cheese, softened
  1 6-ounce package frozen crab meat, thawed and drained
36 won ton skins
    Peanut oil
    Sweet and Sour Sauce (Recipe on page 31)

Mix cream cheese and crab meat in bowl. Place 1 teaspoon in middle of won ton skin; moisten edges with cold water; fold to form triangle; seal edges by pressing together. Prepare remaining won tons in same manner. Heat 2 inches oil in wok until hot. Fry won tons on both sides until golden. Drain on paper towels; keep warm. Serve with Sweet and Sour Sauce for dipping.

Curry Won Tons

Makes 20
Preparation Time: 20 minutes

  1 8-ounce package cream cheese
20 won ton skins
  ⅓ cup chopped green onion
    Curry powder
    Peanut oil

Cut cream cheese into 20 equal pieces. Place 1 cheese cube in center of each won ton skin. Top with some green onion; sprinkle with curry powder. Moisten edges of won ton skins with cold water; fold to form triangle, sealing edges. Heat 2 inches oil in wok until hot. Fry won tons until golden. Drain on paper towels. Serve immediately.

Shrimp Toast

Makes approximately 32 pieces
Preparation Time: 20 minutes; 10 minutes to cook

- 1 6-ounce can shrimp, drained and minced
- 3 ounces ground lean pork
- 1½ teaspoons dry sherry
- 1½ teaspoons soy sauce
- ½ teaspoon salt
- ¼ teaspoon freshly ground black pepper
- ¼ cup finely chopped green onions
- ¾ teaspoon cornstarch
- ½ teaspoon sesame oil
- 2 eggs
- 7 to 8 slices thin white bread
- ⅓ cup fine dry bread crumbs
- 1 cup peanut oil

Mix shrimp with next 8 ingredients and 1 egg. Spread shrimp mixture generously over 1 side of each slice of bread. Beat remaining egg in bowl; brush over bread and filling. Sprinkle bread crumbs over filling. Cut bread diagonally into quarters. Heat oil in wok over high heat until hot. Slide bread triangles, a few at a time, filling-side-down, into hot oil. Fry until golden; turn to brown other side. Drain on paper towels. Serve hot.

Note: Shrimp Toast can be made 30 minutes in advance; keep warm in 200° oven.

Chinese Pancakes

Makes 8
Preparation Time: 30 minutes

- 1 cup flour
- ½ cup boiling water
- 2 tablespoons sesame oil

Stir flour and water in bowl until flour comes away from sides of bowl. Knead on lightly floured board until smooth. Cover; let rest 20 minutes. Knead 1 minute; shape into 1½-inch diameter roll. Cut into 8 equal pieces. Flatten each to thin round pancake. Brush 1 side of each pancake with sesame oil; place 2 pancakes together, oiled sides touching. Roll each to 7-inch circle. Heat griddle; cook pancake on both sides until slightly puffy. Do not brown. Remove; separate 2 pancakes. Store between sheets of foil; wrap entire stack in foil. Place foil packet on rack or in bamboo steamer in wok. Add hot water to within ½-inch of rack or basket. Bring water to boil; cover; steam 10 minutes. For extra flavor, spread pancakes with Duck Sauce before filling. Serve with Mo Shu Pork or any shredded meat or vegetable stir-fry.

Note: Pancakes can be prepared in advance. Re-steam before serving. Pancakes can be frozen. Thaw in foil; steam 20 minutes.

Fried Walnuts

Makes approximately 4 cups
Preparation Time: 5 minutes; overnight to marinate; 10 to 15 minutes to cook

- 1 cup water
- ¾ cup sugar
- 1 pound walnut halves
- Peanut oil

Combine water and sugar in saucepan; cook 5 minutes to make syrup. Place walnuts in jar with cover; top with syrup. Cool; cover; let stand overnight; drain. Heat oil in wok until hot. Add nuts in batches; fry 2 to 3 minutes. Remove from oil with strainer. Drain on paper towels. Serve immediately.

Gingered Pork Balls

Makes 12 to 16
Preparation Time: 20 minutes

- 1 pound ground pork
- 1 cup coarsely chopped water chestnuts
- ½ teaspoon peeled and chopped fresh gingerroot
- 1 egg, lightly beaten
- 1 tablespoon soy sauce
- Cornstarch
- Peanut oil

Mix first 5 ingredients lightly. Shape into bite-size balls; roll lightly in cornstarch. Heat 2 inches oil in wok until hot. Add pork balls, a few at a time; fry until golden brown and cooked through. Drain on paper towels; serve hot with wooden picks.

Nacho Won Tons

Makes 20
Preparation Time: 20 minutes

- 6 ounces sharp Cheddar cheese, shredded
- 20 won ton skins
- 1 4-ounce can chopped mild *or* hot green chilies, drained
- Peanut oil

Dividing cheese equally, place in middle of each won ton skin. Top each with ¼ teaspoon chilies. Moisten edges of won ton skins with cold water; fold to form triangle, sealing edges. Heat 2 inches oil in wok until hot. Fry won tons on both sides until browned. Drain on paper towels. Serve immediately.

Oriental Spareribs

Makes approximately 2 dozen
Preparation Time: 1½ hours

    2 cups water
    ½ cup soy sauce
    1 clove garlic, peeled and minced
    3 pounds spareribs, cut in 2-inch pieces
    2 tablespoons packed light brown sugar
    1 tablespoon cornstarch
    1 tablespoon sesame seed
    2 tablespoons chopped green onion
    1 ¼-inch slice fresh gingerroot, peeled and minced

Mix water, ¼ cup soy sauce and garlic in wok. Add spareribs; bring to boil. Reduce heat; cover; simmer on low heat 1 hour. Remove cover; bring to boil; cook 20 minutes. Drain; reserve ¼ cup cooking liquid. Mix remaining ¼ cup soy sauce and remaining ingredients. Place spareribs and reserved ¼ cup cooking liquid in wok over medium heat. Pour seasoned soy sauce over ribs; cook, spooning sauce over ribs until it thickens and adheres to ribs, about 10 minutes. Serve warm.

Note: These can be made 3 to 4 hours in advance; reheat in microwave oven or in conventional 350° oven 10 minutes.

Egg Rolls

Makes 4 to 5 dozen
Preparation Time: 1 hour

    2 tablespoons peanut oil
    3 ribs celery, cut in 1-inch julienne pieces
    6 green onions, cut in 1-inch julienne pieces
    ¾ teaspoon salt
    ¾ teaspoon sugar
    1½ pounds finely chopped lean pork *or* chicken *or* shrimp
    1 8-ounce can sliced bamboo shoots, drained and coarsely chopped
    2 cups fresh bean sprouts
    2 tablespoons soy sauce
    2 tablespoons dry sherry
    1 1-pound package egg roll skins
    1 egg white, lightly beaten
    Peanut oil
    Sweet and Sour Sauce (Recipe on page 31) *or* Hot Mustard Sauce (Recipe on page 31) *or* Duck Sauce

Heat 1 tablespoon oil in wok until hot. Add next 4 ingredients; stir-fry 2 minutes. Remove to large bowl; set aside. Heat 1½ teaspoons oil in wok until hot; add pork and bamboo shoots; stir-fry 1 minute. Remove to bowl. Heat remaining 1½ teaspoons oil in wok until hot; add bean sprouts;

stir-fry 2 minutes; remove to bowl. Stir soy sauce and sherry into mixture in bowl. Place in strainer to drain thoroughly, at least 10 minutes. Place 1 egg roll skin on counter with a corner toward you. Put 1 tablespoon filling in rectangular mound on center of wrapper. Fold bottom corner of wrapper up over filling; overlap 2 opposite side corners. Moisten 4th or top corner with egg white; fold over to form roll. Heat 2 inches oil in wok until hot. Fry egg rolls, two to three at a time, until golden brown. Drain on paper towels. Serve with sauce of your choice.

Note: After frying, egg rolls can be covered and refrigerated no longer than 24 hours. Heat, uncovered, in 350° oven about 15 minutes or until heated through.

Fried Won Tons

Makes approximately 50
Preparation Time: 30 minutes; 10 minutes to cook

    ¼ pound ground lean pork *or* chicken *or* beef
    1 6-ounce can shrimp, drained and minced
    ¼ cup minced mushrooms
    ¼ cup diced water chestnuts
    1 green onion, finely chopped
    2 egg yolks
    1 tablespoon soy sauce
    1½ teaspoons peanut oil
    ¾ pound won ton skins (about 50)
    Peanut oil
    Won Ton Sauce

Mix first 8 ingredients in wok over medium heat. Cook, stirring often, about 5 minutes. Cool. Place about 1 tablespoon mixture in middle of each won ton skin. Moisten edges of wrapper with cold water; fold in half diagonally to form triangle; press edges together to seal. Fry won tons in hot oil in wok until golden on both sides; drain on paper towels. Serve with sauce.

Note: Can be prepared 1 hour in advance; keep warm in 200° oven.

Won Ton Sauce

    2 tablespoons cornstarch
    3 tablespoons light brown sugar, packed
    ¼ cup soy sauce
    ¾ cup water
    1 clove garlic, peeled and sliced
    1 tablespoon peanut oil

Stir first 4 ingredients until smooth. Fry garlic in hot oil in wok on low heat until light brown. Remove garlic; set aside. Slowly pour cornstarch mixture into hot oil; cook, stirring, until thickened. Top with fried garlic.

Fried Won Tons, this page;
Egg Rolls, this page

Soups

Chinese Cucumber Soup

Makes 6 to 8 servings
Preparation Time: 30 minutes

- 1 tablespoon dry sherry
- 2 tablespoons soy sauce
- 1 tablespoon cornstarch
- ½ pound boned and skinned chicken breast *or* finely shredded lean pork
- 2 tablespoons peanut oil
- 6 cups chicken stock
- 2 green onions, thinly sliced
- 1 medium cucumber, peeled, split lengthwise, seeds removed, diced
- 1½ teaspoons salt
- ¼ teaspoon freshly ground white pepper
- 1 egg, lightly beaten

Mix first 3 ingredients in bowl; add chicken; stir to coat. Heat oil in wok over high heat. Add chicken; stir-fry 3 to 5 minutes. Add chicken stock; reduce heat; simmer 10 to 12 minutes. Add next 4 ingredients; simmer 5 minutes. Increase heat; bring soup to fast boil; remove from heat; stir in egg. Serve immediately.

Egg Drop Soup with Shrimp

Makes 6 to 8 servings
Preparation Time: 20 minutes

- 6 cups chicken stock
  Salt and freshly ground white pepper to taste
  Pinch cayenne pepper
- ½ cup frozen peas
- 16 medium shrimp, shelled and deveined
- 2 tablespoons cornstarch mixed with
  ¼ cup cold water
- 2 eggs, lightly beaten with 1 teaspoon soy sauce
- 2 green onions, thinly sliced

Heat chicken stock, salt, pepper and cayenne pepper in wok over high heat to just under a boil. Add peas; cook 1 minute. Add shrimp; cook until pink. Add cornstarch mixture, stirring until slightly thickened. Remove from heat; swirl in eggs using fork. Garnish with onions; serve immediately.

Hot and Sour Soup

Makes 4 to 6 servings
Preparation Time: 25 minutes; 20 minutes to cook

- 4 cups chicken stock
- 6 ounces lean pork *or* chicken breast, cut in julienne strips
- ½ cup tofu, cut in julienne strips
- ½ cup bamboo shoots, cut in julienne strips
- 6 cloud ear mushrooms, soaked in ½ cup hot water 15 minutes, stems discarded, caps halved
- 6 Chinese dried black mushrooms, soaked in ½ cup hot water 15 minutes, stems discarded, caps thinly sliced
- 1 tablespoon soy sauce
- ¼ teaspoon sugar
- ¾ teaspoon salt
- 2 tablespoons cornstarch mixed with 3 tablespoons water
- 1 egg, beaten until slightly foamy
- 3 tablespoons Chinese red vinegar
- ½ teaspoon ground white pepper
- 2 green onions including tops, thinly sliced

Bring chicken stock to boil in wok over high heat. Add pork, tofu, bamboo shoots, cloud ear and Chinese mushrooms; cook 3 to 5 minutes. Mix soy sauce, sugar, salt and cornstarch mixture; add to soup; stir; cook until soup just comes to a boil. Slowly swirl in egg; remove from heat immediately. Put vinegar and pepper in bowl; add soup and green onions. Stir; serve immediately.

Hot Oriental Mushroom Soup

Makes 4 to 6 servings
Preparation Time: 30 minutes

- 4 cups chicken stock
- 6 Chinese dried black mushrooms, soaked in hot water 20 minutes, drained, stems discarded, caps thinly sliced
- ¼ cup Madeira
  Chopped green onion

Bring stock to boil in wok over high heat. Add mushrooms and wine; reduce heat and cover; simmer 20 minutes. Sprinkle with green onion; serve immediately.

Japanese Soup

Makes 6 to 8 servings
Preparation Time: 25 minutes

    6 cups chicken stock
    ¼ cup dry sherry
    1½ tablespoons soy sauce
    6 to 8 fresh mushrooms, wiped clean and
        thinly sliced
    1 teaspoon lemon juice
    6 green onions, cut in ½-inch diagonal slices
    1 small carrot, pared and cut in thin diagonal slices
    ¼ pound tiny shelled shrimp, optional

Bring stock to simmer in wok over high heat. Stir in sherry and soy sauce; simmer 5 minutes. Add remaining ingredients; bring to boil; simmer 5 minutes. Serve immediately.

Noodles and Vegetables in Broth

Makes 6 servings.
Preparation Time: 20 minutes

    8 ounces wide egg noodles
    6 cups chicken stock
    2 cups cubed cooked chicken, turkey, pork or ham
    1 carrot, pared and cut in thin diagonal slices
    1 large rib celery, cut in thin diagonal slices
    2 green onions, halved lengthwise and cut diagonally
        in 1-inch pieces
    ½ cup thinly sliced bok choy (Chinese cabbage)
    2 tablespoons soy sauce
        Salt and freshly ground white pepper to taste

Cook noodles according to package directions; drain; rinse under cold running water to stop cooking; set aside. Heat chicken stock in wok over high heat. Add next 6 ingredients; season to taste with salt and pepper. Simmer 5 to 10 minutes to just barely cook vegetables. Divide noodles among 6 soup bowls; ladle in soup. Serve immediately.

Oriental Spring Soup

Makes 6 servings
Preparation Time: 10 minutes; 15 minutes to cook

    5 cups chicken stock
    ½ cup julienne-cut carrot
    ½ cup peas, fresh or frozen
    ½ cup fresh spinach leaves, washed, stems discarded,
        shredded
    ¼ cup finely sliced green onion
    2 tablespoons minced fresh parsley
        Salt and freshly ground white pepper to taste

Bring chicken stock to simmer in wok over high heat. Add carrot and peas; cook 5 minutes. Add spinach, green onion and parsley; simmer 2 minutes. Add salt and pepper to taste. Serve immediately.

Spinach Soup with Pork Balls

Makes 4 servings
Preparation Time: 1 hour

    6 cups chicken stock
    2 ¼-inch peeled slices fresh gingerroot
    4 Chinese dried black mushrooms, soaked in
        hot water 20 minutes, drained, stems discarded,
        caps thinly sliced
        Salt and freshly ground white pepper to taste
    2 green onions, minced
    ¼ cup minced water chestnuts
    ½ pound lean ground pork
    1 tablespoon soy sauce
    1 teaspoon dry sherry
    2 teaspoons cornstarch
    ½ cup loosely packed spinach leaves, washed, stems
        discarded, shredded

Bring chicken stock and 2 slices gingerroot to simmer in wok over high heat. Add mushrooms, salt and pepper; simmer 15 minutes. Remove gingerroot. Mix next 6 ingredients; form into 12 1¼-inch balls. Add pork balls to stock; simmer 30 minutes or until cooked through. Add spinach 3 minutes before serving; serve immediately.

Velvet Corn Soup

Makes 6 to 8 servings
Preparation Time: 10 minutes; 15 minutes to cook

    6 cups hot chicken stock
    2 tablespoons cornstarch
    1 tablespoon peanut oil
    4 green onions, white part only, minced
    2 cups cream-style corn, pureed in food processor or
        blender
    ¼ teaspoon salt
    ¼ teaspoon freshly ground white pepper
    1 tablespoon dry sherry
    2 egg whites, lightly beaten until frothy
    2 tablespoons minced cooked ham

Pour ¼ cup chicken stock over cornstarch in small bowl; stir to combine; set aside. Heat oil in wok over high heat. Add onions; stir-fry 30 to 45 seconds. Add remaining stock, corn, salt, pepper and sherry; simmer 15 minutes over medium heat. Increase heat; bring soup to boil; add cornstarch mixture. Stir until soup is slightly thickened, about 3 minutes. Remove from heat; add egg whites; stir to combine. Stir in ham; serve immediately.

Watercress Soup with Ham Shreds

Makes 6 to 8 servings
Preparation Time: 30 minutes

  8 cups chicken stock
  ½ teaspoon five-spice powder
  2 teaspoons salt
  1 teaspoon sugar
  2 tablespoons dry sherry
  2 ¼-inch slices fresh gingerroot, peeled
  4 green onions, sliced
  2 bunches watercress, washed, stems discarded
  ½ cup thinly sliced ham

Put first 7 ingredients in wok over high heat; bring to boil; cook 10 minutes; strain, reserving stock. Return stock to wok over high heat; bring to boil; add watercress and ham; return to boil. Serve immediately.

Won Ton Soup

Makes 6 servings plus leftover won tons
Preparation Time: 1 hour; 10 minutes to cook

  6 Chinese dried black mushrooms, soaked in hot water 20 minutes, drained, stems discarded, caps minced
  ¼ pound ground lean pork
  ¼ pound shrimp, coarsely chopped
  3 teaspoons minced green onion
  2 tablespoons soy sauce
  ½ teaspoon salt
  1 teaspoon sesame oil
    Dash freshly ground white pepper
  1 pound won ton skins
  1 egg white, lightly beaten
  6 cups hot chicken stock
    Finely sliced green onions, optional

Mix first 8 ingredients. Place ½ teaspoon filling in center of each won ton skin. Moisten edges with egg white; fold in triangle; press edges to seal. Moisten the two far points of triangle with water; press together firmly. Makes about 55 won tons. Drop 18 won tons into wok of boiling water; cook 10 minutes; drain. Place 3 won tons in each of 6 soup bowls; fill with hot chicken stock; garnish with green onions, if desired. Serve immediately.

Note: Remaining won tons can be frozen. It is not necessary to thaw before cooking.

Far East Tofu Soup

Makes 4 to 6 servings
Preparation Time: 20 minutes; 30 minutes to cook

  2 tablespoons peanut oil
  1½ cups sliced fresh mushrooms
  3 large cloves garlic, peeled and crushed
  ½ teaspoon peeled and minced fresh gingerroot
  3 tablespoons soy sauce
  2½ cups chicken stock
  1½ cups water
  1 cup uncooked egg noodles
  1 unpeeled medium zucchini, cut in ½-inch pieces
  1 cup cleaned and finely chopped fresh spinach
  ¼ pound tofu, cut in ½-inch cubes
  ⅓ cup finely chopped green onions including tops

Heat oil in wok over high heat. Add next 3 ingredients; stir-fry 2 minutes. Add soy sauce; take off heat. Bring stock and water to boil in another wok over high heat; add noodles; boil 2 minutes; reduce heat to simmer; add zucchini and spinach; simmer 6 to 8 minutes. Add tofu and reserved mushroom mixture; simmer 8 to 10 minutes. Garnish with green onions. Serve immediately.

Zucchini and Pasta Soup

Makes 4 servings
Preparation Time: 15 minutes; 12 minutes to cook

  ¼ cup olive oil
  1 medium onion, peeled and chopped
  1 clove garlic, peeled and crushed
  4 unpeeled medium zucchini, cut in 1½-inch-long julienne strips
  1 tomato, peeled, seeded and chopped
  ½ teaspoon basil
    Salt and freshly ground white pepper to taste
  3 cups chicken stock
  2 cups cold cooked pasta (such as macaroni, small shells *or* bow knots)

Heat oil in wok until hot. Stir-fry onion and garlic 30 seconds. Add next 5 ingredients; cover; simmer 10 minutes. Stir in pasta; heat thoroughly. Serve immediately.

Clockwise, from top:
Won Ton Soup, this page;
Japanese Soup, page 13;
Egg Drop Soup with Shrimp, page 12

Tofu

Tofu with Oyster Sauce

Makes 4 servings
Preparation Time: 5 minutes; 4 minutes to cook

> 2 tablespoons peanut oil
> ½ teaspoon minced garlic
> 2 green onions, thinly sliced
> ½ pound tofu, cut in ½-inch cubes
> ½ cup chicken stock
> 2 tablespoons oyster sauce
> 1 teaspoon cornstarch mixed with
>   2 teaspoons cold water

Heat oil in wok until hot. Add garlic and green onions; stir-fry 30 seconds. Add tofu; gently stir-fry 1 minute. Add stock and oyster sauce; cover; cook 1 minute. Uncover; stir cornstarch mixture; add to wok; stir until slightly thickened. Serve immediately.

Fried Tofu

Makes 4 servings
Preparation Time: 20 minutes

> 1 pound tofu
> ¼ teaspoon salt
> 3 eggs, lightly beaten
> ¼ cup flour
> 2 tablespoons water
>   Peanut oil
> ¼ teaspoon crushed fresh gingerroot
> 1 green onion including top, finely chopped
> 1 tablespoon soy sauce

Cut tofu in half horizontally; sprinkle with salt; let stand 10 minutes. Pat dry; cut tofu in 1 x 2-inch pieces. Mix next 3 ingredients in bowl until smooth. Heat 1 tablespoon oil in wok until hot. Dip tofu pieces, one at a time, in batter; fry, three to four at a time, in oil until golden brown. (Add more oil if necessary.) Heat 2 tablespoons oil in wok. Add gingerroot and green onion; stir-fry 10 seconds. Return tofu to wok with soy sauce; cover; cook 1 minute. Serve immediately.

Scrambled Tofu

Makes 4 servings
Preparation Time: 5 minutes; 4 minutes to cook

> 1½ tablespoons peanut oil
> 1 pound tofu, cut in ½-inch cubes
>   Juice of ½ lemon
>   Salt and freshly ground black pepper to taste
> 1 medium onion, peeled, halved, and thinly sliced
> ½ pound snow peas, ends and strings removed
> ½ teaspoon dried thyme

Heat oil in wok until hot. Add tofu; gently stir-fry 2 minutes. Add remaining ingredients; stir-fry 2 minutes. Serve immediately.

Spicy Tofu

Makes 4 servings
Preparation Time: 5 minutes; 4 minutes to cook

> 3 tablespoons hot bean paste
> 1 tablespoon dry sherry
> 1 teaspoon sesame oil
> 2 tablespoons peanut oil
> 1 teaspoon salt
> 2 onions, peeled, halved and thinly sliced
> 1 pound tofu, cut in ½-inch cubes

Mix first 3 ingredients; set aside. Heat oil in wok until hot. Add salt and onions; stir-fry 2 minutes. Add tofu; gently stir-fry 1 minute. Add bean paste mixture; stir-fry to coat. Serve immediately.

Stir-Fried Tofu and Vegetables

Makes 4 servings
Preparation Time: 10 minutes; 5 minutes to cook

> 2 tablespoons peanut oil
> 1 clove garlic, peeled and crushed
> ¼ pound fresh mushrooms, wiped clean and thinly sliced
> 1 carrot, pared and cut in thin diagonal slices
> 1 onion, peeled, halved and thinly sliced
> 1 green pepper, cored, seeded and cut in ½-inch pieces
> 3 tablespoons soy sauce
> ½ teaspoon sugar
> 1 pound tofu, cut in ½-inch cubes
> 1 teaspoon cornstarch mixed with
>   2 teaspoons cold water

Heat oil in wok until hot. Add garlic and mushrooms; stir-fry 30 seconds. Add next 3 ingredients; stir-fry 2 minutes. Add soy sauce, sugar and tofu; stir-fry 10 seconds. Cover; cook 1 minute. Uncover; stir cornstarch mixture; add to wok. Stir-fry until slightly thickened. Serve immediately.

Flavored Rice

Makes 4 servings
Preparation Time: 10 minutes; 5 minutes to cook

1 tablespoon sesame oil
3 tablespoons toasted sesame seed
3 green onions, minced
2 cloves garlic, peeled and crushed
1½ cups fresh bean sprouts
2 cups hot cooked rice
2 tablespoons soy sauce

Heat oil in wok until hot. Add next 3 ingredients; stir-fry until onions soften, about 1 minute. Add bean sprouts; stir-fry until heated through. Add rice and soy sauce; toss to combine. Heat through. Serve immediately.

Pork Fried Rice

Makes 4 servings
Preparation Time: 15 minutes; 7 minutes to cook

2 tablespoons peanut oil
½ pound lean pork, cut in thin strips
½ teaspoon sugar
½ teaspoon salt
½ cup thinly sliced green onions including tops
½ cup thinly sliced celery
2 cups cold cooked rice
1 cup fresh bean sprouts
3 tablespoons soy sauce
3 eggs, lightly beaten

Heat oil in wok until hot. Add next 3 ingredients; stir-fry 2 to 3 minutes. Add green onions and celery; stir-fry 1 minute. Add rice and bean sprouts; stir-fry 30 seconds. Add soy sauce; stir to mix. Make well in center of rice; pour in beaten eggs; allow to set; scramble with spatula; stir into rice. Serve immediately.

Vegetarian Fried Rice

Makes 4 to 6 servings
Preparation Time: 10 minutes; 5 minutes to cook

2 tablespoons peanut oil
½ teaspoon salt
2 eggs, lightly beaten
⅔ cup thinly sliced green onions
1 cup fresh bean sprouts
3 tablespoons soy sauce
3 cups cold cooked rice
Freshly ground black pepper to taste

Heat oil in wok until hot. Add salt and eggs; scramble quickly, breaking into small pieces with spatula. Add onions; stir-fry 2 minutes. Add bean sprouts; stir-fry 1 minute. Add soy sauce, rice and pepper; stir-fry until heated through, about 1 minute. Serve immediately.

Stir-Fried Noodles

Makes 4 servings
Preparation Time: 20 minutes; 2 to 3 minutes to cook

3 tablespoons peanut oil
1 1-inch piece fresh gingerroot, peeled and finely chopped
6 Chinese dried black mushrooms, soaked in hot water 20 minutes, drained, stems discarded, caps thinly sliced
3 green onions, thinly sliced
½ teaspoon salt
8 ounces Chinese noodles, cooked and drained
2 tablespoons soy sauce
1 teaspoon sesame oil
1 tablespoon dry sherry

Heat oil in wok until hot. Add next 4 ingredients; stir-fry 30 seconds. Add remaining ingredients; stir-fry to combine and heat. Serve immediately.

Subgum Fried Rice

Makes 4 servings
Preparation Time: 15 minutes; 5 minutes to cook

2 tablespoons peanut oil
¼ cup thinly sliced green onions including tops
¼ cup frozen peas
¼ cup diced cooked shrimp
¼ cup diced cooked lean ham
2 eggs, lightly beaten
½ teaspoon salt
2 cups cold cooked rice
2 tablespoons soy sauce

Heat oil in wok until hot. Add onions; stir-fry 30 seconds. Add next 3 ingredients; stir-fry 1 minute. Push to one side of wok; add eggs; sprinkle with salt; scramble; cut apart with spatula; mix in with other ingredients. Add rice and soy sauce; stir-fry to mix and heat through, about 2 minutes. Serve immediately.

Rice and Noodles

Spicy Noodles and Ham

Makes 6 servings
Preparation Time: 5 minutes; 2 minutes to cook

- 1½ quarts water
- ½ teaspoon salt
- 1 pound Chinese egg noodles
- 1 teaspoon sesame oil
- 3 tablespoons soy sauce
- 1½ tablespoons vinegar
- 1 teaspoon sugar
- ½ teaspoon hot pepper sauce
- 3 tablespoons chopped green onion
- ½ cup chicken stock
- 1 cup shredded cooked ham

Bring water and salt to boil in wok. Add noodles; boil 2 minutes, stirring constantly. Drain; rinse under cold running water to stop cooking. Drain; pour into bowl; stir in sesame oil. Mix next 6 ingredients; pour over noodles; toss to combine. Add ham; toss. Serve cold or at room temperature.

Fried Rice with Ham

Makes 4 servings
Preparation Time: 15 minutes; 5 minutes to cook

- 2 tablespoons peanut oil
- ⅓ cup thinly sliced green onions including tops
- ½ teaspoon peeled and minced fresh gingerroot
- ½ teaspoon minced garlic
- 2 eggs, lightly beaten
- ¼ teaspoon salt
- ¼ teaspoon sugar
- ⅓ pound finely diced cooked lean ham
- ½ cup frozen tiny peas
- 2 tablespoons soy sauce
- 2 cups cold cooked rice
- ½ teaspoon sesame oil

Heat oil in wok until hot. Add next 3 ingredients; stir-fry 1 minute. Add eggs; scramble loosely; break up with spatula. Add next 5 ingredients; stir-fry 2 minutes. Add rice; stir-fry 30 seconds. Add sesame oil; stir and serve immediately.

Note: Leftover fried rice can be refrigerated and reheated as well as frozen, thawed and reheated. For best results with fried rice recipes, be sure rice is cold before stir-frying.

Red Pepper Rice

Makes 4 servings
Preparation Time: 20 minutes; 20 minutes to cook

- 3 tablespoons olive oil
- 4 cloves garlic, peeled, split lengthwise
- 2 onions, peeled and chopped
  Pinch dried red pepper flakes
- 1 cup long-grain rice
- ½ small red pepper, cored, seeded and diced
- 1 small tomato, cored, peeled and chopped
- 1½ cups chicken stock
  Salt to taste

Heat oil in wok until hot. Add garlic; swirl around in hot oil 30 seconds; remove and discard. Add onions; stir-fry 1 minute. Add pepper flakes; stir-fry 10 seconds. Add rice; stir-fry 2 to 3 minutes or until all grains are coated with oil. Add next 3 ingredients; stir and bring to boil. Cover; reduce heat and simmer 15 minutes. Fluff rice with fork; season with salt. Serve immediately.

Noodle Salad with Oriental Dressing

Makes 4 servings
Preparation Time: 20 minutes

- ½ pound thin egg noodles *or* linguine
  Oriental Dressing
- 1 cup fresh bean sprouts
- 2 cups shredded lettuce
- 3 tablespoons sesame seed

Cook noodles in boiling salted water in wok until al dente or just tender; drain; toss with Dressing to prevent sticking. Just before serving, toss noodles with bean sprouts and lettuce. Sprinkle with sesame seed; serve immediately.

Oriental Dressing

- 2 tablespoons peanut butter
- 2 tablespoons water
- 2 tablespoons soy sauce
- 2 tablespoons vinegar
- 2 tablespoons peanut oil
- 1 tablespoon sesame oil
- 2 tablespoons minced green onion tops
- ½ teaspoon minced garlic
- ½ teaspoon peeled and minced fresh gingerroot
- 1 teaspoon salt

Combine all ingredients in jar; cover; shake to combine.

Flavored Rice, page 17;
Fried Rice with Ham, this page

Rice and Noodles

Sticky Rice

Makes 3 cups
Preparation Time: 20 minutes

  2 cups cold water
  1 teaspoon salt
  1 cup short-grain rice

Bring water to boil in wok; add salt and rice; stir. Reduce heat to medium; cover; cook 15 minutes or until water has evaporated.

Note: Cooked rice can be frozen and reheated in a microwave oven. Allow 1 minute on high power per 1 cup thawed rice.

Noodles in Oyster Sauce

Makes 4 servings
Preparation Time: 10 minutes

  ½ pound Chinese egg noodles
  ¼ cup peanut oil
  4 ¼-inch slices fresh gingerroot, peeled and grated
  4 green onions including tops, diagonally sliced in 1-inch pieces
  ½ cup chicken stock
  Oyster sauce to taste

Cook noodles in boiling water about 3 minutes; drain. Heat oil in wok until hot. Add gingerroot and green onions; stir-fry 2 minutes. Add stock; stir-fry over high heat until stock is reduced to 3 to 4 tablespoons. Add noodles; stir-fry until heated through. Stir in oyster sauce. Serve immediately.

Spanish Rice

Makes 6 to 8 servings
Preparation Time: 40 minutes

  4 cups chicken stock
  1 cup tomato sauce
  1 teaspoon salt
  1 tablespoon whole pickling spice
  2 cups long-grain rice
  2 tablespoons oil
  Chopped fresh tomato
  Chopped fresh green pepper

Mix first 3 ingredients in wok. Place pickling spice in cheesecloth bag; add to wok. Bring to boil; reduce heat; simmer 10 minutes. Sauté rice in hot oil in skillet or another wok until lightly browned. Add to stock mixture. Bring to boil; cover; simmer about 25 minutes or until rice is tender. Remove spice bag. Serve immediately garnished with chopped tomato and pepper.

Exotic Noodles

Makes 4 servings
Preparation Time: 15 minutes

  ¼ cup unsalted butter
  ½ pound Chinese egg noodles, cooked and drained
  ¼ cup toasted sesame seed
  ¼ cup soy sauce
  2 green onions, thinly sliced

Melt butter in wok over medium heat. (Do not use high heat or butter will burn.) Add next 3 ingredients; toss to combine; heat through. Sprinkle with green onions. Serve immediately.

Shrimp Fried Rice

Makes 4 servings
Preparation Time: 15 minutes; 7 minutes to cook

  2 tablespoons peanut oil
  ½ pound small shrimp, shelled
  ½ teaspoon sugar
  ½ teaspoon salt
  ½ cup thinly sliced green onions including tops
  ½ cup diced bamboo shoots
  2 cups cold cooked rice
  1 cup fresh bean sprouts
  3 tablespoons soy sauce
  3 eggs, lightly beaten

Heat oil in wok until hot. Add next 3 ingredients; stir-fry 2 to 3 minutes. Add green onions and bamboo shoots; stir-fry 1 minute. Add rice and bean sprouts; stir-fry 30 seconds. Add soy sauce; stir to mix. Make well in center of rice; pour in eggs; allow to set; scramble with spatula; stir into rice. Serve immediately.

Sesame Rice

Makes 4 servings
Preparation Time: 20 minutes

  1 tablespoon unsalted butter
  1 tablespoon peanut oil
  1 cup raw long-grain rice
  ¼ cup sesame seed
  2 cups chicken stock
  1 teaspoon salt
  ¼ teaspoon peeled and minced fresh gingerroot
  1 tablespoon soy sauce *or* more to taste

Melt butter in oil in wok over medium heat. Add rice and sesame seed; cook, stirring constantly, over low heat until light brown. Add stock, salt and gingerroot. Stir; bring to boil; cover; reduce heat to low; simmer 15 minutes. Uncover; stir in soy sauce. Serve immediately.

TEMPURA

Tempura is a Japanese frying technique in which small pieces or slices of food are dipped in a thin batter and fried in hot oil in a wok. The result is tender-crisp vegetables, seafood and meat encased in a delicate crunchy coating. The food can be cooked by one or two people in the kitchen just before serving, or the cooking can be done in an electric wok at the table. A variety of garnishes and dipping sauces are served.

To Prepare Tempura:

1. Have all foods for tempura frying cut in bite-size or thin strips, arranged attractively on a platter. Be sure foods are at room temperature before cooking.
2. Prepare the dipping sauces and seasonings to be served. These can be prepared hours in advance. They should be at room temperature when served.
3. Prepare either Batter I (it must stand at room temperature 1 hour) or Batter II (it must be prepared just before using and kept cold) or prepare both batters, if desired.
4. Heat 1 quart peanut oil in electric wok to 400° or so that oil reaches 365°. (If an electric wok is not available, use a wok on the stove and heat the oil to the prescribed temperature.) Fit the wok with a tempura ring if available. If not, line a plate with paper towels for draining excess oil from foods.
5. Using tongs or chopsticks, coat foods to be fried, one by one, with batter; drop into hot oil. Fry 3 or 4 items at a time, browning on all sides, 2 to 3 minutes. It will be necessary to increase the temperature of the oil during frying because its temperature will be lowered as foods are added. Remove cooked food with slotted spoon or strainer; place on tempura ring or paper towels to drain; serve while hot.
6. Each person dips the tempura-fried foods in the desired sauces. Food can be cooked by one person or everyone at the table. Divide batter so that each person has his own dish. If using the batter containing ice water, place individual bowls of this batter in bowls of crushed ice to keep it cold.

Suggested Ingredients:

Sweet potato, peeled, cut into ¼-inch-wide slices
Spanish onion, peeled, cut in ¼-inch-wide slices without separating into rings
Green or red pepper, cut in ½-inch-wide strips
Zucchini, unpeeled, cut in ⅛-inch-wide strips
Green beans, ends trimmed
Cucumber, peeled, thinly sliced
Parsley sprigs
Mushrooms, halved if particularly large
Eggplant, unpeeled, cut in thin strips
Celery, cut in 3-inch-long strips
Carrot, cut in 3-inch-long strips
Snow peas, ends and strings removed
Flounder or sole, cut in 2-inch pieces
Sea scallops, halved if particularly large
Shrimp, shelled except for tails, deveined
Chunks of lobster, 1½ inches
Chunks of boneless, skinned chicken breast, ½ inch
Chicken livers, halved

Dipping Sauces and Seasonings:

Soy sauce
Grated white radish
Lemon juice
Sweet and Sour Sauce (recipe on page 31)
Hot Mustard Sauce (recipe on page 31)
Plum Sauce (recipe on page 31)
Tempura Sauce (recipe on page 31)

Tempura

Batter I

2 eggs
1⅓ cups flour
1 teaspoon salt
1 cup flat beer

Beat eggs in bowl; add ⅓ cup flour and salt. Add beer alternately with remaining flour, beating after each addition. Let batter stand at room temperature 1 hour.

Batter II

⅔ cup flour
3 tablespoons cornstarch
½ teaspoon salt
2 eggs
¾ cup ice water

Stir first 3 ingredients together in bowl. Beat eggs and ice water in another bowl until blended. Add to flour mixture; stir until just moistened. Batter will be lumpy. Do not stir again. Keep batter cold by placing it in a bowl set in a larger bowl of crushed ice.

CHINESE HOT POT

A Chinese hot pot dinner is a fun way to entertain. To be authentic, a Mongolian hot pot should be used, but an electric wok will serve the purpose perfectly well. Chicken stock is heated to boiling in a wok. Guests then dip meat, seafood and vegetables into the stock using chopsticks or spearing food on bamboo skewers. These foods are then eaten with an assortment of sauces.

Then cellophane noodles are cooked in the stock, and the noodles and stock are ladled into serving bowls as the last course of the dinner. All of the preparation is done in advance, making this an almost effortless party menu. It's best to serve this to no more than four people at a time so each will have easy access to the wok.

Suggested Vegetables:

Broccoli flowerets, sliced ¼ inch thick
Cauliflowerets, sliced ¼ inch thick
Carrots, pared, cut in ⅛-inch-thick diagonal slices
Snow peas, ends and strings removed
Spinach leaves, washed, stems removed
Mushrooms, wiped clean, sliced ¼ inch thick
Green onions, roots removed, cut in 1½-inch-long pieces
Red or green pepper strips, ¼ inch wide

Suggested Proteins:

Pork tenderloin, beef top sirloin, lean lamb; all cut across grain in ⅛-inch-thick slices
Chicken breast, skinned and boned, cut across grain in ¼-inch-thick slices
Chicken livers, halved
Medium to large shrimp, shelled and deveined, halved lengthwise
Sea scallops, halved if particularly large
Tofu or bean curd, cut in ½- to 1-inch cubes

Other Ingredients:

3 to 4 ounces cellophane noodles
3 to 4 cups warm water
6 to 8 cups richly flavored chicken stock
Soy sauce
Teriyaki Sauce (recipe page 31)
Plum Sauce (recipe page 31)
Hoisin Sauce (recipe page 31)
Mustard Sauce (recipe page 31)

To Prepare Hot Pot:

Arrange vegetables and proteins attractively in overlapping layers on serving trays. Cover; refrigerate until serving time. Cover cellophane noodles with warm water; let stand 30 minutes. Drain; cut in 6-inch lengths. When ready to serve, put enough stock in wok to fill halfway. Heat to boiling. Let guests cook vegetables and proteins to desired doneness, 1 to 4 minutes. Serve with dipping sauces. It may be necessary to add additional stock to wok. As the last course, heat noodles in stock; ladle into bowls.

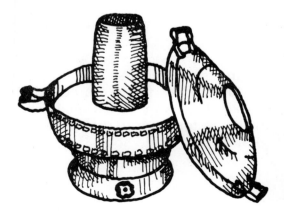

Vegetables

Harvest Vegetable Stir-Fry

Makes 6 to 8 servings
Preparation Time: 15 minutes; 15 minutes to cook

- **2 tablespoons peanut oil**
- **1 ¼-inch slice fresh gingerroot, peeled**
- **2 cups small broccoli flowerets, blanched 3 minutes**
- **2 cups small cauliflowerets, blanched 3 minutes**
- **2 cups sliced fresh mushrooms**
- **1 green pepper, cored, seeded and cut in ¼-inch-wide strips**
- **2 cups thin diagonal celery slices**
- **1 large clove garlic, peeled and minced**
- **1 teaspoon salt**
- **1 teaspoon freshly ground black pepper**
- **2 tablespoons soy sauce**
- **½ cup grated sharp Cheddar cheese**

Heat oil in wok until hot. Add gingerroot; swirl around sides of wok; discard. Add broccoli, cauliflower, mushrooms, green pepper and celery in that order. Add garlic, salt and pepper. Cover; cook 10 minutes or until vegetables are tender-crisp. Add soy sauce; toss. Sprinkle with cheese; cook until cheese melts. Serve immediately.

Julienne Vegetable Stir-Fry

Makes 6 servings
Preparation Time: 10 minutes; 4 minutes to cook

- **2 tablespoons peanut oil**
- **1 small green pepper, cut in 1½-inch-long julienne strips**
- **2 small carrots, pared, cut in 1½-inch-long julienne strips**
- **½ rib celery, cut in 1½-inch-long julienne strips**
- **1 unpeeled zucchini, cut in 1½-inch-long julienne strips**
- **2 tablespoons chicken stock**
- **20 snow peas, ends trimmed, strings removed**
  Salt and freshly ground black pepper to taste

Heat oil in wok until hot. Add green pepper and carrots; stir-fry 1 minute. Add celery and zucchini; stir-fry 1 minute. Add stock; cover; cook 30 seconds. Add snow peas; cook 1 minute. Season with salt and black pepper. Serve immediately.

Stir-Fried Asparagus

Makes 4 servings
Preparation Time: 10 minutes; 6 minutes to cook

- **2 tablespoons peanut oil**
- **2 cloves garlic, peeled and minced**
- **1 cup chicken stock**
- **1 pound asparagus, cut in 2-inch diagonal pieces, leaving tips whole**
- **2 tablespoons dry sherry**
- **2 tablespoons soy sauce**
- **2 teaspoons cornstarch**
- **¼ teaspoon sugar**
- **¾ teaspoon salt**
- **¼ teaspoon black pepper**

Heat oil in wok until hot. Add garlic; stir-fry 10 seconds. Add stock and asparagus; bring to boil. Cover; cook 5 minutes or until asparagus is tender-crisp. Meanwhile, mix remaining ingredients. Uncover; stir cornstarch mixture; add to wok; stir-fry until sauce thickens. Serve immediately.

Stir-Fried Broccoli

Makes 4 servings
Preparation Time: 10 minutes; 3 minutes to cook

- **2½ tablespoons peanut oil**
- **1 clove garlic, peeled and split lengthwise**
- **1 pound broccoli, cut in 1½-inch pieces**
- **½ teaspoon salt**
- **¼ teaspoon freshly ground black pepper**
- **2 1-inch-long dried chilies, crushed**
- **2 tablespoons cold water**
- **½ teaspoon sesame oil**

Heat oil in wok until hot. Add garlic; swirl around wok 30 seconds; discard. Add next 4 ingredients; stir-fry 1 minute. Add water; cover; cook 1 minute. Uncover; add sesame oil; stir-fry 30 seconds. Serve immediately.

Stir-Fried Spinach

Makes 3 to 4 servings
Preparation Time: 10 minutes; 3 minutes to cook

- **2 tablespoons peanut oil**
- **1 clove garlic, peeled**
- **1 pound fresh spinach, washed, stems discarded**
- **½ teaspoon salt**
  Pinch sugar

Heat oil in wok until hot. Add garlic and spinach; stir-fry 1 minute. Discard garlic. Add salt and sugar; stir-fry 1 minute. Serve immediately.

Sweet and Sour Zucchini

Makes 4 servings
Preparation Time: 10 minutes; 10 minutes to cook

2 tablespoons peanut oil
3 unpeeled medium zucchini, cut in ½-inch slices
2 tablespoons sugar dissolved in
2 tablespoons vinegar
Salt and freshly ground white pepper to taste

Heat oil in wok until hot. Add zucchini; stir-fry until tender-crisp. Add remaining ingredients; simmer 3 minutes. Serve immediately.

Stir-Fried Green Beans

Makes 4 servings
Preparation Time: 10 minutes; 4 minutes to cook

2 tablespoons peanut oil
2 small cloves garlic, peeled and finely chopped
2 ¼-inch slices fresh gingerroot, peeled and finely chopped
2 green onions, thinly sliced
1 pound green beans, ends removed, blanched 4 minutes
Salt to taste

Heat oil in wok until hot. Add next 3 ingredients; stir-fry 30 seconds. Add beans; stir-fry 2 to 3 minutes or until tender-crisp. Add salt. Serve immediately.

Stir-Fried Vegetables on Rice Sticks

Makes 4 servings
Preparation Time: 20 minutes; 7 minutes to cook

¼ cup peanut oil
3 to 4 ounces rice sticks, torn into 2 batches
2 ribs celery, cut in thin diagonal slices
20 snow peas, ends and strings removed
10 Chinese dried black mushrooms, soaked in hot water 20 minutes, drained, stems discarded, caps thinly sliced
2 cups fresh bean sprouts
1 tablespoon curry powder mixed with
1 cup chicken stock
Salt to taste

Heat oil in wok until hot. Add 1 batch rice sticks; cook until puffed; turn; cook 10 seconds on other side. Remove to paper towel to drain. Cook remaining batch rice sticks in same manner. Remove all but 1 tablespoon oil from wok. Heat oil in wok until hot. Add celery, snow peas, mushrooms and bean sprouts; stir-fry 2 minutes. Add curry powder mixture and salt. Pour over rice sticks. Serve immediately.

Vegetable Stir-Fry

Makes 4 servings
Preparation Time: 10 minutes; 6 minutes to cook

2 tablespoons peanut oil
1 clove garlic, peeled and minced
1 ¼-inch slice fresh gingerroot, peeled and minced
1 small onion, peeled and cut into thin rings
1 cup small cauliflowerets, blanched in boiling water until almost tender
1 cup small broccoli flowerets, blanched in boiling water until almost tender
4 to 5 fresh mushrooms, wiped clean, halved
Salt to taste

Heat oil in wok until hot. Add garlic, gingerroot and onion; stir-fry until onion is limp, about 2 minutes. Add cauliflower, broccoli and mushrooms; stir-fry 3 to 4 minutes or until vegetables are tender-crisp. Add salt; serve immediately.

Vegetable Stir-Fry Deluxe

Makes 6 servings
Preparation Time: 20 minutes; 7 minutes to cook

2 tablespoons peanut oil
2 onions, peeled, halved vertically and sliced
2 green peppers, cored, seeded and cut in thin strips
2 carrots, pared and cut in thin diagonal slices
2 ribs celery, cut in thin diagonal slices
1 ¼-inch slice fresh gingerroot, peeled and minced
3 cloves garlic, peeled and finely chopped
2 tablespoons soy sauce
2 tablespoons dry sherry
1 pound broccoli flowerets, blanched 3 minutes
½ pound cauliflowerets, blanched 3 minutes
1 cup shredded bok choy (Chinese cabbage)
1 cup fresh bean sprouts
2 tablespoons fresh lemon juice
Salt and freshly ground black pepper to taste

Heat oil in wok until hot. Add next 3 ingredients; stir-fry 3 minutes. Add next 5 ingredients; stir-fry 2 minutes. Add broccoli and cauliflower; stir-fry 1 minute. Add cabbage; stir-fry 30 seconds. Add bean sprouts and lemon juice; stir-fry to heat through. Season with salt and pepper. Serve immediately.

Snow Peas with Water Chestnuts

Makes 4 servings
Preparation Time: 10 minutes; 2 minutes to cook

 2 tablespoons peanut oil
 1 ¼-inch slice fresh gingerroot, peeled
 1 pound snow peas, ends and strings removed
 1 teaspoon salt
 1 tablespoon water
 1 8-ounce can sliced water chestnuts, drained
 ½ teaspoon sugar

Heat oil in wok until hot. Add gingerroot; swirl around wok 30 seconds; discard. Add snow peas; stir-fry 30 seconds. Add salt and water; cover; cook 30 seconds. Uncover; add water chestnuts and sugar; stir-fry 30 seconds. Serve immediately.

Vegetables and Cashew Nuts

Makes 4 servings
Preparation Time: 15 minutes; 4 minutes to cook

 2 tablespoons peanut oil
 1 cup diagonally sliced celery
 1 small red onion, peeled and sliced
 1 cup sliced water chestnuts, drained
20 snow peas, ends and strings removed
 1 clove garlic, peeled and crushed
 1 teaspoon sugar
 1 tablespoon soy sauce
 ½ cup chicken stock
 1 cup unsalted cashew nuts
 1 teaspoon cornstarch mixed with
   1 tablespoon cold water

Heat oil in wok until hot. Stir-fry celery and onion 15 seconds. Add next 6 ingredients; stir-fry 1 minute. Add nuts. Stir cornstarch mixture; add to wok. Stir-fry until thickened. Serve immediately.

Stir-Fried Zucchini

Makes 4 servings
Preparation Time: 5 minutes; 10 minutes to cook

 2 tablespoons peanut oil
 2 medium onions, peeled and thinly sliced
 4 unpeeled medium zucchini, cut in
   ½-inch diagonal slices
   Salt and freshly ground black pepper to taste
 ½ teaspoon dried basil
 ½ teaspoon dried oregano
 1 clove garlic, peeled and crushed
 1 tablespoon chopped fresh parsley

Heat oil in wok until hot. Add onion; stir-fry until limp. Add zucchini; cook 4 minutes. Add remaining ingredients; lower heat; cook 4 minutes. Serve immediately.

Ginger Stir-Fried Vegetables, this page;
Vegetable Stir-Fry Deluxe, page 25

Ginger Stir-Fried Vegetables

Makes 4 servings
Preparation Time: 10 minutes; 5 minutes to cook

 2 tablespoons peanut oil
 1 teaspoon peeled and minced fresh gingerroot
 1 clove garlic, peeled and minced
 ¼ pound caulifloweretts, cut in ¼-inch slices
 1 cup pared and thinly sliced carrots
 ⅓ cup chicken stock
 ¼ pound asparagus, cut in 1½-inch pieces
 ¼ pound snow peas, ends and strings removed
 ½ teaspoon salt
 ½ teaspoon sesame oil

Heat oil in wok until hot. Add gingerroot and garlic; stir-fry 30 seconds. Add cauliflower, carrots and chicken stock; cover; cook 2 minutes. Uncover; add asparagus; cover; cook 1 minute. Uncover; add snow peas; stir-fry 30 seconds. Add salt and sesame oil; stir-fry 30 seconds. Serve immediately.

Mushroom and Broccoli Stir-Fry

Makes 8 servings
Preparation Time: 15 minutes; 20 minutes to cook

 3 tablespoons peanut oil
 ½ cup chopped onion
 1 pound fresh mushrooms, wiped clean, halved
 1 pound small broccoli flowerets
 1 clove garlic, peeled and minced
 ⅓ cup sliced water chestnuts, drained
 1 tablespoon cornstarch
 ½ teaspoon salt
 1 ¼-inch slice fresh gingerroot, peeled and minced
 1 tablespoon soy sauce
 ¾ cup chicken stock

Heat 1 tablespoon oil in wok until hot. Add onion; stir-fry 2 minutes. Add mushrooms; stir-fry 3 minutes. Remove from wok; set aside. Heat 2 tablespoons oil in wok until hot. Add broccoli and garlic; stir-fry 3 minutes. Add water chestnuts; stir-fry 2 minutes. Blend remaining ingredients; pour in wok. Cook until mixture thickens. Reduce heat; simmer, covered, until broccoli is tender-crisp, about 5 minutes. Return sautéed mushrooms to wok. Heat through. Serve immediately.

Vegetables

Green Beans with Water Chestnuts

Makes 4 servings
Preparation Time: 15 minutes; 8 minutes to cook

- 1 teaspoon peanut oil
- 1 teaspoon sesame oil
- ½ pound green beans, cut diagonally in 1½-inch pieces
- ½ cup sliced water chestnuts, drained
- ½ cup sliced fresh mushrooms
- 1 small clove garlic, peeled and crushed
- 2 tablespoons soy sauce
- 2 tablespoons cold water
- ½ teaspoon salt
- ¼ teaspoon freshly ground black pepper
- 2 teaspoons sesame seed

Heat both oils in wok until hot. Add next 4 ingredients; stir-fry 1 minute. Add remaining ingredients; cover; cook until beans are tender, 5 to 7 minutes. Serve immediately.

Stir-Fried Broccoli and Carrots

Makes 6 servings
Preparation Time: 15 minutes; 5 minutes to cook

- 2 tablespoons peanut oil
- 2 ¼-inch slices gingerroot, peeled and finely chopped
- 1 clove garlic, peeled and finely chopped
- 1½ cups small broccoli flowerets
- 1½ cups pared and thinly sliced carrots
- 1 small onion, peeled, sliced and separated into rings
- ¾ cup chicken stock
- 1 teaspoon salt
- 1 tablespoon cornstarch mixed with 2 tablespoons cold water
- 1 8-ounce can sliced water chestnuts, drained
- 1 cup sliced fresh mushrooms
- 2 tablespoons oyster sauce

Heat oil in wok until hot. Add gingerroot and garlic; stir-fry 15 seconds. Add next 3 ingredients; stir-fry 1 minute. Add chicken stock and salt; cover; cook until carrots are tender-crisp, about 3 minutes. Stir cornstarch mixture; add to vegetable mixture. Cook, stirring, until slightly thickened, about 10 seconds. Add remaining ingredients; stir-fry 30 seconds. Serve immediately.

Green Bean and Zucchini Stir-Fry

Makes 4 servings
Preparation Time: 10 minutes; 10 minutes to cook

- 2 tablespoons peanut oil
- 1 pound fresh green beans, cut in 2-inch pieces
- 3 cups unpeeled sliced zucchini
- ¼ cup chopped celery
- 1 tablespoon fresh lemon juice
- 1½ teaspoons salt
- ⅓ cup chicken stock
- 1 teaspoon cornstarch dissolved in 1 tablespoon water

Heat oil in wok until hot. Add beans; stir-fry 3 minutes or until tender-crisp. Add next 4 ingredients; stir-fry 3 minutes. Add stock; cover; simmer 3 minutes. Stir cornstarch mixture; add to wok. Serve immediately.

Broccoli and Cauliflower with Garlic

Makes 4 servings
Preparation Time: 10 minutes; 5 minutes to cook

- 2 tablespoons peanut oil
- 2 small cloves garlic, peeled and crushed
- 2 cups small broccoli flowerets, blanched 3 minutes
- 2 cups small cauliflowerets, blanched 3 minutes
- 1 cup chicken stock
- 2 teaspoons cornstarch mixed with 2 teaspoons cold water

Heat oil in wok until hot. Add garlic; stir-fry 30 seconds. Add broccoli and cauliflower; stir-fry 2 minutes. Add stock; cover; cook 2 minutes or until vegetables are tender-crisp. Stir cornstarch mixture; add to wok; stir-fry until sauce thickens slightly. Serve immediately.

Broccoli Cantonese

Makes 4 servings
Preparation Time: 10 minutes; 5 to 7 minutes to cook

- 2 tablespoons peanut oil
- 1½ pounds small broccoli flowerets
- 1 cup chicken stock
- 2 teaspoons cornstarch
- 2 teaspoons cold water
- 1 ¼-inch slice fresh gingerroot, peeled and minced
- ½ teaspoon salt
- ¼ teaspoon sesame oil

Heat oil in wok until hot. Add broccoli and stock; bring to boil. Cover; cook 3 to 5 minutes or until broccoli is tender-crisp. Meanwhile, mix next 4 ingredients. Uncover wok; stir cornstarch mixture; add to wok. Stir-fry until sauce thickens. Add sesame oil; stir-fry 10 seconds. Serve immediately.

Stir-Fried Peppers

Makes 4 servings
Preparation Time: 15 minutes; 7 minutes to cook

   2 tablespoons olive oil
   2 green peppers, cored, seeded, cut in ½-inch-wide
      lengthwise strips
   2 red peppers, cored, seeded, cut in ½-inch-wide
      lengthwise strips
   1 large clove garlic, peeled and crushed
   1 medium onion, peeled, thinly sliced and separated
      into rings
   ½ teaspoon crumbled oregano
      Pinch cayenne pepper
   3 to 4 dashes hot pepper sauce
      Salt and freshly ground black pepper to taste

Heat oil in wok until hot. Add pepper strips; stir-fry
2 minutes. Add remaining ingredients; stir-fry 30
seconds. Cover; simmer 3 to 4 minutes or until
peppers are tender-crisp. Serve immediately.

Note: If red peppers are not available, substitute
green peppers.

Garden Stir-Fry

Makes 4 servings
Preparation Time: 20 minutes; 8 minutes to cook

   2 tablespoons peanut oil
   ½ pound fresh mushrooms, wiped clean, thinly sliced
      Salt and freshly ground black pepper to taste
   1 tablespoon fresh lemon juice
   2 small onions, peeled, halved vertically and sliced
   1 large green pepper, cored, seeded and
      cut in thin strips
   2 large cloves garlic, peeled and crushed
   1 teaspoon dried rosemary, crumbled
   1 teaspoon dried basil
   ½ teaspoon dried marjoram
      Salt and freshly ground black pepper to taste
   2 tablespoons dry red wine
   2 medium unpeeled zucchini, cut in
      thin diagonal slices
   2 small tomatoes, cored, each cut in 6 wedges

Heat 1 tablespoon oil in wok until hot. Add mushrooms; sprinkle with salt and pepper to taste and
lemon juice. Stir-fry 2 minutes; remove; set aside.
Heat remaining 1 tablespoon oil in wok until hot.
Add next 3 ingredients; stir-fry 2 minutes. Add
seasonings, wine, zucchini, tomatoes and mushrooms; stir-fry 2 minutes. Serve immediately.

Bean Sprout and Mushroom Stir-Fry

Makes 4 servings
Preparation Time: 20 minutes; 6 minutes to cook

   2 tablespoons peanut oil
   6 to 8 Chinese dried black mushrooms, soaked in hot
      water 20 minutes, drained, stems discarded, caps
      thinly sliced
   3½ cups fresh bean sprouts
   1 clove garlic, peeled and finely chopped
   1 teaspoon peeled and finely chopped fresh
      gingerroot
   ½ cup water
   2 teaspoons cornstarch mixed with
      1 tablespoon cold water
   1 tablespoon soy sauce
   2 green onions, cut in 1-inch pieces

Heat oil in wok until hot. Add mushrooms, bean
sprouts, garlic and gingerroot; stir-fry 2 minutes.
Add water; bring to boil. Stir cornstarch mixture;
add to wok with soy sauce. Stir until thickened.
Garnish with green onions. Serve immediately.

Cauliflower Stir-Fry

Makes 4 servings
Preparation Time: 5 minutes; 15 minutes to cook

   3 tablespoons peanut oil
   1 small head cauliflower, separated into
      small flowerets
   2 tablespoons fresh lemon juice
   2 tablespoons water
   4 green onions, thinly sliced
   1 clove garlic, peeled and crushed
      Salt and freshly ground white pepper to taste

Heat 1 tablespoon oil in wok until hot. Add next 3
ingredients; cover; cook on medium heat 7 to 10
minutes or until crisp-tender. Remove from wok
with strainer; set aside. Heat remaining 2 tablespoons oil in wok until hot. Add green onions;
stir-fry 30 seconds. Add garlic; stir-fry 30 seconds. Add cauliflower, salt and pepper. Stir-fry 1
minute. Cook 2 minutes. Serve immediately.

Hot Mustard Sauce I

Makes 1 cup
Preparation Time: 15 minutes

¼ cup dry mustard
2 tablespoons peanut oil
2 tablespoons water
¼ cup sugar
1 tablespoon cornstarch
½ teaspoon salt
½ cup water
¼ cup white vinegar

Mix mustard and oil in small bowl. Gradually add 2 tablespoons water, stirring constantly, to form smooth paste. Stir together sugar, cornstarch and salt in wok; gradually add ½ cup water and vinegar. Blend thoroughly. Cook over medium heat, stirring constantly, until mixture thickens. Gradually add to mustard mixture, stirring constantly, until blended. Refrigerate until serving time. Stir before serving. Serve at room temperature.

Hot Mustard Sauce II

Makes approximately ⅓ cup
Preparation Time: 2 minutes; 30 minutes for flavors to blend

3 tablespoons dry mustard
2 tablespoons water
1 tablespoon soy sauce

Stir all ingredients together until smooth; let set 30 minutes for flavors to blend before serving.

Plum Sauce

Makes approximately 1 cup
Preparation Time: 15 minutes

1 cup plum jam, jelly *or* preserves
½ cup applesauce
½ teaspoon ground ginger
2 teaspoons cornstarch
2 teaspoons soy sauce
2 teaspoons wine vinegar

Mix plum jam and applesauce in wok; bring to boil over medium heat. Combine ginger, cornstarch, soy sauce, vinegar; stir into jam mixture. Cook, stirring constantly, until mixture thickens. Cool. Refrigerate until serving time. Bring to room temperature before serving.

Ginger Sauce

Makes approximately ¾ cup
Preparation Time: 2 minutes

1 tablespoon ground ginger
1 small clove garlic, peeled and crushed
¼ cup water
2 tablespoons sugar
½ cup soy sauce

Mix all ingredients. Use as dipping sauce.

Sweet and Sour Sauce

Makes approximately 1¼ cups
Preparation Time: 5 minutes

½ cup pineapple juice
½ cup white wine vinegar
2 tablespoons peanut oil
2 tablespoons packed light brown sugar
1 tablespoon soy sauce
½ teaspoon freshly ground black pepper
2 teaspoons cornstarch mixed with
4 teaspoons cold water

Mix first 6 ingredients in wok; bring to boil. Stir cornstarch mixture; add to wok, stirring until sauce is clear and slightly thickened.

Tempura Sauce

Makes approximately ½ cup
Preparation Time: 10 minutes

¼ cup chicken stock
1 tablespoon soy sauce
1 tablespoon cream sherry
1 tablespoon grated daikon (Japanese radish)
1 tablespoon peeled and grated fresh gingerroot

Combine first 3 ingredients. Just before serving, stir in daikon and gingerroot.

Teriyaki Sauce

Makes approximately ⅔ cup
Preparation Time: 10 minutes

½ cup pineapple juice
¼ cup packed light brown sugar
2 tablespoons soy sauce
1 tablespoon peanut oil
¾ teaspoon ground ginger
¼ teaspoon salt
1 clove garlic, peeled and minced

Mix all ingredients in wok; heat to blend flavors.

Clockwise, from top:
Plum Sauce, this page;
Sweet and Sour Sauce, this page;
Hot Mustard Sauce, this page

Beef

Asparagus and Beef Stir-Fry

Makes 2 servings
Preparation Time: 15 minutes; 6 minutes to cook

- 1 tablespoon cornstarch
- ½ teaspoon sugar
- 1 tablespoon cold water
- 1 tablespoon hot bean sauce
- 1 clove garlic, peeled and crushed
- 3 tablespoons peanut oil
- ½ pound flank steak, thinly sliced across grain and cut in 1½-inch-long strips
- 1 pound asparagus, cut in ½-inch diagonal slices, blanched 2 minutes and drained
- 1½ teaspoons salt

Mix first 3 ingredients; set aside. Mix bean sauce and garlic; set aside. Heat 2 tablespoons oil in wok until hot. Add beef; stir-fry 1 minute; remove with strainer. Add remaining 1 tablespoon oil to wok; heat until hot. Add bean mixture; stir-fry 10 seconds. Add asparagus and salt; stir-fry 1 minute. Return meat to wok; stir cornstarch mixture; add to wok; stir-fry until slightly thickened. Serve immediately.

Beef Kwangton

Makes 4 servings
Preparation Time: 15 minutes; 4 minutes to cook

- 2 tablespoons peanut oil
- 1 ½-inch piece fresh gingerroot, peeled
- 1 pound lean flank *or* sirloin steak, thinly sliced across grain and cut in 1½-inch-long strips
- ½ cup sliced bamboo shoots, drained
- 4 large fresh mushrooms, wiped clean, thinly sliced
- 20 snow peas, ends and strings removed
- ½ cup chicken stock
- 2 tablespoons oyster sauce
- ½ teaspoon soy sauce
- ¼ teaspoon sesame oil
- ¼ teaspoon sugar
- ½ teaspoon salt
- 1 tablespoon cornstarch mixed with 1 tablespoon cold water

Heat oil in wok until hot. Swirl gingerroot in oil around wok 30 seconds; discard gingerroot. Add beef; stir-fry 2 minutes. Add next 4 ingredients; cover; cook 2 minutes. Meanwhile, mix next 5 ingredients. Uncover; add oyster sauce mixture and cornstarch mixture; stir-fry until sauce thickens. Serve immediately.

Cauliflower and Beef Chinoise

Makes 4 to 6 servings
Preparation Time: 20 minutes; 6 minutes to cook

- 3 tablespoons peanut oil
- 1 pound lean flank *or* sirloin steak, thinly sliced across grain and cut in 1½-inch-long strips
- 1 small onion, peeled, halved and thinly sliced
- 2 cloves garlic, peeled and minced
- 1 cup beef stock
- 1 small head cauliflower, cut into uniform-size flowerets
- 1 cup frozen peas
- ½ cup fresh bean sprouts
- ½ cup sliced bamboo shoots, drained
- 1 teaspoon salt
- 2 tablespoons cornstarch
- 1 tablespoon soy sauce
- ½ cup water
- 2 teaspoons dry sherry

Heat oil in wok until hot. Add beef, onion and garlic; stir-fry until meat begins to brown. Add next 6 ingredients; cover; cook until vegetables are barely tender, about 6 minutes. Mix remaining ingredients. Stir; add to wok; stir-fry until sauce thickens slightly. Serve immediately.

Chinese Pepper Steak

Makes 4 servings
Preparation Time: 15 minutes; 5 minutes to cook

- 1 tablespoon cornstarch
- 1 cup beef stock
- 1 tablespoon soy sauce
- 2 tablespoons peanut oil
- 1 pound round steak, thinly sliced and cut in 1½-inch-long strips
- 1 clove garlic, peeled and minced
- 2 small onions, peeled and each cut into 6 wedges
- 2 green peppers, cored, seeded and cut into thin 1½-inch-long strips
- 1 teaspoon salt
- ¼ teaspoon freshly ground black pepper
- ½ teaspoon peeled and minced fresh gingerroot

Mix first 3 ingredients; set aside. Heat oil in wok until hot. Add meat and garlic; stir-fry 1 minute. Add onion and peppers; stir-fry 1 to 2 minutes. Add next 3 ingredients. Stir cornstarch mixture; add to wok; stir-fry until sauce thickens slightly. Serve immediately.

Stir-Fried Beef and Snow Peas in Oyster Sauce

Makes 4 servings
Preparation Time: 30 minutes; 5 minutes to cook

    12 ¼-inch-thick slices beef tenderloin from large end,
        thinly sliced into strips
     2 tablespoons soy sauce
     2 tablespoons dry sherry
     ½ teaspoon ground Szechwan peppercorns
     ½ teaspoon peeled and grated fresh gingerroot
     ¼ cup oyster sauce
     2 tablespoons water
     2 tablespoons soy sauce
     2 tablespoons dry sherry
     1 teaspoon cornstarch
     1 teaspoon sesame oil
     2 tablespoons peanut oil
     1 ¼-inch slice fresh gingerroot, peeled
     ½ pound snow peas, ends and strings removed
     2 green onions, thinly sliced
     3 tablespoons water
     1 tablespoon dry sherry
     ½ teaspoon sugar
     ½ teaspoon salt
     1 teaspoon cornstarch mixed with
        1 teaspoon cold water

Mix first 5 ingredients in bowl; set aside to marinate 30 minutes. Mix next 6 ingredients; set aside. Heat oil in wok until hot. Add gingerroot slice; swirl around wok 30 seconds; discard. Add meat mixture and reserved oyster sauce mixture; stir-fry until meat loses pinkness, 2 to 3 minutes. Add next 6 ingredients; stir-fry 1 minute. Stir cornstarch mixture; add to wok; stir-fry until sauce thickens slightly. Serve immediately.

Stir-Fried Broccoli and Beef

Makes 4 servings
Preparation Time: 15 minutes; 8 minutes to cook

     2 teaspoons dry sherry
     ⅛ teaspoon freshly ground black pepper
     2 teaspoons soy sauce
     ½ teaspoon salt
     ½ teaspoon sugar
     ¾ cup water
     2 teaspoons cornstarch
     ¼ cup peanut oil
     ¾ pound broccoli, flowerets removed and reserved;
        stalks cut diagonally into ¼-inch slices
     ½ pound flank steak, thinly sliced across grain and cut
        in 1½-inch-long strips

Mix first 5 ingredients and ½ cup water; set aside. Mix cornstarch with remaining ¼ cup water; set aside. Heat 2 tablespoons oil in wok until hot. Add broccoli stalk slices; cover; cook 2 minutes. Add flowerets; cover; cook 2 minutes or until tender-crisp. Remove broccoli to hot platter. Add remaining 2 tablespoons oil to wok; heat until hot. Add meat; stir-fry 1 minute. Add soy sauce mixture; stir-fry 2 minutes. Return broccoli to wok; mix. Add cornstarch mixture; stir until slightly thickened. Serve immediately.

Sukiyaki

Makes 6 servings
Preparation Time: 20 minutes; 6 minutes to cook

     3 tablespoons peanut oil
     2 pounds top sirloin *or* boned and trimmed rib steak,
        cut in thin strips
        Sukiyaki Sauce
     3 bunches green onions, cut in 1½-inch-long strips
     2 pounds onions, peeled and sliced lengthwise into
        thin wedges
     2 bunches spinach, washed and stems discarded
     ¼ pound tofu, cut in small cubes
     ½ cup sliced bamboo shoots, drained
     ½ pound fresh bean sprouts
     ½ pound fresh mushrooms, sliced
     6 ribs celery, cut in thin diagonal slices

Heat oil in wok until hot. Add meat; stir-fry 1 minute. Add one-half of Sukiyaki Sauce and remaining ingredients. Stir-fry 3 to 4 minutes or until vegetables are tender-crisp. Add remaining sauce; stir-fry 1 minute. Serve immediately.

Sukiyaki Sauce

     ⅔ cup soy sauce
     ⅔ cup beef consommé
     1 tablespoon sugar
     ¼ cup sake *or* dry sherry

Stir all ingredients in bowl until sugar dissolves.

Tenderloin Stir-Fry

Makes 4 servings
Preparation Time: 15 minutes; 5 minutes to cook

     1 tablespoon cornstarch
     ½ cup cold water
     1 teaspoon soy sauce
     ½ teaspoon oyster sauce
     1 tablespoon peanut oil
     1 pound beef tenderloin, cut in 1-inch cubes
     8 large fresh mushrooms, wiped clean and sliced
     ½ teaspoon salt
     4 water chestnuts, sliced
     ¼ pound snow peas, ends and strings removed
     ¼ cup chicken stock

Mix first 4 ingredients; set aside. Heat oil in wok until hot. Add next 3 ingredients; stir-fry 2 minutes. Add remaining ingredients; stir-fry 1 minute. Stir cornstarch mixture; add to wok; stir-fry 1 to 2 minutes. Serve immediately.

Beef

Curried Beef and Vegetables

Makes 6 servings
Preparation Time: 20 minutes; 6 minutes to cook

- ¼ teaspoon peeled and minced fresh gingerroot
- ½ teaspoon sugar
- 1 tablespoon soy sauce
- 1 tablespoon curry powder
- ½ cup beef stock
- 2 tablespoons peanut oil
- 1 pound tenderloin, cut in ¼-inch-thick slices, cut across the grain in thin strips
- 1 medium onion, peeled, quartered and separated into layers
- 1 medium tomato, cored and cut in 6 wedges
- 1 green pepper, halved, cored, seeds removed and cut in thin 1½-inch-long strips
- 2 teaspoons cornstarch mixed with 1 tablespoon cold water

Mix first 5 ingredients; set aside. Heat oil in wok over high heat until hot. Add meat; stir-fry 30 seconds; remove; set aside. Add next 3 ingredients; stir-fry 1 minute. Add curry mixture; cover; cook 2 to 3 minutes. Return meat to wok; stir together. Stir cornstarch mixture; add to wok; stir-fry until slightly thickened. Serve immediately.

Curry Beef

Makes 4 servings
Preparation Time: 15 minutes; 3½ minutes to cook

- 2 tablespoons peanut oil
- ½ pound lean flank steak, thinly sliced across grain and cut in 1½-inch-long strips
- 1 medium onion, peeled, quartered and cut in thin strips
- 1 small green pepper, cored, seeded and cut in thin 1½-inch-long strips
- 2 medium tomatoes, cored and each cut into 6 wedges
- ¼ cup chicken stock
- 1 teaspoon curry powder
- 1½ teaspoons sugar
- ½ teaspoon salt
- 1 tablespoon cornstarch mixed with 1 tablespoon cold water

Heat oil in wok until hot. Add beef; stir-fry 30 seconds. Add next 4 ingredients; cover; cook on medium heat 2 minutes. Uncover; add curry powder, sugar and salt; stir-fry 30 seconds. Stir cornstarch mixture; add to wok. Stir-fry until sauce thickens. Serve immediately.

Hot and Spicy Beef

Makes 4 to 6 servings
Preparation Time: 20 minutes; 4 minutes to cook

- 1 pound flank steak, thinly sliced across grain and cut in 1½-inch-long strips
- 1 egg, lightly beaten
- 1 teaspoon baking soda
- 3 tablespoons peanut oil
- 1 tablespoon cornstarch mixed with 1 tablespoon cold water
- 2 tablespoons peanut oil
- 1 small red pepper, cored, seeded and cut into thin 1½-inch-long strips
- 1 small green pepper, cored, seeded and cut into thin 1½-inch-long strips
- ½ cup sliced water chestnuts, drained
- 1 tablespoon dry sherry
- 2 small dried chilies, crushed
- 1 tablespoon soy sauce
- ½ teaspoon sugar
- ½ teaspoon salt
- ¼ teaspoon sesame oil
- 1 tablespoon cornstarch mixed with 1 tablespoon cold water

Mix meat with next 4 ingredients in small bowl; set aside to marinate at least 20 minutes. Heat oil in wok until hot. Add meat mixture; stir-fry 1 minute. Add next 3 ingredients; stir-fry 1 minute. Add next 6 ingredients; stir-fry 1 minute. Stir cornstarch mixture; add to wok. Stir-fry until sauce thickens. Serve immediately.

Mongolian Beef

Makes 4 servings
Preparation Time: 15 minutes; 3½ minutes to cook

- 1 pound lean flank *or* sirloin steak, thinly sliced across grain and cut in 1½-inch-long strips
- 2 tablespoons soy sauce
- ½ teaspoon salt
- 1 tablespoon dry sherry
- ½ teaspoon dried red pepper flakes
- 3 tablespoons peanut oil
- 1 tablespoon sesame oil
- ½ teaspoon chopped garlic
- 1 bunch green onions, each cut in half lengthwise, then cut diagonally in 1-inch-long pieces

Put meat strips in bowl; add 1 tablespoon soy sauce, next 3 ingredients and 2 tablespoons oil; set aside. Mix remaining 1 tablespoon soy sauce with sesame oil; set aside. Heat remaining 1 tablespoon oil in wok until hot. Add garlic; stir-fry 10 seconds. Add beef; stir-fry 1 minute. Add onion and sesame oil mixture; stir-fry until heated through, 1 to 2 minutes. Serve immediately.

Oriental Beef with Vegetables, page 37

Beef

Oriental Meatball Dinner

Makes 4 servings
Preparation Time: 30 minutes; 6 to 7 minutes to cook

- ½ pound very lean ground beef
- ½ pound mild pork sausage
- 1 cup beef stock
- ½ cup water chestnuts, drained and chopped
- 1 egg, lightly beaten
- ⅓ cup quick-cooking rolled oats
- 2 tablespoons chopped onion
- 1½ teaspoons toasted sesame seed
- 1 teaspoon salt
- ¾ teaspoon peeled and minced fresh gingerroot
- 2 tablespoons peanut oil
- 1 unpeeled small zucchini, thinly sliced
- 1 small green pepper, cored, seeded and cut into thin 1-inch-long strips
- 1 small onion, peeled, sliced and separated into rings
- 2 ribs celery, cut in thin diagonal slices
- 2 cloves garlic, peeled and minced
- 1 cup fresh bean sprouts
- ⅓ cup water
- 2 tablespoons soy sauce mixed with 1½ tablespoons cornstarch

Preheat oven to 450°. Mix beef, sausage, ½ cup stock and next 7 ingredients in bowl. Use 2 tablespoons mixture to shape into smooth ball; place on ungreased baking sheet. Repeat with remaining meat mixture, placing meatballs on sheet so they do not touch. Bake 30 minutes; remove; keep warm. Heat oil in wok until hot. Add next 5 ingredients; stir-fry 3 minutes. Add bean sprouts; stir-fry 1 minute. Add meatballs, remaining ½ cup stock and water; bring to simmer. Stir cornstarch mixture; add to wok; stir gently until sauce thickens slightly. Serve immediately.

Stir-Fried Beef and Bean Sauce

Makes 2 servings
Preparation Time: 15 minutes; 4 minutes to cook

- 1 small red or green pepper, cored, seeded and cut in 1-inch pieces
- 1 small onion, peeled and cut into rings
- 2 ¼-inch slices fresh gingerroot, peeled and minced
- 1 clove garlic, peeled and minced
- 1 tablespoon dry sherry
- 1 tablespoon water
- 1 tablespoon cornstarch
- ½ cup beef stock
- 2 tablespoons peanut oil
- ½ pound flank or sirloin steak, thinly sliced across grain and cut in 1½-inch-long strips
- 2 tablespoons bean sauce

Combine pepper and onion; set aside. Combine

gingerroot and garlic; set aside. Mix next 4 ingredients; set aside. Heat oil in wok until hot. Add gingerroot and garlic; stir-fry 30 seconds. Add pepper and onion; stir-fry 2 minutes. Add beef; stir-fry 1 minute or until beef is browned. Add bean sauce; stir-fry 30 seconds. Stir cornstarch mixture; add to wok; stir-fry until slightly thickened. Serve immediately.

Stir-Fried Round Steak and Vegetables

Makes 4 servings
Preparation Time: 15 minutes; 4 minutes to cook

- 2 tablespoons peanut oil
- 1 pound round steak, thinly sliced across grain and cut in 1½-inch-long strips
- 3 tablespoons soy sauce
- 1 head bok choy, thinly sliced (Chinese cabbage)
- ¼ pound fresh mushrooms, sliced
- 1 8-ounce can sliced water chestnuts, drained
- 2 teaspoons cornstarch mixed with 2 teaspoons cold water

Heat oil in wok until hot. Add beef; stir-fry 1 minute. Add next 4 ingredients; stir-fry 1 minute. Stir cornstarch mixture; add to wok; stir-fry until sauce thickens slightly. Serve immediately.

Note: Cook round steak quickly over high heat or it will toughen.

Stir-Fried Beef and Onions

Makes 2 servings
Preparation Time: 10 minutes; 4 minutes to cook

- 1 tablespoon cornstarch
- 2 tablespoons soy sauce
- 4 tablespoons dry sherry
- ½ pound lean flank or sirloin steak, thinly sliced across grain and cut in 1½-inch-long strips
- ½ teaspoon sugar
- ½ teaspoon salt
- 2 tablespoons peanut oil
- 2 medium onions, peeled, sliced and separated into rings

Mix cornstarch, 1 tablespoon soy sauce and 2 tablespoons sherry in bowl. Add meat; stir to coat; set aside to marinate 10 minutes. Stir together remaining soy sauce, remaining sherry, sugar and salt; set aside. Heat oil in wok until hot. Add onions; stir-fry 2 minutes. Add beef and soy sauce mixture; stir-fry 2 minutes. Serve immediately.

Stir-Fried Beef and Pineapple

Makes 4 servings
Preparation Time: 1 hour; 5 minutes to cook

　　2 tablespoons water
　　1 teaspoon baking soda
　　1 pound beef tenderloin, thinly sliced across grain
　　　and cut in 1½-inch-long strips
　1½ tablespoons cornstarch
　　2 tablespoons soy sauce
　½ teaspoon sesame oil
　　1 tablespoon water
　　2 drops sesame oil
　　1 teaspoon soy sauce
　　2 tablespoons peanut oil
　½ small red pepper, cored, seeded and cut in thin
　　　1½-inch-long strips
　½ small green pepper, cored, seeded and cut in thin
　　　1½-inch-long strips
　　2 ¼-inch slices fresh gingerroot, peeled and minced
　　2 small cloves garlic, peeled and minced
　½ teaspoon sugar
　　1 pineapple, quartered lengthwise through frond,
　　　fruit removed and cubed (reserve shells)

Mix water and baking soda; pour over meat; marinate 1 hour. Mix next 3 ingredients; toss with meat. Mix next 3 ingredients; set aside. Heat oil in wok until hot. Add next 5 ingredients; stir-fry 1 minute. Add beef and reserved soy sauce mixture; stir-fry 2 minutes. Add cubed pineapple and heat through. Divide among 4 pineapple shells. Serve immediately.

Oriental Beef with Vegetables

Makes 4 servings
Preparation Time: 15 minutes; 9 minutes to cook

　　1 pound lean flank *or* sirloin steak, thinly sliced across
　　　grain and cut in 1½-inch-long strips
　　2 tablespoons peanut oil
　　2 tablespoons soy sauce
　　2 tablespoons dry sherry
　½ teaspoon sugar
　　1 clove garlic, peeled and crushed
　½ teaspoon peeled and finely grated fresh gingerroot
　　2 teaspoons cornstarch
　　2 tablespoons water
　　3 tablespoons peanut oil
　　1 small onion, peeled, halved and thinly sliced
　　1 small green pepper, cored, seeded and cut in thin
　　　1½-inch long strips
　　1 small red pepper, cored, seeded and cut in thin
　　　1½-inch-long strips
　½ cup sliced bamboo shoots, drained

Put meat in shallow dish with next 8 ingredients; mix to coat meat. Heat 2 tablespoons oil in wok until hot. Add remaining ingredients; stir-fry 3 to 5

minutes or until vegetables are tender-crisp. Remove from wok; set aside. Wipe out wok with paper towel. Heat remaining 1 tablespoon oil in wok until hot. Add meat; stir-fry 2 minutes or until no longer pink. Return vegetables to wok; stir-fry to heat through. Serve immediately.

Beef and Snow Peas

Makes 3 servings
Preparation Time: 15 minutes; 3 minutes to cook

　¼ cup soy sauce
　　1 tablespoon cornstarch
　　1 tablespoon dry sherry
　　1 teaspoon sugar
　　1 pound flank *or* sirloin steak, fat trimmed, thinly
　　　sliced across grain and cut in 1½-inch-long strips
　　2 tablespoons peanut oil
　½ teaspoon salt
　20 snow peas, ends and strings removed
　½ cup sliced water chestnuts, drained

Mix first 4 ingredients in bowl. Add meat; stir to coat; marinate 15 minutes. Heat oil in wok until hot. Add meat; stir-fry 2 minutes. Add salt, snow peas and water chestnuts; stir-fry 1 minute. Serve immediately.

Beef with Green Peppers and Tomatoes

Makes 4 to 6 servings
Preparation Time: 15 minutes; 12 minutes to cook

　　2 tablespoons peanut oil
　　1 clove garlic, peeled and crushed
　½ teaspoon salt
　½ teaspoon freshly ground black pepper
　½ teaspoon peeled and minced fresh gingerroot
　　1 pound round steak, fat trimmed, thinly sliced and
　　　cut in 1½-inch-long strips
　¼ cup soy sauce
　½ teaspoon sugar
　　2 green peppers, cored, seeded and cut in thin
　　　1½-inch-long strips
　　2 tomatoes, cored and quartered
　　3 tablespoons cornstarch mixed with
　　　¼ cup cold water
　　　Hot cooked rice

Heat oil in wok until hot. Add garlic, salt, pepper and gingerroot; stir-fry 3 seconds. Add beef; stir-fry 2 minutes. Add soy sauce, sugar, green peppers; cover; cook 3 minutes. Add tomatoes; cover; cook 2 minutes. Add cornstarch mixture; stir-fry until sauce thickens slightly. Serve immediately with hot cooked rice.

Pork

Mo Shu Pork

Makes 4 servings
Preparation Time: 20 minutes; 4 minutes to cook

- 4 tablespoons peanut oil
- 3 eggs, lightly beaten
- ½ pound pork butt, fat trimmed and cut into thin 1½-inch-long strips
- 1 cup sliced bamboo shoots, drained and thinly sliced into strips
- 10 Chinese dried black mushrooms, soaked in hot water 20 minutes, drained, squeezed dry, stems discarded and caps thinly sliced
- 1 tablespoon soy sauce
- 2 green onions, diagonally cut in ½-inch pieces
- 8 to 10 prepared Chinese Pancakes (Recipe on page 9)
  Duck sauce, optional

Heat 2 tablespoons oil in wok until hot. Add eggs; scramble without overcooking. Turn out onto plate. Heat remaining 2 tablespoons oil in wok until hot. Stir-fry pork 2 minutes. Add bamboo shoots, mushrooms and eggs; stir well, breaking up eggs somewhat. Add soy sauce and green onions; stir-fry 15 seconds. Serve immediately with Chinese Pancakes. Spread some duck sauce on pancakes before filling, if desired. Put a spoonful of pork on a pancake and roll up.

Oriental Pork and Chinese Cabbage

Makes 4 servings
Preparation Time: 10 minutes; 7 minutes to cook

- 3 tablespoons soy sauce
- 1 tablespoon packed light brown sugar
- 1½ teaspoons salt
- ½ teaspoon peeled and minced fresh gingerroot
- 3 tablespoons peanut oil
- 1 pound 1-inch lean pork cubes
- 1 small green pepper, cored, seeded and cut in thin 1-inch-long strips
- 1 small onion, peeled and cut into wedges
- 4 cups loosely packed shredded Chinese cabbage
- ½ cup cold water
- 1 tablespoon cornstarch mixed with 2 teaspoons cold water

Mix first 4 ingredients; set aside. Heat oil in wok until hot. Add pork; stir-fry 3 minutes. Add pepper and onion; stir-fry 1 minute. Add soy sauce mixture, cabbage and water; toss to combine; cover; cook 1 minute. Uncover; stir cornstarch mixture; add to wok; stir-fry until slightly thickened. Serve immediately.

Stir-Fried Pork with Cashews

Makes 4 servings
Preparation Time: 15 minutes; 6 minutes to cook

- 2 tablespoons soy sauce
- 1 tablespoon dry sherry
- 1 teaspoon salt
  Pinch sugar
- 2 tablespoons peanut oil
- ½ teaspoon crushed garlic
- 3 green onions including tops, thinly sliced
- 1 pound lean boneless pork, cut in 1½-inch-long thin strips
- ½ cup sliced bamboo shoots, drained
- ½ cup sliced water chestnuts, drained
- 1 cup fresh bean sprouts
- 2 teaspoons cornstarch mixed with 2 teaspoons cold water
- ⅓ cup unsalted raw cashews

Mix soy sauce, sherry, salt and sugar; set aside. Heat oil in wok until hot. Add garlic and onions; stir-fry 1 minute. Add pork; stir-fry until pinkness is gone, about 3 minutes. Add next 3 ingredients and reserved soy sauce mixture; stir-fry 1 minute. Stir cornstarch mixture; add to wok. Stir-fry until sauce thickens. Add cashews; toss to coat. Serve immediately.

Spicy Pork with Vegetables

Makes 2 servings
Preparation Time: 15 minutes; 6 minutes to cook

- 2 tablespoons black bean sauce
- 1 tablespoon soy sauce
- 1 tablespoon dry sherry
- 2 tablespoons peanut oil
- 1 ¼-inch-thick slice fresh gingerroot, peeled and finely minced
- 2 cloves garlic, peeled and minced
- ¼ teaspoon dried red pepper flakes
- 1 large carrot, pared and very thinly sliced on diagonal
- 1 green pepper, cored, seeded and cut in thin 1½-inch-long strips
- ½ pound thinly sliced 1½-inch-long lean pork strips
- ½ cup sliced bamboo shoots, drained
- ½ cup chicken stock
- 2 teaspoons cornstarch mixed with 2 teaspoons cold water

Mix first 3 ingredients; set aside. Heat oil in wok until hot. Add next 3 ingredients; stir-fry 30 seconds. Add carrot and green pepper; stir-fry 1 minute. Add pork and bean sauce mixture; stir-fry 2 minutes. Add bamboo shoots and stock; cover; cook 1 minute or until carrots are tender-crisp. Uncover; stir cornstarch mixture; add to wok; stir-fry until sauce thickens. Serve immediately.

Spicy Pork with Vegetables, this page

Pork

Pork Strips with Szechwan Sauce

Makes 4 servings
Preparation Time: 15 minutes; 5 minutes to cook

- 1 pound lean boneless pork, cut in thin 1½-inch-long strips
- 1 teaspoon minced garlic
- 4 tablespoons soy sauce
- 1 egg, lightly beaten
- 2 tablespoons cornstarch
- 1 tablespoon dry sherry
- 2 tablespoons vinegar
- ½ cup peanut oil
- ½ teaspoon dried red pepper flakes
- 4 green onions including tops, thinly sliced

Mix pork, ½ teaspoon garlic, 2 tablespoons soy sauce, egg, cornstarch and sherry in bowl; set aside. Mix remaining 2 tablespoons soy sauce and vinegar; set aside. Heat oil in wok until hot. Add pork mixture; stir-fry until pork loses its pinkness, 2 to 3 minutes; remove from wok using strainer; set aside. Drain all but 1 tablespoon oil from wok. Heat until hot. Add red pepper flakes, remaining ½ teaspoon garlic and onions; stir-fry 30 seconds. Return pork to wok with vinegar mixture; stir-fry 1 minute. Serve immediately.

Pork Szechwan

Makes 2 servings
Preparation Time: 15 minutes; 10 minutes to cook

- 1 cup peanut oil
- 1 unpeeled small eggplant, cut in 2-inch cubes
- 2 cloves garlic, peeled and finely chopped
- 2 green onions, tops discarded, thinly sliced
- ¼ teaspoon dried red pepper flakes
- ½ pound lean pork butt, cut in thin 1½-inch-long strips
- 1 teaspoon dry sherry
- 2 teaspoons hot bean sauce
- ½ teaspoon sugar
- ¼ cup chicken stock
- 1 tablespoon vinegar
- ¼ cup sesame oil
- 1 teaspoon cornstarch mixed with 2 tablespoons water

Heat oil in wok until hot. Add eggplant cubes; fry until golden brown, 4 to 5 minutes. Remove with strainer; drain on paper toweling. Pour all but 1 tablespoon oil from wok. Heat oil in wok until hot. Add garlic, onions and red pepper flakes; stir-fry 10 seconds. Add pork; stir-fry until it loses its pinkness. Add sherry and eggplant; stir-fry 10 seconds. Add next 5 ingredients; stir-fry 15 seconds. Stir cornstarch mixture; add to wok. Stir-fry until sauce thickens. Serve immediately.

Sliced Pork with Philippine Sauce

Makes 4 servings.
Preparation Time: 5 minutes; 15 minutes to cook

- 2 tablespoons peanut oil
- 1 small onion, peeled and finely chopped
- 1 clove garlic, peeled and crushed
- 3 tablespoons packed light brown sugar
- ½ cup lime juice
- ½ cup water
- ½ teaspoon peeled and minced fresh gingerroot
- ½ teaspoon salt
  Dash cayenne pepper
- ½ teaspoon cornstarch mixed with 1 tablespoon cold water
  Hot *or* cold sliced cooked pork roast

Heat oil in wok until hot. Add onion and garlic; stir-fry 1 minute. Add next 6 ingredients; cover; simmer 10 minutes. Stir cornstarch mixture; add to wok and stir. Serve immediately with pork.

Twice-Cooked Pork with Spicy Vegetables

Makes 2 small servings
Preparation Time: 1 hour; 5 minutes to cook

- ½ pound pork butt
- 6 Chinese dried black mushrooms, soaked in hot water 20 minutes, drained (reserve water), stems discarded and caps thinly sliced
- 1 tablespoon soy sauce
  Pinch sugar
- 1 teaspoon salt
- 2 tablespoons peanut oil
- 2 cloves garlic, peeled and minced
- 1 teaspoon peeled and minced fresh gingerroot
- ⅛ teaspoon dried red pepper flakes
- 1 small green pepper, cored, seeded and cut in thin 1-inch-long strips
- 1 large carrot, pared and cut in thin diagonal slices
- ¼ cup sliced bamboo shoots, drained
- 1 teaspoon cornstarch mixed with 1 teaspoon cold water

Cover pork with water in wok; simmer 30 minutes, adding more hot water if level goes below pork. Cool pork in cooking liquid. Remove; cut in thin 1-inch-long strips; set aside. Mix ⅓ cup mushroom water with soy sauce, sugar and salt; set aside. Heat oil in wok until hot. Add garlic, gingerroot, red pepper flakes and mushrooms; stir-fry 30 seconds. Add next 3 ingredients and pork strips; stir-fry 1 minute. Add mushroom liquid mixture; cover; cook 2 minutes. Stir cornstarch mixture; add to wok; stir-fry until sauce thickens. Serve immediately.

Pork Cubes in Hot Bean-Paste Sauce

Makes 4 servings
Preparation Time: 20 minutes; 6 minutes to cook

     1 pound ½-inch cubes lean pork
     2 teaspoons soy sauce
  2½ teaspoons cornstarch
     1 small egg, lightly beaten
     2 tablespoons soy sauce
     1 teaspoon minced fresh garlic
     1 teaspoon peeled and minced fresh gingerroot
     1 tablespoon sugar
     1 tablespoon water
     1 tablespoon vinegar
     ½ cup peanut oil
   10 Chinese dried black mushrooms, soaked in hot
        water 10 minutes, drained, stems discarded and
        caps thinly sliced
     ¼ cup sliced water chestnuts, drained
     1 teaspoon hot bean paste
     1 green onion including top, thinly sliced
     ½ teaspoon sesame oil

Mix pork, 2 teaspoons soy sauce, cornstarch and egg; set aside. Mix 2 tablespoons soy sauce, garlic, gingerroot, sugar, water and vinegar; set aside. Heat oil in wok until hot. Add pork mixture, mushrooms and water chestnuts; stir-fry until pork loses pinkness, about 3 minutes. Remove pork, mushrooms and water chestnuts with strainer. Pour off all but 1 tablespoon oil. Heat oil until hot. Add bean paste and meat mixture; stir-fry 30 seconds. Add reserved soy sauce mixture and green onions; stir-fry 10 seconds. Stir in sesame oil. Serve immediately.

Pork Stir-Fry

Makes 4 servings
Preparation Time: 10 minutes; 7 minutes to cook

     2 tablespoons peanut oil
     2 medium onions, peeled and thinly sliced
     1 10-inch celery rib, thinly sliced
     2 cloves garlic, peeled and crushed
     1 pound thin 1½-inch-long lean pork strips
     ¼ cup chicken stock
     2 tablespoons dry sherry
     ½ teaspoon salt
        Freshly ground black pepper to taste
     2 teaspoons cornstarch mixed with
        2 teaspoons cold water
     2 tablespoons soy sauce

Heat oil in wok until hot. Add onions and celery; stir-fry 2 minutes or until tender-crisp. Add garlic and pork; stir-fry until pork loses its pinkness, 2 to 3 minutes. Add next 4 ingredients; stir-fry 30

seconds. Stir cornstarch mixture; add to wok with soy sauce; stir-fry until sauce thickens. Serve immediately.

Mandarin Ham Stir-Fry

Makes 4 servings
Preparation Time: 10 minutes; 7 minutes to cook

     ¾ cup packed light brown sugar
     ¼ teaspoon dry mustard
     1 tablespoon cornstarch
     1 teaspoon peeled and minced fresh gingerroot
     ¼ teaspoon ground cloves
     1 small clove garlic, peeled and crushed
     ¼ cup vinegar
     ½ cup water
     2 cups 1-inch ham cubes

Mix all ingredients except ham in wok. Heat; cook 5 minutes. Add ham; stir-fry to heat ham through. Serve immediately.

Pork and Vegetables with Almonds

Makes 4 servings
Preparation Time: 10 minutes; 12 minutes to cook

     1 teaspoon peanut oil
     ½ cup slivered blanched almonds
     1 pound lean pork, cut in ½-inch cubes
     1 egg white, lightly beaten
     4 tablespoons cornstarch
     ½ teaspoon salt
     2 tablespoons dry sherry
  1¼ cups chicken stock
     2 tablespoons peanut oil
     1 teaspoon peeled and minced fresh gingerroot
     1 cup thinly sliced carrot
     1 small green pepper, cored, seeded and cut into thin
        1½-inch-long strips
     1 8-ounce can sliced water chestnuts, drained
        Slivered blanched almonds, for garnish

Heat 1 teaspoon oil in wok until hot. Add almonds; stir-fry until evenly browned. Remove with strainer; drain thoroughly on paper towel; set aside. Toss pork with egg white, 2 tablespoons cornstarch and salt to thoroughly coat; set aside. Mix remaining 2 tablespoons cornstarch, sherry and ¼ cup chicken stock; set aside. Heat 2 tablespoons oil in wok until hot. Add pork mixture; stir-fry until pork loses pinkness, 2 to 3 minutes. Add gingerroot, remaining 1 cup chicken stock and carrot; cover; cook 5 minutes or until carrot is tender. Uncover; add green pepper; cover; cook 2 minutes. Add water chestnuts. Stir cornstarch mixture; add to wok; stir-fry until sauce thickens. Sprinkle with almonds. Serve immediately.

Pork with Green Onions and Water Chestnuts

Makes 4 servings
Preparation Time: 15 minutes; 5 minutes to cook

    4 tablespoons soy sauce
    2 tablespoons cold water
    4 teaspoons cornstarch
    1 teaspoon sugar
    1½ pounds boneless lean pork, cut in 2 x 2 x ⅛-inch slices
    2 tablespoons dry sherry
    2 teaspoons rice vinegar
    1 teaspoon sesame oil
    2 tablespoons peanut oil
    2 cloves garlic, peeled and finely minced
    4 green onions including tops, cut in ½-inch-long slices
    ½ cup sliced bamboo shoots, drained

Mix 2 tablespoons soy sauce, cold water, corn-starch and sugar in bowl; add pork; set aside 15 minutes. Mix remaining 2 tablespoons soy sauce, sherry, vinegar and sesame oil; set aside. Heat oil in wok over high heat until hot. Add garlic; stir-fry 10 seconds. Add pork; stir-fry 3 minutes. Add onions and bamboo shoots; stir-fry 30 seconds. Add sherry mixture; stir until smooth. Serve immediately.

Pork and Straw Mushroom Stir-Fry

Makes 4 servings
Preparation Time: 30 minutes; 7 minutes to cook

    1 tablespoon cornstarch
    ½ teaspoon salt
    ½ teaspoon sugar
    1 pound lean pork, cut in ½-inch cubes
    2 tablespoons soy sauce
    1 tablespoon dry sherry
    4 tablespoons peanut oil
    1 teaspoon peeled and minced fresh gingerroot
    2 to 3 thin carrots, pared and sliced diagonally ⅛ inch thick
    1 15-ounce can baby ears of corn, drained and rinsed
    ¼ cup chicken stock
    1 15-ounce can straw mushrooms, drained and rinsed
    ¼ pound snow peas, ends and strings removed

Mix first 3 ingredients in bowl; add meat; toss to coat well. Add soy sauce and wine; toss again; marinate 30 minutes. Heat 2 tablespoons oil in wok until hot. Add pork; stir-fry until pinkness is gone; remove with strainer; set aside. Remove oil; wipe wok with paper towel. Heat remaining 2 tablespoons oil in wok until hot. Add gingerroot and carrots; stir-fry 2 minutes. Add corn; stir-fry 10 seconds. Return pork mixture to wok with stock; stir. Add mushrooms and snow peas; stir-fry 30 seconds. Serve immediately.

Sweet and Sour Pork

Makes 6 servings
Preparation Time: 20 minutes; 15 minutes to cook

    2 pounds boneless pork loin, cut in ½-inch cubes
    ¼ cup soy sauce
    1 egg, lightly beaten
      Cornstarch
      Vegetable oil
    1 large onion, peeled and cut in 8 wedges
    1 green pepper, cored, seeded and cut in 1-inch pieces
    1 cup pineapple chunks, drained and juice reserved
    2 small tomatoes, cored and cut in wedges
      Sweet and Sour Sauce

Toss pork with soy sauce; roll in egg; roll in corn-starch, shaking off excess cornstarch. Heat oil in wok until hot. Add pork in batches, stir-frying until golden brown. Drain on paper towels; keep warm in preheated 200° oven. Drain all but 1 table-spoon oil from wok; heat until hot. Add onion; stir-fry 2 minutes. Add green pepper; stir-fry 2 minutes. Add pineapple and tomatoes; stir-fry 1 minute. Return pork to wok; add Sweet and Sour Sauce; stir-fry to coat all ingredients with sauce. Serve immediately.

Sweet and Sour Sauce

    ½ cup reserved pineapple juice
    ½ cup white wine vinegar
    2 tablespoons peanut oil
    2 tablespoons packed light brown sugar
    1 tablespoon soy sauce
    ½ teaspoon freshly ground black pepper
    2 teaspoons cornstarch mixed with
      4 teaspoons cold water

Mix first 6 ingredients in wok; bring to boil. Stir cornstarch mixture; add to wok, stirring until sauce is clear and slightly thickened.

Sweet and Sour Pork, this page;
Pork and Straw Mushroom Stir-Fry, this page

Chicken

Stir-Fried Chicken and Vegetables

Makes 4 servings
Preparation Time: 15 minutes; 5 minutes to cook

- ½ cup cold water
- 2 teaspoons cornstarch
- ½ teaspoon peeled and finely minced fresh gingerroot
- 2 teaspoons soy sauce
- 2 tablespoons peanut oil
- 1 medium onion, peeled, halved and sliced
- 1 teaspoon minced garlic
- 1 whole chicken breast, split, skinned, boned and cut in ¾-inch pieces
- 1 green pepper, cored, seeded and cut in thin 1½-inch-long strips
- 2 tomatoes, cored and each cut in 6 wedges

Mix water, cornstarch, gingerroot and soy sauce; set aside. Heat oil in wok until hot. Add onion and garlic; stir-fry 1 minute. Add chicken and green pepper; stir-fry 3 minutes. Add tomatoes; stir-fry 1 minute. Stir cornstarch mixture; add to wok; cook until sauce thickens. Serve immediately.

Szechwan Chicken

Makes 4 servings
Preparation Time: 15 minutes; 6 minutes to cook

- 1 tablespoon cornstarch
- 3 tablespoons soy sauce
- 2 whole chicken breasts, split, skinned, boned and cut in ½-inch cubes
- 1 tablespoon dry sherry
- 2 teaspoons sugar
- 1 teaspoon vinegar
- ¼ cup peanut oil
- ½ to 1 teaspoon dried red pepper flakes
- 2 green onions including tops, sliced
- ½ teaspoon peeled and minced fresh gingerroot
- ½ cup dry-roasted peanuts
  Hot cooked rice

Blend cornstarch and 1 tablespoon soy sauce in bowl. Mix in chicken; set aside. Mix remaining 2 tablespoons soy sauce, sherry, sugar and vinegar; set aside. Heat oil in wok over high heat. When hot, add red pepper flakes; stir-fry until black, 10 seconds. Add chicken; stir-fry 2 minutes. Remove chicken with strainer; set aside. Add green onions and gingerroot; stir-fry 1 minute. Add chicken; stir-fry 2 minutes. Add sherry mixture; stir-fry 1 minute. Stir in peanuts. Serve with hot rice.

Stir-Fried Chicken and Broccoli

Makes 4 servings
Preparation Time: 15 minutes; 10 minutes to cook

- 1 whole chicken breast, split, skinned, boned and thinly sliced
- 3 tablespoons cornstarch
- ¼ cup soy sauce
- 2 tablespoons peanut oil
- ½ pound broccoli, cut in small pieces
- 1 medium onion, peeled and thinly sliced
- ¼ pound mushrooms, wiped clean and sliced
- 2 cups fresh bean sprouts
- 1 cup hot chicken stock

Stir first 3 ingredients in bowl until chicken is thoroughly coated; set aside 15 minutes. Heat 1 tablespoon oil in wok until hot. Add chicken; stir-fry 3 minutes; remove from wok with strainer. Add 1 tablespoon oil to wok; heat until hot. Add broccoli and onion; stir-fry 2 minutes. Add mushrooms, bean sprouts, chicken and stock; cover; cook 5 minutes or until vegetables are tender-crisp. Serve immediately.

Walnut Chicken

Makes 4 servings
Preparation Time: 20 minutes; 8 minutes to cook

- ½ cup water
- 2 tablespoons cornstarch
- 1 tablespoon soy sauce
- ½ teaspoon sugar
- ½ teaspoon salt
- 3 tablespoons peanut oil
- 1 cup walnut halves
- 1 whole chicken breast, split, skinned, boned and slivered
- 6 Chinese dried black mushrooms, soaked in hot water 20 minutes, drained, stems discarded, caps quartered
- 12 snow peas, ends and strings removed
- 6 fresh mushrooms, wiped clean and sliced
- ½ cup sliced water chestnuts, drained
- ½ cup sliced bamboo shoots, drained

Mix first 5 ingredients; set aside. Heat 1 tablespoon oil in wok; add walnuts; stir-fry 1 minute. Do not let burn. Remove walnuts with strainer; drain on paper towel. Discard oil in wok. Heat remaining 2 tablespoons oil in wok until hot. Add chicken; stir-fry 3 minutes. Add next 5 ingredients; stir-fry 3 minutes. Add cornstarch mixture; cook until thickened. Serve immediately topped with walnuts.

Chicken with Button Mushrooms

Makes 2 servings
Preparation Time: 10 minutes; 7 minutes to cook

 1 teaspoon cornstarch mixed with
    1 teaspoon cold water
 1 tablespoon dry sherry
 1 tablespoon oyster sauce
 1 teaspoon water
 ½ teaspoon salt
 1 whole chicken breast, split, skinned, boned and
    cubed
 2 teaspoons dry white wine *or* dry vermouth
 1 egg white, lightly beaten
 1 teaspoon cornstarch
    Salt and freshly ground white pepper to taste
 2 tablespoons peanut oil
 ¼ pound snow peas, ends and strings removed
 ¼ cup sliced water chestnuts, drained
 ¼ cup sliced bamboo shoots, drained
 24 fresh button mushrooms

Stir cornstarch mixture; add next 4 ingredients; mix well; set aside. Mix next 4 ingredients; season with salt and pepper. Heat oil in wok until hot. Add chicken; stir-fry until opaque. Add snow peas, water chestnuts, bamboo shoots and mushrooms; stir-fry 3 minutes. Stir sherry mixture; add to wok. Cook, stirring, 1 minute. Serve immediately.

Spiced Orange Chicken

Makes 4 servings
Preparation Time: 15 minutes; 6 to 7 minutes to cook

 2 whole chicken breasts, split, skinned, boned and
    cut in 1-inch cubes
 1 teaspoon salt
 1 egg, lightly beaten
 2 tablespoons cornstarch
 5 tablespoons peanut oil, divided
 2 tablespoons soy sauce
 1 tablespoon sugar
 1 teaspoon sesame oil
 1 tablespoon dry sherry
 1 teaspoon white vinegar
    Grated peel from 2 tangerines
 ¼ teaspoon dried red pepper flakes
 4 ¼-inch slices fresh gingerroot, peeled and
    coarsely chopped
 3 to 4 green onions, cut diagonally in ¼-inch slices

Mix chicken, salt, egg, 1 tablespoon cornstarch and 1 tablespoon oil in bowl until chicken is coated; set aside. Mix next 5 ingredients and remaining 1 tablespoon cornstarch; set aside. Heat 3 tablespoons oil in wok until hot. Stir-fry chicken until opaque, about 3 minutes. Remove with strainer; set aside. Heat 1 tablespoon oil in wok until hot; add tangerine peel and red pepper

flakes. Cook until blackened, about 10 seconds, stirring constantly. Add gingerroot, green onions and chicken; stir-fry 10 seconds. Stir soy mixture; add to wok; stir-fry 1 minute. Serve immediately.

Chicken with Oyster Sauce

Makes 4 servings
Preparation Time: 15 minutes; 6 minutes to cook

 1 tablespoon soy sauce
 ½ teaspoon sugar
 ½ teaspoon salt
 1 tablespoon oyster sauce
 2 tablespoons peanut oil
 1 clove garlic, peeled and split
 1 large green pepper, cored, seeded and
    cut in 1-inch pieces
 1 onion, peeled and cut in 1-inch cubes
 2 whole chicken breasts, split, skinned, boned and
    cut in 1-inch cubes

Mix soy sauce, sugar, salt and oyster sauce; set aside. Heat oil in wok until hot. Swirl garlic around sides and bottom of wok about 30 seconds; discard. Add pepper and onion; stir-fry 1 minute. Add chicken; stir-fry 3 minutes or until opaque. Add soy sauce mixture; stir well. Serve immediately.

Chicken with Hoisin Sauce and Nuts

Makes 4 servings
Preparation Time: 20 minutes; 7 minutes to cook

 1 tablespoon cornstarch
 2 tablespoons dry sherry
 2 whole chicken breasts, split, skinned, boned and
    cut into 1-inch cubes
 3 tablespoons peanut oil
 6 large Chinese dried black mushrooms, soaked in
    hot water 20 minutes, drained, stems discarded,
    caps quartered
 1 small green pepper, cored, seeded and cut in thin
    1½-inch-long strips
 ½ cup sliced water chestnuts, drained
 ½ teaspoon salt
 1 tablespoon sugar mixed with
    3 tablespoons hoisin sauce
 ¼ cup unsalted raw cashews, almonds, pecans *or*
    peanuts

Mix cornstarch and sherry in bowl; add chicken; stir; set aside. Heat 1 tablespoon oil in wok until hot; add mushrooms; stir-fry 1 minute. Add pepper and water chestnuts; stir-fry 1 minute. Add salt; mix. Remove vegetables from wok with strainer; set aside. Add remaining 2 tablespoons oil to wok; heat until hot. Add chicken; stir-fry 3 minutes or until opaque. Add sugar-hoisin mixture; toss well. Return vegetables to wok; mix. Add nuts; mix. Serve immediately.

Hot Shredded Chicken

Makes 2 servings
Preparation Time: 1 hour, 15 minutes

    3 chicken thighs
    4 teaspoons dry mustard
    ¼ cup cold water
    1 cup peanut oil
    2 ounces rice sticks, pulled apart slightly
    ½ teaspoon five-spice powder
    ½ teaspoon salt
    3 tablespoons soy sauce
    4 teaspoons sesame seed oil
    6 to 8 green onions including 2-inches of tops, cut in
      3-inch lengths, then cut lengthwise in thin strips

Put chicken on rack over boiling water in wok. Cover; steam 1 hour, adding boiling water if needed. Blend mustard with water; let stand 15 to 20 minutes. Heat oil in wok until hot. Add chicken thighs; fry until crisp, 5 to 8 minutes. Drain on paper towels; cool; cut meat in thin lengthwise strips. Add rice sticks to oil heated to 325°. Sticks will puff immediately; turn with tongs; cook 30 seconds on other side. Remove to paper towels to drain; place on platter. Blend five-spice powder, salt, soy sauce and sesame seed oil into mustard mixture. Add onions and chicken; toss to coat. Spoon mixture over rice sticks. Serve within 30 minutes.

Shredded Chicken Hunan-Style

Makes 4 servings
Preparation Time: 15 minutes; 3 to 4 minutes to cook

    ⅓ cup dry sherry
    ¼ teaspoon salt
    ¼ teaspoon sugar
    ¼ cup chicken stock
    4 green onions including tops, cut in ½-inch pieces
    2 ¼-inch slices fresh gingerroot, peeled and diced
    1 tablespoon cornstarch mixed with
      2 tablespoons cold water
    1 whole chicken breast, split, skinned, boned and cut
      in ⅛-inch-thick slices
    2 egg whites
    ½ teaspoon salt
    2 tablespoons dry sherry
    3 tablespoons cornstarch
    1½ cups peanut oil
    12 snow peas, ends and strings removed
    2 cups fresh bean sprouts

Mix ⅓ cup dry sherry and next 6 ingredients; set aside. Put chicken shreds in bowl with next 3 ingredients; mix with fork vigorously until chicken is coated. Add cornstarch; mix with fork until smooth. Heat oil in wok to 280°. Add chicken mixture; stir-fry 1 minute, breaking up chicken with spatula. Remove chicken with strainer; pour all but 1 tablespoon oil from wok; heat oil in wok until hot. Add snow peas and bean sprouts; stir-fry 15 seconds. Return chicken to wok; add sherry mixture; cook until sauce is thickened. Serve immediately.

Note: Slicing chicken is easier when chicken is partially frozen.

Chicken with Cashews and Snow Peas

Makes 2 servings
Preparation Time: 15 minutes; 5 minutes to cook

    1 whole chicken breast, split, skinned, boned and cut
      in 1-inch cubes
    2 cloves garlic, peeled and minced
    1 tablespoon soy sauce
    1 tablespoon dry sherry
    2 tablespoons cornstarch
    1 teaspoon hoisin sauce
    1 tablespoon peanut oil
    20 snow peas, ends and strings removed
    ½ cup sliced water chestnuts, drained
    ½ cup hot chicken stock
    ½ teaspoon salt
    ½ cup unsalted raw cashews

Marinate chicken 15 minutes in mixture of next 5 ingredients. Heat oil in wok until hot. Add chicken mixture; stir-fry 3 minutes. Add snow peas and water chestnuts; stir-fry 30 seconds. Add stock and salt; stir-fry until slightly thickened. Stir in cashews. Serve immediately.

Chicken Livers Chinese-Style

Makes 4 servings
Preparation Time: 10 minutes; 10 minutes to cook

    2 tablespoons soy sauce
    2 tablespoons water
    1 tablespoon cornstarch
    3 slices bacon
    1 pound chicken livers, fat trimmed, each cut in
      3 pieces
    4 green onions including tops, chopped
    1 medium green pepper, cored, seeded and chopped

Mix first 3 ingredients; set aside. Fry bacon in wok until crisp; drain; crumble; set aside. Brown livers and onions in fat in wok, about 3 minutes. Near end of browning, add green pepper. Stir soy mixture; add to wok. Stir until sauce thickens slightly. Stir in reserved bacon. Serve immediately.

Chicken with Cashews and Snow Peas,
this page

Chicken

Almond Chicken

Makes 4 servings
Preparation Time: 15 minutes; 7 minutes to cook

  2 tablespoons peanut oil
  1 whole chicken breast, split, skinned, boned and
    thinly sliced
  ½ cup sliced bamboo shoots, drained
  ½ teaspoon salt
  ½ cup sliced water chestnuts, drained
  ½ cup slivered almonds
  2 tablespoons soy sauce
  1 cup chicken stock
  3 tablespoons cornstarch mixed with
    ½ cup cold water

Heat oil in wok until hot. Add chicken; stir-fry 3 minutes or until chicken is opaque. Add next 6 ingredients; cover; cook 3 minutes. Stir cornstarch mixture; add to wok. Stir-fry until slightly thickened. Serve immediately.

Chicken Delicious

Makes 4 servings
Preparation Time: 20 minutes; 4 minutes to cook

  2 whole chicken breasts, split, skinned, boned and
    cut in 1-inch cubes
  1 tablespoon cornstarch
  1 tablespoon dry sherry
  1 tablespoon soy sauce
  2 tablespoons peanut oil
  ¼ pound fresh mushrooms, wiped clean and sliced
  1 green pepper, cored, seeded and
    cut in 1-inch pieces
  1 heaping tablespoon hoisin sauce
    Salt to taste
  ⅓ cup unsalted raw cashews

Sprinkle chicken with cornstarch; toss to coat thoroughly. Add sherry and soy sauce; marinate 15 minutes at room temperature. Heat oil in wok until hot. Add chicken; stir-fry 3 minutes. Add mushrooms and green pepper; stir-fry 45 seconds. Add remaining ingredients; toss to mix. Serve immediately.

Lemon Chicken

Makes 2 to 4 servings
Preparation Time: 40 minutes

  1 chicken
    Chicken stock
    Juice of 3 lemons
  ½ cup sugar
  ½ cup boiling water

Simmer chicken in chicken stock to cover in wok until nearly tender, about 20 minutes. Remove;

halve lengthwise; place on broiler rack. Broil 4 to 5 inches from heat 10 minutes; turn; broil another 10 minutes or until golden brown. Meanwhile, mix lemon juice, sugar and boiling water in saucepan. Bring to boil; simmer 2 to 3 minutes. Remove from heat; set aside. Arrange chicken halves on platter; spoon lemon sauce over chicken.

Chinese Chicken and Shrimp Salad

Makes 6 servings
Preparation Time: 20 minutes

    Peanut oil
  6 ounces rice sticks
  2 whole chicken breasts, cooked, skinned, boned and
    shredded
  ½ pound medium shrimp, shelled, deveined and
    cooked
  1 cup thinly sliced celery
  1 cup slivered almonds
  1 large zucchini, cut in 2-inch-long julienne strips
  1 head iceberg lettuce, shredded
  1 cup thinly sliced red radishes
  1 cup chopped green onions
    Dressing

Heat at least 1½ cups oil in wok to 375°. Drop rice sticks, 1 ounce at a time, into oil. After they puff (about 30 seconds), remove immediately. Do not brown. Drain on paper towels. Cool; store in airtight container until serving time. To serve, toss rice sticks, chicken, shrimp, celery, almonds and zucchini in bowl. Toss remaining ingredients except Dressing in large bowl; top with ingredients in other bowl; toss. Add desired amount of Dressing; toss. Serve immediately.

Dressing

Makes approximately 1¼ cups.

  2 tablespoons sesame oil
  ¼ cup peanut oil
  ½ cup cider vinegar
  ¼ cup soy sauce
  ½ teaspoon sugar
  1 teaspoon five-spice powder
  1 clove garlic, peeled and minced
  2 tablespoons toasted sesame seed

Place all ingredients in jar with tight-fitting lid; let stand at room temperature at least 1 hour to blend flavors. Shake before serving.

Steamed Chicken with Vegetables

Makes 4 servings
Preparation Time: 20 minutes; 45 minutes to cook

- 1 chicken, cut into serving pieces
- 2 unpeeled zucchini, cut in thick diagonal slices
- 2 large carrots, pared and cut in thick diagonal slices
- 2 potatoes, peeled and sliced diagonally
- 1 large rib celery, sliced diagonally
- 2 sprigs parsley
- ½ teaspoon dried tarragon
- 1 bay leaf
     Salt to taste
     Sauce

Place chicken pieces on steamer rack in wok. Top with next 7 ingredients. Season with salt. Cover; steam over hot water 45 minutes or until chicken and vegetables are tender. Remove bay leaf. Serve with Sauce.

Sauce

Makes approximately 1 cup

- 1 cup dry white wine *or* dry vermouth
- 1 shallot, peeled and minced
- 1 tablespoon unsalted butter
- 1 cup chicken stock
     Freshly ground white pepper to taste

Boil wine in wok until reduced by half. In another wok or saucepan, sauté shallot in butter 4 to 5 minutes over low to medium heat. Do not brown. Add to wok with stock; cook until reduced by one-third. Season with pepper.

Eight Delicious Chicken

Makes 4 servings
Preparation Time: 20 minutes; 10 minutes to cook

- 1½ cups peanut *or* vegetable oil
- 1 whole chicken breast, split, skinned, boned and cut into ½-inch cubes
- ½ cup small shelled shrimp
- 1 tablespoon peeled and diced fresh gingerroot
- 1 clove garlic, peeled and finely chopped
- ¼ cup sliced bamboo shoots, drained
- ¼ cup sliced water chestnuts, drained
- 6 canned Chinese baby corn, drained
- ½ cup button mushrooms
- 8 to 10 Chinese dried black mushrooms, soaked in hot water 20 minutes, drained, stems discarded, caps quartered
- 2 tablespoons dry sherry
- 1 tablespoon sugar
- 3 tablespoons soy sauce
- 2 teaspoons hoisin sauce
- ½ cup unsalted peanuts

Heat oil in wok to 325°. Add chicken; stir-fry 3 minutes. Add shrimp; stir-fry until pink. Remove chicken and shrimp with strainer; set aside. Drain all but 2 tablespoons oil from wok. (Oil can be reserved for future use.) Increase heat; add gingerroot and garlic; stir-fry 10 seconds. Add bamboo shoots, water chestnuts, baby corn, button and black mushrooms; stir-fry until vegetables are tender-crisp, about 3 minutes. Mix sherry, sugar, soy and hoisin sauce; pour over vegetables. Add chicken and shrimp; stir-fry 2 minutes. Add peanuts; stir. Serve immediately.

Crisp Chicken Salad

Makes 4 servings
Preparation Time: 20 minutes; 3 hours to marinate

- 2 whole chicken breasts, split, skinned and boned
- 1½ cups chicken stock
- ½ cup sliced green onions
- ½ cup sliced water chestnuts, drained
- ¼ cup sesame seed, lightly toasted
- ¼ pound snow peas, ends and strings removed, cut in julienne strips
     Dressing
     Salt and freshly ground black pepper to taste

Simmer chicken breasts in chicken stock 15 minutes. Let cool in broth; remove; cut meat in ¼-inch strips. Mix chicken, green onions, water chestnuts, sesame seed and snow peas in large bowl. Toss with enough Dressing to coat ingredients. Season with salt and pepper. Serve immediately.

Dressing

Makes 1 cup

- 1 ¼-inch slice fresh gingerroot, peeled
- 2 tablespoons dry sherry
- 1 egg yolk
- 1 tablespoon Dijon mustard
- 1½ teaspoons fresh lemon juice
- ½ cup peanut oil *or* ¼ cup peanut oil and ¼ cup olive oil
- 1 tablespoon soy sauce
     Salt and freshly ground white pepper to taste

Marinate gingerroot in sherry 3 hours. Beat yolk with mustard. Add lemon juice; beat to combine. Add oil in thin stream, whisking constantly until thickened and smooth. Remove gingerroot from sherry; add soy sauce, whisking constantly. Season with salt and pepper.

Fish and Seafood

Jade Fish

Makes 4 servings
Preparation Time: 15 minutes; 20 minutes to cook

    1 2-pound bass *or* red snapper, cleaned, head and tail
      intact *or* 1-inch-thick fillets
      Hot water
      Lettuce leaves
    ¼ cup peanut oil
   20 snow peas, ends and strings removed
    ½ pound sliced fresh mushrooms
   1½ cups fish stock
    5 green onions including tops, cut in
      1½-inch diagonal slices
    2 teaspoons soy sauce
    1 tablespoon oyster sauce
    ¼ teaspoon dried red pepper flakes, optional
    1 teaspoon vinegar
    ½ teaspoon salt
    ½ teaspoon sugar
    2 tablespoons cornstarch mixed with
      ¼ cup cold water

Put fish on rack in wok or in steamer basket. Add hot water; cover; steam 10 to 15 minutes or until fish is opaque. Meanwhile, line deep platter with lettuce leaves. Carefully lift fish from water using slotted spatula; place on lettuce. Clean wok. Heat oil in wok until hot. Add snow peas; stir-fry 30 seconds; remove with strainer; set aside. Add mushrooms; stir-fry 1 minute. Add next 8 ingredients; bring to boil. Stir cornstarch mixture; add to wok; stir until slightly thickened. Add snow peas; reheat. Arrange snow peas around fish; pour sauce over all. Serve immediately.

Oriental Scallops

Makes 6 servings
Preparation Time: 10 minutes; 5 minutes to cook

    ¼ cup cold water
    2 tablespoons cornstarch
    1 tablespoon soy sauce
    ½ teaspoon salt
    ⅛ teaspoon freshly ground white pepper
    2 tablespoons peanut oil
    2 pounds scallops, halved if large
   30 snow peas, ends and strings removed
    2 medium tomatoes, cored and each cut into
      6 wedges

Mix first 5 ingredients; set aside. Heat oil in wok until hot. Add scallops; stir-fry 2 to 3 minutes until opaque. Add snow peas and tomatoes; stir-fry 1 minute. Stir cornstarch mixture; add to wok. Stir until thickened. Serve immediately.

Poor Man's Lobster

Makes 6 servings
Preparation Time: 20 minutes

    2 pounds cod fillets
      Water
    1 teaspoon salt
    1 bay leaf
    1 small onion, peeled and sliced
    1 slice lemon
    ½ cup dry vermouth
      Hot melted butter
      Chopped fresh parsley

Place fish in wok. Cover with water and next 5 ingredients; bring to boil. Reduce heat; simmer 8 to 10 minutes or until fish is opaque. Carefully remove fish from wok with slotted spatula. Serve hot with melted butter and chopped parsley.

Shrimp and Vegetable Stir-Fry

Makes 6 servings
Preparation Time: 15 minutes; approximately 6 minutes to cook

    2 tablespoons peanut oil
    2 ¼-inch slices fresh gingerroot,
      peeled and minced
    1 clove garlic, peeled and finely chopped
   1½ cups small broccoli flowerets
   1½ cups thin diagonal carrot slices
    1 small onion, peeled and sliced into thin rings
    1 small green pepper *or* ½ green pepper and ½ red
      pepper, cored, seeded and cut vertically into thin
      1½-inch-long strips
    ¾ cup chicken stock
    1 teaspoon salt
    ½ pound large shrimp, shelled and deveined
    1 tablespoon cornstarch mixed with
      2 tablespoons cold water
    1 8-ounce can sliced water chestnuts, drained
    1 cup thinly sliced fresh mushrooms
    2 tablespoons oyster sauce

Heat oil in wok until hot. Add gingerroot and garlic; stir-fry 15 seconds. Add broccoli, carrots, onion and pepper; stir-fry 1 minute. Add chicken stock and salt; toss to combine; cover; cook until carrots are tender-crisp, 2 to 3 minutes. Uncover; add shrimp; stir-fry 1 minute or until pink. Stir cornstarch mixture; add to wok with remaining ingredients; stir-fry 30 to 45 seconds or until heated thoroughly. Serve immediately.

Fish and Seafood

Shrimp Egg Foo Yung

Makes 4 servings
Preparation Time: 5 minutes; 20 to 30 minutes to cook

  1 cup fresh bean sprouts
  ½ cup sliced water chestnuts, drained and chopped
  1 6¼-ounce can small shrimp, drained
  4 eggs, lightly beaten
  1 teaspoon salt
  ½ teaspoon freshly ground white pepper
  3 tablespoons peanut oil
    Sauce

Mix all ingredients except oil and Sauce in bowl. Heat 1 tablespoon oil in wok until hot. Pour ¼ of mixture into wok; form into round cake; brown on both sides. Remove; keep warm. Brown remaining cakes using remaining oil as needed. Serve immediately with Sauce.

Sauce

  1½ teaspoons packed light brown sugar
  ¼ cup boiling beef stock
  1 tablespoon cornstarch mixed with
    2 tablespoons cold water
  1 tablespoon soy sauce
  1 tablespoon dark molasses
    Pinch freshly ground black pepper

Dissolve brown sugar in beef stock in saucepan. Stir cornstarch mixture; add to saucepan with remaining ingredients; stir over moderate heat until thickened.

Shrimp in Bean Sauce

Makes 4 servings
Preparation Time: 15 minutes; 6 minutes to cook

  1 tablespoon dry sherry
  2 teaspoons peeled and minced fresh gingerroot
  1 tablespoon soy sauce
  ¼ teaspoon freshly ground white pepper
  1 pound large shrimp, shelled except for tail, deveined
  4 tablespoons peanut oil
  1 small onion, peeled, halved and sliced
  1 cup frozen tiny peas
  ½ small green pepper, cored, seeded and cut in
    ½-inch-long strips
  ½ small red pepper, cored, seeded and cut in
    ½-inch-long strips
  2 cloves garlic, peeled and minced
  2 tablespoons bean sauce
  2 teaspoons cornstarch mixed with
    2 tablespoons cold water

Mix first 4 ingredients; pour over shrimp; marinate 15 minutes; drain. Heat 2 tablespoons oil in wok until hot. Stir-fry next 4 ingredients 2 min-utes; remove with strainer; set aside. Add remaining 2 tablespoons oil; stir-fry garlic and bean sauce 10 seconds. Add shrimp; stir-fry until pink, about 2 minutes. Return vegetables to wok; stir cornstarch mixture; add to wok. Stir-fry until sauce thickens. Serve immediately.

Steamed Fish Chinois

Makes 4 servings
Preparation Time: 1 hour; 10 to 15 minutes to cook

  3 tablespoons soy sauce
  ½ cup dry sherry
  2 tablespoons fresh lemon juice
  1 clove garlic, peeled and crushed
  2 pounds halibut, salmon, haddock or cod fillets
    Water

Mix first 4 ingredients in shallow baking dish. Add fillets; marinate 1 hour. Heat water in wok until simmering. Place fillets in steamer basket or on steamer ring in 1 layer over simmering water. Cover; steam fish until opaque, 10 minutes per 1-inch thickness of fish. Serve immediately.

Fish and Snow Peas

Makes 4 servings
Preparation Time: 15 minutes; 4 minutes to cook

  1 pound cod fillets, cut in 1 x 3 x ½-inch pieces
  2 tablespoons cornstarch
  1 egg white, lightly beaten
  1 clove garlic, peeled and crushed
  1 green onion, thinly sliced
  ½ cup sliced water chestnuts, drained
  20 to 30 snow peas, ends and strings removed
  ¼ cup dry sherry
  1 teaspoon sugar
  ½ teaspoon salt
  ½ teaspoon sesame oil
  1 tablespoon cold water
  2 tablespoons peanut oil

Toss fish, 1 tablespoon cornstarch and egg white in bowl; set aside. Combine garlic and onion; set aside. Combine water chestnuts and snow peas; set aside. Mix next 5 ingredients with remaining 1 tablespoon cornstarch; set aside. Heat 1 table-spoon oil in wok until hot. Add garlic mixture; stir-fry 15 seconds. Add snow pea mixture; stir-fry 30 seconds; remove from wok using strainer; set aside. Heat remaining 1 tablespoon oil in wok until hot. Add fish; gently stir-fry 1 minute. Return vegetables to wok; stir-fry 15 seconds. Stir corn-starch mixture; add to wok. Stir gently until sauce thickens slightly. Serve immediately.

Stir-Fried Shrimp

Makes 4 servings
Preparation Time: 25 minutes; 4½ minutes to cook

- 2 ¼-inch slices fresh gingerroot, peeled
- 1 large clove garlic, peeled
- 2 tablespoons soy sauce
- 1 tablespoon dry sherry
- 2 tablespoons catsup
- 1 teaspoon sugar
  Pinch cayenne pepper
- 2 tablespoons peanut oil
- 1 pound raw shrimp, shelled, deveined and patted dry
- 2 green onions including tops, cut diagonally in 1-inch pieces

Crush gingerroot and garlic together; set aside. Mix next 5 ingredients; set aside. Heat oil in wok until hot. Add gingerroot and garlic; stir-fry 10 seconds. Add shrimp; stir-fry 3 minutes or until pink. Add green onion; stir-fry 30 seconds. Add soy sauce mixture; stir-fry 30 seconds. Serve immediately.

Note: For hotter taste, use ⅛ teaspoon cayenne pepper.

Stir-Fried Smelt with Sauce

Makes 4 servings
Preparation Time: 20 minutes; 15 to 20 minutes to cook

- 1½ pounds smelts, heads, tails and fins removed
  Salt and freshly ground black pepper to taste
- 3 tablespoons fresh lemon juice
- ¼ cup milk
- 1 tablespoon peanut oil
- ½ cup flour
- 1 cup peanut oil
- 4 anchovy fillets, mashed
- 1 tablespoon bread crumbs
- 1 tablespoon chopped fresh parsley

Lay smelts in 1 layer on counter. Season with salt and pepper. Sprinkle with 2 tablespoons lemon juice. Mix milk and 1 tablespoon oil. Dip smelts, one at a time, into milk mixture, then into flour to coat well; set aside. Heat oil in wok until hot. Fry smelts on both sides until brown and crisp; remove with strainer to warm platter; keep warm. Pour all but 1 teaspoon oil from wok. Add remaining 1 tablespoon lemon juice and remaining ingredients to wok. Stir-fry 30 seconds to heat sauce; pour over warm fish. Serve immediately.

Spicy Shrimp

Makes 3 servings
Preparation Time: 10 minutes; 3 minutes to cook

- ½ teaspoon soy sauce
- ½ teaspoon sugar
- ½ teaspoon ground coriander
- ½ cup chicken stock
- 1 pound shrimp, shelled and deveined
- 1 teaspoon dry sherry
- 1 egg white, lightly beaten
- 1½ teaspoons cornstarch
- 2 tablespoons peanut oil
- ½ teaspoon dried red pepper flakes
- ½ cup thin diagonal celery slices
- 8 Chinese dried black mushrooms, soaked in ½ cup hot water 20 minutes, drained, stems discarded, caps cut in thin strips
- 1 teaspoon cornstarch mixed with 1 teaspoon cold water

Mix first 4 ingredients; set aside. Put next 4 ingredients in bowl; toss to coat. Heat oil in wok until hot; add pepper; stir-fry 30 seconds. Add shrimp; stir-fry 1 minute. Add celery and mushrooms; stir-fry 1 minute. Add soy sauce mixture; stir-fry 30 seconds. Add cornstarch mixture; stir until slightly thickened. Serve immediately.

Steamed Bass

Makes 4 servings
Preparation Time: 10 minutes; 20 minutes to cook

- 1 sea bass *or* striped bass (about 3 pounds cleaned) with head and tail intact
- 1 tablespoon salt
  Water
- 1 tablespoon peanut oil
- 2 ¼-inch slices fresh gingerroot, peeled and minced
- 4 small cloves garlic, peeled and crushed
- 3 green onions including tops, cut in 1-inch pieces
- 2 tablespoons dry sherry
- ¼ cup soy sauce
- 1 teaspoon sesame oil

Rinse and pat fish dry; sprinkle with salt. Place fish on heatproof plate. Place plate on rack inside wok, or place fish in steamer basket. Add enough water to wok around plate or steamer basket to come within ½ inch of plate or basket. Bring water to boil. Meanwhile, heat oil in another wok until hot. Add next 4 ingredients; stir-fry 30 seconds. Add remaining ingredients; stir. Pour over fish; cover wok or put top on steamer basket. Let water boil 15 minutes or until fish is steamed to desired doneness. Serve immediately.

Fish and Seafood

Kung Pao Scallops

Makes 4 servings
Preparation Time: 50 minutes; 5 minutes to cook

    1 pound scallops
    1 egg white, lightly beaten
    1 tablespoon cornstarch
    1 tablespoon dry sherry
    2 tablespoons soy sauce
 1½ teaspoons hot bean sauce
 1½ teaspoons sugar
 1½ teaspoons vinegar
    1 teaspoon dry sherry
    2 cups peanut oil
    2 teaspoons peeled and minced fresh gingerroot
    1 clove garlic, peeled and minced
    4 green onions including tops, thinly sliced
   10 water chestnuts, halved
   20 snow peas, ends and strings removed
    ½ cup unsalted roasted peanuts
    1 teaspoon cornstarch mixed with
       3 tablespoons chicken stock *or* water

Mix first 4 ingredients; set aside to marinate 30 minutes. Mix next 5 ingredients; set aside. Heat oil in wok until hot. Add scallops; stir-fry 1 minute. Remove with strainer; let drain in colander. Remove all but 1 teaspoon oil from wok. Heat oil in wok until hot. Add next 3 ingredients; stir-fry 30 seconds. Add next 3 ingredients; stir-fry 10 seconds. Add scallops with reserved soy sauce mixture; toss to combine. Stir cornstarch mixture; add to wok; stir-fry until thickened. Serve immediately.

Walnut Shrimp

Makes 4 servings
Preparation Time: 10 minutes; 7 minutes to cook

    1 pound medium shrimp, shelled, deveined,
       cut in thirds
    2 teaspoons soy sauce
    2 teaspoons dry sherry
    ¼ teaspoon freshly ground white pepper
    1 teaspoon cornstarch
    3 tablespoons peanut oil
    ½ cup sliced bamboo shoots, drained
    ½ cup walnuts
    1 ¼-inch slice fresh gingerroot, peeled
    2 green onions including tops, sliced diagonally in
       1-inch pieces
    1 teaspoon salt
    ½ teaspoon sesame oil

Toss first 5 ingredients and 1 tablespoon oil in bowl; set aside. Heat 1 tablespoon oil in wok until hot. Add bamboo shoots and walnuts; stir-fry 1 minute; set aside. Wipe out wok with paper towels. Heat remaining 1 tablespoon oil in wok. Swirl gingerroot slice around wok 30 seconds; discard.

Add onions and shrimp mixture; stir-fry 2 minutes. Add bamboo shoots and walnuts; stir to combine. Add salt and sesame oil; stir to combine. Serve immediately.

Crab Stir-Fry with Cashews

Makes 4 servings
Preparation Time: 15 minutes; 5 minutes to cook

    1 tablespoon cornstarch
    1 tablespoon soy sauce
    1 tablespoon fresh lemon juice
    ¾ cup chicken stock
    2 tablespoons peanut oil
    ¼ pound fresh mushrooms, wiped clean and
       thinly sliced
    1 6-ounce can crab meat, drained
    4 green onions including tops, cut in
       thin diagonal slices
    ¼ cup sliced water chestnuts, drained
   20 snow peas, ends and strings removed
    ⅓ cup unsalted cashews

Mix first 4 ingredients; set aside. Heat oil in wok until hot. Add mushrooms; stir-fry 1 minute. Add next 3 ingredients; stir-fry 1 minute. Add snow peas; stir-fry 1 minute. Stir cornstarch mixture; add to wok; stir-fry until slightly thickened. Add nuts; toss to combine. Serve immediately.

Fried Squid

Makes 6 servings
Preparation Time: 20 minutes; 15 to 20 minutes to cook

    3 pounds squid
    3 tablespoons fresh lemon juice
 1½ teaspoons salt
    ⅛ teaspoon freshly ground white pepper
    2 eggs, lightly beaten
    3 tablespoons milk
 1½ cups flour
       Peanut oil
       Lemon wedges

Cut through squid just behind eyes; squeeze out inedible beak located near cut; reserve tentacles. Feel inside body for internal shell; grasp firmly; remove from body. Rinse under cold water; peel off speckled membrane that covers body; drain body. Cut body crosswise into ½-inch rings. Cut tentacles in 1-inch pieces. Sprinkle pieces with lemon juice, salt and pepper. Mix egg and milk. Dip squid pieces in egg mixture; dredge in flour. Heat oil in wok to 350°. Fry squid pieces 3 to 5 minutes on 1 side; turn; fry 3 to 5 minutes on other side or until lightly browned. Remove using strainer; drain on paper towels. Serve immediately with lemon wedges.

Kung Pao Scallops, this page

Fish and Seafood

Sweet and Sour Salmon

Makes 4 servings
Preparation Time: 15 minutes; 40 minutes to cook

- 1½ cups water
- 1 carrot, pared and thinly sliced
- 1 tablespoon peanut oil
- 1 onion, peeled and thinly sliced
- 1 teaspoon fresh lemon juice
- 2 tablespoons sugar
- ½ cup vinegar
- 10 whole peppercorns
- 2 ribs celery, cut in 4-inch pieces
- 3 whole cloves
- 2 pounds salmon steaks, each 1-inch thick
- ⅓ to ½ cup vinegar
- 10 gingersnaps, crumbled
- ¾ cup packed light brown sugar
- ¼ cup seedless raisins
- ¼ cup dry sherry
- ¼ cup slivered almonds

Mix first 7 ingredients in wok. Tie peppercorns, celery and cloves in cheesecloth bag; add to wok. Bring to boil; reduce heat; simmer 20 minutes. Add salmon steaks; poach gently 10 minutes. Remove steaks with slotted spatula to warm serving platter; keep warm. Remove cheesecloth bag from wok. Pour enough vinegar over gingersnap crumbs to dissolve them. Add to liquid in wok with next 3 ingredients; boil 4 minutes. Add almonds; pour over fish. Serve immediately.

Sweet and Sour Shrimp

Makes 4 servings
Preparation Time: 15 minutes; 9 minutes to cook

- ½ cup flour
- 2 tablespoons cornstarch
- ½ teaspoon baking powder
- ½ teaspoon salt
- 1 egg
- 1½ cups water
- 1 cup plus 2 teaspoons peanut oil
- 16 large shrimp, shelled except for tail portion, deveined
- ½ cup catsup
- 2 tablespoons white vinegar
- 3 tablespoons sugar
- 1 large green pepper, cored, seeded and cut in 1-inch chunks
- 1 large onion, peeled, cut in eighths, separated into pieces
- 1 15½-ounce can pineapple chunks, drained
- 2 teaspoons cornstarch mixed with 2 teaspoons cold water

Mix flour, cornstarch, baking powder, salt, egg, ½ cup water and 1 teaspoon oil in bowl until smooth;

set aside. Heat 1 cup oil in wok until hot. Holding shrimp by tail, dip one at a time into batter, letting excess drip back into bowl. Slide shrimp into hot oil; fry until golden brown, 1 to 2 minutes each. Fry two or three at a time. Drain on paper towels. Pour out all oil except 1 tablespoon. Add remaining 1 cup water, 1 teaspoon oil, catsup, vinegar and sugar to wok; bring to boil. Add green pepper and onion; return to boil. Stir-fry 2 minutes. Add pineapple; return to boil. Stir cornstarch mixture; add to wok; stir to thicken. Add shrimp; stir gently until heated through. Serve immediately.

Shrimp and Lobster Stir-Fry

Makes 6 servings
Preparation Time: 20 minutes; 8½ minutes to cook

- 2 tablespoons peanut oil
- 2 cloves garlic, peeled and finely chopped
- 2 ¼-inch slices fresh gingerroot, peeled and minced
- 3 green onions including tops, thinly sliced
- 1 8-ounce can sliced water chestnuts, drained
- 1 8-ounce can sliced bamboo shoots, drained
- ¼ pound fresh mushrooms, wiped clean, thinly sliced
- ¾ pound large shrimp, shelled except for tail, deveined and patted dry
- ¾ pound lobster tails, thin undershells cut away, meat and shells cut crosswise in segments
- ⅓ pound snow peas, ends and strings removed
- 1½ cups chicken stock
- 2 tablespoons cornstarch
- 2 tablespoons soy sauce
- 1 teaspoon salt
- 1 teaspoon sugar
- ¼ teaspoon freshly ground white pepper

Heat oil in wok until hot. Add next 3 ingredients; stir-fry 1 minute. Add next 3 ingredients; stir-fry 2 minutes. Add next 3 ingredients; stir-fry 2 minutes. Add ¾ cup chicken stock; cover; cook 1 minute. Mix remaining ¾ cup chicken stock with remaining ingredients; add to wok; stir-fry until slightly thickened, about 30 seconds. Cover; cook 1 minute. Serve immediately.

Note: Shell is left on tail of shrimp and on lobster segments because it adds flavor. Meat of both shellfish can be removed easily with fork. Use the lobster meat in body, legs and claws for salads.

International Dishes

Brandied Beef

Makes 6 servings
Preparation Time: 1 hour, 45 minutes

  1 teaspoon salt
  1 teaspoon paprika
  ½ teaspoon dried basil
  ¼ teaspoon dried thyme
  2 tablespoons flour
  2 pounds beef stew meat
  2 tablespoons peanut oil
  1 clove garlic, peeled and crushed
  1 large onion, peeled and cut in 8 wedges
  ½ cup beef stock
  ½ cup brandy
  2 cups fresh mushrooms, wiped clean and
    halved if large
    Hot buttered cooked egg noodles

Mix first 5 ingredients. Lightly dredge meat in flour mixture. Heat oil in wok until hot. Brown meat in batches, removing to plate. Add garlic and onion; stir-fry 30 seconds. Return meat to wok with stock and brandy. Reduce heat to medium; cover; simmer 1 hour. Add mushrooms; stir; cook 10 minutes, covered. Serve immediately with buttered egg noodles.

Chicken Cacciatore

Makes 6 servings
Preparation Time: 1 hour, 30 minutes

  ¼ cup peanut oil
  2 chickens, cut into serving pieces and patted dry
  2 onions, peeled and chopped
  1 green pepper, cored, seeded and chopped
  1 red pepper, cored, seeded and chopped
  3 cloves garlic, peeled and crushed
  1½ cups tomato puree
  ¼ cup dry red wine
  1½ teaspoons salt
  ¼ teaspoon freshly ground black pepper
  ¼ teaspoon ground allspice
  3 tablespoons tomato paste
  1 teaspoon dried oregano
  1 teaspoon dried basil
    Hot cooked spinach noodles

Heat oil in wok until hot. Brown chicken pieces on both sides, a few at a time; place on plate. Add onions, peppers and garlic; stir-fry 2 minutes. Add remaining ingredients except chicken and noodles; bring to boil; simmer 10 minutes. Return chicken to wok; simmer, covered, 15 to 20 minutes. Uncover; simmer 10 minutes. Serve immediately with spinach noodles.

Portuguese Codfish

Makes 4 servings
Preparation Time: 1 hour; overnight to soak fish

  1 pound dried codfish, soaked overnight in cold
    water, drained
    Water
  3 potatoes
  ¼ cup peanut oil
  2 large onions, peeled and sliced
  1 clove garlic, peeled and crushed
  ¼ cup finely chopped ripe olives
  ½ teaspoon dried dillweed
  ⅓ cup dry vermouth
    Freshly ground black pepper to taste
    Fresh parsley, chopped

Place fish in wok; cover with cold water; bring to boil; boil 20 minutes or until fish is opaque. Remove; set aside to cool; remove skin and bones if necessary. Cook potatoes in same water in wok until tender; remove; discard water. Peel and slice potatoes; set aside. Heat oil in clean wok; add onions; stir-fry until limp but not brown. Add fish, potatoes and next 5 ingredients. Gently stir-fry 3 minutes. Cover; cook on low heat 10 to 15 minutes. Garnish with parsley. Serve immediately.

Veal and Mushrooms

Makes 4 to 6 servings
Preparation Time: 1¼ hours

  2 tablespoons peanut oil
  2 pounds lean veal, cut in 1½-inch cubes
  ¾ pound fresh mushrooms, sliced
  2 tablespoons flour
  1½ cups chicken stock
    Salt and freshly ground black pepper to taste
  ⅓ cup dry vermouth
  2 tablespoons chopped fresh parsley
    Hot cooked rice or noodles

Heat oil in wok until hot. Sear veal cubes in batches over medium heat; do not crowd; remove to bowl. Return veal to wok with mushrooms; stir-fry 3 minutes. Sprinkle with flour; toss to combine. Reduce heat; add stock and salt and pepper; mix well. Cover; simmer 50 minutes or until meat is tender. Add vermouth; toss. Sprinkle with parsley. Serve immediately on rice.

Ratatouille

Makes 6 servings
Preparation Time: 30 minutes; 10 to 12 minutes
to cook

    1 unpeeled large eggplant, cubed
    2 tablespoons olive oil
    3 tomatoes, cored, peeled, seeded and chopped
    3 unpeeled zucchini, thinly sliced
    2 onions, peeled and diced
    1 clove garlic, peeled and crushed
    2 tablespoons chopped fresh parsley

Place eggplant cubes in colander; sprinkle generously with salt. Let stand 30 minutes; rinse under cold running water; spread out cubes on towel and pat dry. Heat oil in wok until hot. Add all ingredients except parsley; stir-fry until vegetables are soft but not browned. Stir in parsley. Serve immediately.

Continental Calves' Liver

Makes 4 servings
Preparation Time: 20 minutes

    1 pound calves' liver, skinned, sliced 1½-inch-thick
      and cut in 1-inch pieces
      Salt and freshly ground black pepper to taste
    ¼ cup flour
    ¼ cup peanut oil
    2 medium onions, peeled and thinly sliced
    ½ cup dry vermouth
    2 tablespoons tomato puree
    2 tablespoons chopped fresh parsley

Sprinkle liver with salt and pepper; lightly dredge in flour. Heat oil in wok until hot. Add onion; stir-fry until limp but not brown. Increase heat; add liver; stir-fry 3 to 4 minutes. Drain off excess oil from wok. Add vermouth and puree; toss to mix. Cook 2 to 3 minutes. Sprinkle with parsley; serve immediately.

Italian Shrimp and Vegetables

Makes 4 servings
Preparation Time: 15 minutes; 10 minutes to cook

    2 tablespoons peanut oil
    1 pound large shrimp, shelled and deveined
    1 pound unpeeled zucchini, thinly sliced
    1 large onion, peeled and thinly sliced
    2 cloves garlic, peeled and crushed
    ¼ cup minced fresh parsley
    1 teaspoon salt
    ¼ teaspoon freshly ground black pepper
    1½ teaspoons fresh lemon juice
    ¼ cup freshly grated Parmesan cheese

Heat oil in wok until hot. Add shrimp; stir-fry 3

minutes or until pink; remove with strainer. Add zucchini, onion and garlic; stir-fry until tender-crisp. Add next 3 ingredients and shrimp. Cover; simmer 2 minutes. Uncover; sprinkle with lemon juice and cheese. Toss to combine thoroughly. Serve immediately.

Favorite Chili

Makes 4 servings
Preparation Time: 5 minutes; 2 to 3 hours to cook

    1 pound coarsely ground lean beef
    1 large clove garlic, peeled and crushed
    2 tablespoons flour
    1 teaspoon ground cumin
    1 to 2 tablespoons chili powder
    ½ teaspoon salt
    ¼ teaspoon freshly ground black pepper
    1½ cups vegetable cocktail juice
    ½ teaspoon Worcestershire sauce
    1 15-ounce can red kidney beans, drained, optional

Stir-fry meat and garlic in wok over medium heat until meat is browned and crumbled. Add flour; stir to blend. Add next 6 ingredients; bring to boil. Reduce heat to low; cover; cook 2 to 3 hours, stirring occasionally. Mixture should not cook dry; reduce heat and add more vegetable juice if needed. Add beans 1 hour before end of cooking time, if desired. Serve immediately.

Note: This freezes well.

Greek Lamb Stew

Makes 6 servings
Preparation Time: 20 minutes; 1½ hours to cook

    2 tablespoons peanut oil
    2 pounds boned, cubed lean lamb
      Salt and freshly ground black pepper to taste
    3 small onions, peeled and chopped
    2 ribs celery, chopped
    3 carrots, pared and thinly sliced
    2 small cloves garlic, peeled and crushed
    2 cups water
    4 eggs, separated
    ¼ cup fresh lemon juice

Heat oil in wok until hot. Brown meat in batches; season with salt and pepper. Reduce heat; add onion; stir-fry until translucent. Return meat to wok with next 4 ingredients; simmer, covered, 1 hour or until meat is tender. Add more water if needed. Remove from heat; skim off any fat. Beat egg whites until they hold peaks; gradually beat in yolks. Slowly add lemon juice, beating constantly. Pour over stew; stir to combine and heat thoroughly. Serve immediately.

Desserts

Custard with Oriental Sauce

Makes 6 servings
Preparation Time: 10 minutes; 30 to 40 minutes to bake; 3 to 4 hours to chill

     3 eggs
     3 tablespoons sugar
  ⅛ teaspoon salt
  ¼ teaspoon almond extract
  ½ teaspoon vanilla extract
2¼ cups scalded milk
     Oriental Fruit

Preheat oven to 350°. Beat eggs, sugar, salt, almond and vanilla extracts together in bowl. Gradually add milk, stirring constantly. Divide equally among 6 custard cups. Place cups in large shallow pan; fill pan with boiling water that reaches to level of custard in cups. Bake 30 to 40 minutes or until knife inserted in center of custard comes out clean. Cool at room temperature 10 minutes; cover; chill thoroughly. Prepare Oriental Fruit. To serve, run knife around outside edges of custards; invert onto serving dishes; top with Oriental Fruit.

Oriental Fruit

  ⅓ cup sugar
  1 tablespoon cornstarch
  1 cup fresh orange juice
  1 11-ounce can mandarin orange segments, drained
  1 11-ounce can litchi nuts, drained

Stir sugar and cornstarch together in 2-quart saucepan. Place over low heat; gradually add orange juice, stirring constantly. Bring to boil, stirring constantly until thickened. Remove from heat; stir in orange segments and nuts. Cover and chill.

Fresh Pineapple with Grand Marnier

Makes 4 servings
Preparation Time: 15 minutes

  1 large pineapple
  ¼ cup Grand Marnier

Cut pineapple in half lengthwise through top crown. Cut halves lengthwise, making 4 wedges. With sharp knife, cut out core that runs length of each wedge. Cut pineapple from shell in 1 piece; cut into bite-size pieces; pile back onto shell. Repeat with remaining pineapple wedges. Pour 1 tablespoon Grand Marnier over each serving; serve immediately.

Note: Pineapple can be cut, wrapped in plastic wrap and refrigerated 4 to 6 hours in advance; pour on Grand Marnier just before serving.

Fortune Cookies

Makes 48
Preparation Time: 15 minutes; 10 minutes to bake

     5 to 6 egg whites (¾ cup)
1⅔ cups sugar
  ¼ teaspoon salt
  1 cup unsalted butter, melted
  1 cup flour
  ¾ cup very finely chopped blanched almonds
  ½ teaspoon vanilla
  48 fortunes written on 3 x ¾-inch strips of paper

Preheat oven to 350°. Mix first 3 ingredients in bowl until sugar dissolves. Stir in remaining ingredients, one at a time, until well blended. Drop dough by level teaspoonfuls onto ungreased baking sheet; allow 6 cookies per sheet, spacing well apart. Bake 10 minutes or until edges are golden brown. Remove cookies, one at a time, from baking sheet. Place 1 fortune in center of each cookie; fold cookie in half; pinch sides together. Work quickly before cookies cool and harden.

Almond Custard with Mandarin Oranges

Makes 6 to 9 servings
Preparation Time: 10 minutes; overnight to chill

  2 cups water
  1 stick (about ¼ ounce) agar-agar, cut in small pieces
  1 cup evaporated milk
  ⅓ cup sugar
  1 tablespoon almond extract
  1 11-ounce can mandarin orange segments, drained

Bring 1 cup water to boil in saucepan; add agar-agar; stir until dissolved, about 3 minutes. Add milk and sugar; return to boil. Boil 1 minute, stirring constantly. Add extract and remaining 1 cup hot water. Cook, stirring constantly, until mixture returns to boil. Strain into 9-inch square glass pan. Cool at room temperature; cover with plastic wrap; refrigerate overnight to set. To serve, cut into 1-inch cubes; divide among 6 to 9 bowls; top with orange segments. Serve immediately.

Hong Kong Sundae

Makes enough sauce for 6 to 8 servings
Preparation Time: 10 minutes; 3 to 4 hours to chill

    1 8½-ounce can crushed pineapple with juice
    2 tablespoons cornstarch
    1 11-ounce can mandarin orange segments with liquid
    6 to 8 preserved kumquats, drained and chopped
    2 tablespoons chopped preserved ginger
      Vanilla ice cream

Mix 2 tablespoons of the pineapple juice with cornstarch; set aside. Place pineapple and remaining juice, orange segments and liquid, kumquats and ginger in top of double boiler over medium heat. Heat to just below boiling. Stir cornstarch mixture; add to double boiler. Stir until thickened. Pour into bowl; refrigerate until completely cold. Serve as sauce over ice cream.

Note: This sauce can be made several days in advance.

Melon Balls in Liqueur

Makes 3 servings
Preparation Time: 30 minutes plus chilling time

    ½ cup watermelon balls, seeds removed
    ½ cup honeydew melon balls
    ½ cup cantaloupe melon balls
    3 tablespoons melon-flavored liqueur

Mix melon balls gently in glass bowl; chill thoroughly. To serve, divide melon balls equally among 3 glass serving bowls; drizzle 1 tablespoon liqueur over each bowl. Serve immediately.

Red Wine Oranges

Makes 6 servings
Preparation Time: 10 minutes; 3 to 4 hours to chill

    ¾ cup sugar
    1 cup water
    1 cup dry red wine
    5 whole cloves
    2 cinnamon sticks
    4 strips lemon peel
    6 large naval oranges, peeled and sectioned

Mix first 6 ingredients in wok; bring to boil. Lower heat; simmer 10 minutes to make light syrup. Strain to remove cloves, cinnamon sticks and lemon peel. Pour over oranges in bowl; refrigerate until completely chilled.

Almond Cookies

Makes 4 dozen
Preparation Time: 15 minutes; 20 minutes to bake

    1 cup sugar
    1⅓ cups shortening
    1 egg
    1 teaspoon almond extract
    3 cups flour
    1 teaspoon baking soda
    ½ teaspoon salt
    48 blanched whole almonds

Preheat oven to 350°. Cream butter and shortening until fluffy. Add egg and almond extract; beat 1 minute. Sift flour, baking soda and salt together; add to creamed mixture gradually, beating constantly. Roll dough into 1-inch balls; place 1 inch apart on greased baking sheet. Press center of each ball down gently; fill depression with 1 almond. Bake 20 minutes. Remove to wire rack to cool.

Note: Cookies can be frozen.

Fruit Stir-Fry

Makes 4 servings
Preparation Time: 15 minutes; 10 to 15 minutes to cook

    2 firm pears (preferably Bosc), peeled, cored and cut in crosswise slices
    3 cups semidry white wine (such as Riesling)
      Pinch salt
    12 strawberries, hulled and cut in crosswise slices
    2 ripe mangoes, peeled and sectioned
    1 kiwi fruit, peeled and sliced
    3 tablespoons unsalted butter
    1 pint raspberries, rinsed gently

Combine pears, wine and salt in wok; simmer 2 to 3 minutes or until pears are just tender. Add strawberries; simmer 1 minute. Add mangoes; simmer 1 minute. Add kiwi fruit; simmer 1 minute. Fruit should be tender, but not falling apart. Carefully remove fruit with strainer; keep warm. Boil liquid in wok over highest heat to reduce by one-half. Lower heat; swirl in butter. Return cooked fruit to sauce. Add raspberries; mix gently just until raspberries are warmed through. Remove fruit to individual bowls using strainer; boil sauce further if it seems too thin. Spoon sauce over fruit.

Note: This makes a luscious sauce for vanilla ice cream.

Bamboo Shoots Young shoots of tropical bamboo. Sold whole or sliced in cans. After opening, rinse in cold water. Store in water in refrigerator up to 1 week. Change water every 2 days.

Bean Curd Also known as tofu. A nutritious, low-calorie source of protein. Made of pressed pureed soybeans formed into cakes. It is white and has the consistency of firm custard. Bland in taste, it absorbs the flavor of other ingredients. Can be fried, simmered, baked, steamed, or used in stir-frying. Store in water in refrigerator up to 1 week. Change water daily.

Bean Sauce* Made of soybeans, flour, salt and water. Hot bean sauce is a more spicy version used in Szechwan dishes. After opening, refrigerate in tightly covered jar. Keeps indefinitely.

Bean Sprouts Tiny sprouts that are white, sweet, plump and crunchy. Fresh sprouts are preferable to canned sprouts. Rinse in cold water before using. Store in water in refrigerator up to 1 week. Change water daily.

Black Beans* Salted and fermented, these beans season fish and meat dishes. Store in tightly covered container indefinitely.

Bok Choy Green vegetable with long white stalks and ruffled leaves. Store in plastic wrap in refrigerator up to 1 week.

Cellophane Noodles* Also known as bean thread or vermicelli. Made of mung bean flour and look as if they are made from cellophane. Must be presoaked if used in soups; not necessary to presoak for deep-frying. Keep indefinitely.

Chicken Stock Interchangeable with canned chicken broth although homemade chicken stock is preferable.

Dried Orange or Tangerine Peel* Used for flavoring meat and poultry. Keeps indefinitely.

Dried Red Pepper Flakes* Made from dried orange or red hot peppers. Include seed which are essential for hotness. Keep indefinitely.

Ears of Baby Corn Tiny ears of corn, 2 to 3 inches long, sold in cans. Store in liquid in covered can in refrigerator up to 6 days.

Egg Roll Skins Squares of egg noodle dough in which to place filling. Store in refrigerator up to 5 days. May be frozen.

Five-Spice Powder* Combination of 5 ground spices—cinnamon, fennel, star anise, cloves and Szechwan peppercorns. Used for stewing and barbecuing meats. Reddish brown in color. Keeps indefinitely.

Garlic Do not substitute garlic powder. Never burn garlic while cooking, or it will impart bitter taste. Store in dry place.

Ginger, preserved* Used in sweet and sour dishes for color and flavoring. Store in tightly covered jar in refrigerator. Keeps indefinitely.

Gingerroot, fresh Very important seasoning in stir-fry cooking. There is no substitute. Sold by the piece or by weight, fresh gingerroot is knobby in appearance. Always peel before using. Wrap in plastic; keep at room temperature 2 to 3 weeks. Never refrigerate. Can be peeled, sliced and frozen; do not thaw before using.

Green Onion Also called scallion. Long, thin onion with white and green part.

Hoisin Sauce* Spicy reddish-brown sauce with creamy consistency, made of Chinese pumpkin, sugar, spices and soy sauce. After opening, store in covered jar several weeks.

Lychee* Subtropical fruit. Delicious in sweet and sour sauce. Used in desserts. Store in tightly covered jar in refrigerator several days.

Mushrooms, Chinese Dried Black* Rinse and soak in hot water 20 minutes before using. Use caps, discard tough stems. Keep indefinitely.

Mushrooms, Cloud Ear* Also known as tree ears or fungus mushrooms. Black and crinkled, they expand two to three times their dried size when soaked. Soft in texture, subtle in taste. Must be soaked in hot water before using. Cook with vegetables, chicken, meat or soup.

Mushrooms, Straw* Delicious with crab meat. After opening, refrigerate, covered with water, in jar. Change water every 2 days. Keep several weeks.

Mustard, Chinese Used for dipping sauce. Make in small amounts; mix powdered or dry mustard with cold water and allow to mellow 30 minutes to remove harsh, bitter taste. Hot and pungent. Keeps indefinitely.

Oyster Sauce* Thick Cantonese sauce made from oyster extract, but has no fishy taste or odor. Adds flavor to meat, poultry and noodles. Store covered in refrigerator

Peanut Oil Preferred for stir-frying. Can be reused if strained and refrigerated. Discard when dark and full of residue. Oil for cooking fish should be kept separate and reused only for fish. Refrigerate after use.

Plum Sauce* Made of plums, ginger, apricots, chilies, vinegar, sugar and water. Used as condiment. Store in covered container in refrigerator a few months.

Rice, glutinous* Also known as sweet rice. Round grains that become soft and sticky when cooked. Used for making dumplings, sweet dishes and poultry stuffing.

Rice Sticks Also called rice noodles. White, thin, fragile and slightly wavy, these sticks are made from ground rice. Used deep-fried and in soups. Store on shelf indefinitely.

Sesame Seed Oil* Reddish brown, made from roasted sesame seed. Generally used as seasoning; the thicker the oil, the better the flavor. Keeps indefinitely.

Snow Peas Also known as pea pods. Flat, light green, crisp and sweet. Always select thin snow peas. Avoid frozen pea pods because they give up too much moisture in stir-fried dishes. Remove ends and strings. Slice through stem end, but do not sever string. Pull stem end and attached string down pod. Repeat on opposite end for other string. Usually left whole for cooking and eating. Store in refrigerator 1 to 3 days.

Soy Sauce One of the most important seasonings in stir-fry cookery. There are two kinds. Thin soy sauce has a clear brown color and a beanlike aroma. Use it for delicate dishes. Dark soy sauce is very dark in color, has a sheen and is slightly thicker than light soy sauce. Dark soy sauce is slightly sweet and the bean aroma is muted. Store on shelf indefinitely.

Star Anise* Reddish-brown Chinese spice resembling 8-pointed star. Smells like licorice. Flavors meat and poultry. Store in covered jar indefinitely.

Tofu See bean curd.

Water Chestnuts Used as vegetable with meat and poultry. Delicious with snow peas. Sold whole or sliced in cans. After opening, cover with water and refrigerate. Change water twice a week. Keeps several weeks.

Wine, Chinese Rice wine fortified to the strength of sherry. Use dry sherry as substitute, but never cooking sherry.

Won Ton Skins Small squares or rounds of egg noodle dough in which fillings are placed. Sold in 1-pound packages. Keep refrigerated 1 week. Can be frozen.

*denotes items found in Oriental and/or specialty food stores

Clockwise, from top:
Almond Cookies, page 61
Fruit Stir-Fry, page 61
Melon Balls in Liqueur, page 61

Index

Taste of
ISRAEL
A MEDITERRANEAN FEAST

AVI GANOR   RON MAIBERG

with Zachi Bukshester and Kenneth R Windsor

Galahad Books

New York

Published in 1993 by

Galahad Books
A division of Budget Book Service, Inc.
386 Park Avenue South
New York, NY 10016

Galahad Books is a registered trademark of Budget Book Service, Inc.

Published by arrangement with Multimedia Books Limited.

Photography & Art Direction   *Avi Ganor*
Text & Recipes   *Ron Maiberg*
Design   *Kenneth R Windsor, Metamark International*
Food Stylist & Consultant   *Zachi Bukshester*
Production   *Arnon Orbach, Hugh Allan*
Research   *Stella Korin-Liber*
Project Coordination   *Sarah Elergant*
Ceramics   *Dafna Botzer*

Library of Congress Catalog Card Number: 89 - 43582
ISBN: 0-88365-844-5

Printed in Hong Kong by Imago

This book was devised and produced in the United Kingdom by
Multimedia Books Limited, 32–34 Gordon House Road, London NW5 1LP

PHOTOGRAPHS, PAGES 1-8

1. Jaffa oranges, Israel's ambassadors of goodwill. In the background a stretch of seascape in Jaffa.

2. Onion fields in the Golan. Abundance from a fertile land.

3. Labaneh cheese balls in olive oil. Stored in olive oil, labaneh keeps for a long time.

4. Granite mountains in the Judean desert.

5. A colorful display of summer and winter squash.

6. Almond trees in full bloom in Central Galilee.

7. Traditional preparation of zhoug, a fiery Yemenite relish.

8. Strawberries forever. Each year the season is longer and the strawberries bigger.

Above: Goat's cheese with mint and carrots.

CONTENTS

$\mathcal{I}$ NTRODUCTION

When asked to write about Israeli cuisine, foreign food critics usually resort to the Israeli breakfast. It is a subject they can be enthusiastic about without compromising their integrity. In most instances, the setting for this much admired meal is a kibbutz - the pioneering spirit is somehow a fitting backdrop for it. In a kibbutz, the foreign food critic finds himself caught up in an experience which is at once esthetic and gastronomic. He is impressed with the rich display of creams, cheeses, yogurts and buttermilks, set off by a

◆ Lahuhua,

Yemenite

spongy

pancakes.

lush barrage of vegetables. It is an attractive sight, wholesome and full of vitality. It is hard not to respond to it. This, then, is the archetypal scene that has made breakfast, in the eyes of more than one critic, "Israel's main contribution to world cuisine." While in Israel, recommended one critic, eat once a day. Preferably breakfast. Preferably in a kibbutz.

Most of the food we eat in Israel is not indigenous to the Eastern Mediterranean, but it is Israeli by virtue of the fact that it is grown, prepared and eaten here. However, an educated palate can easily identify the major influences at work in Israeli kitchens. There is the North African or Mahgrebi influence. Jews have lived in North Africa for centuries and few surveys of Moroccan food fail to mention the contribution made by the Jewish population. Other influences come from Eastern Europe, where Jews once flourished and prospered. Israel's Arab population has contributed yet other influences. But Arabs and Jews have not assimilated in Israel. They represent two opposing and sometimes hostile cultures, each with its distinctive flavor.

What is Israeli cuisine? To some Israelis, the question is meaningless. How can one describe something that is neither homogeneous nor coherent? But this attitude completely misses the point. Israeli cuisine is unique and deserving of attention precisely because of the plurality of ethnic and cultural influences that compose it. All of these influences - Moroccan, Yemenite, Russian, Arab, Polish - are equally important and the existence of such a wide selection of cuisines in such a small country is what makes Israeli food worthy of discussion.

The existence of an Israeli cuisine is much debated in Israel today. The population is just about equally divided into those who believe there is no such thing and those who believe there is. Giving world-renowned dishes Hebrew names is not Israeli cuisine. Filet mignon with blue cheese under a new name is still filet mignon with blue cheese. But those brave chefs who are slowly teaching us to be proud of what we have achieved claim that they are "Israeli" when they combine avocados, oranges and biblical hyssop. They feel they are breaking new ground with their version of St. Peter's fish with *tahini*.

◆ *A Yemenite dancer in the robe traditionally worn on festive occasions such as weddings.*

In fact Israeli cuisine went nouvelle before it had a chance to define itself. Local experts claim, for example, that Israel's main contribution to world cuisine is not breakfast but barbecued *foie gras*. We were the first to expose this expensive and rare delicacy to the rigors of open fire. Since *foie gras* is largely fat, its preparation is classically conservative and careful. If not watched like a hawk, it can easily melt away. Usually it is made into pâté or cooked whole and served warm or cold. Grilling goose liver on a spit is therefore either a demonstration of courage or an act of defiance against the order of the old world. And what could be more outrageously Israeli than serving *foie gras* in *pita* bread?

At this particular moment, Israel is in culinary ferment, still assimilating the influx of new cuisines - French, Italian, American - introduced in the early eighties, but beginning to realize that it has its own character. Anomalies abound. We have, for instance, a white desert truffle which is inedible. We have an artichoke named after Jerusalem, which is not an artichoke

◆ Head shot of a carp, Israel's national fish.

and has nothing to do with Jerusalem. Hyssop, an herb mentioned in the Bible, is now a protected plant, so nobody is allowed to pick it. We now raise more lamb than we can eat, so we are having to educate Jews to like chops, roast leg of lamb and lamb fries rather than beef. Until five years ago, we had only sweet red wine and respectable table wines were termed "sour" and shunned.

Our grandmothers did more than most to formulate an Israeli cuisine, although recent influences have obscured their achievement. They cooked according to their respective backgrounds but adapted their creativity to local produce and weather conditions.

My Russian grandmother used to bake a brown and fragrant *cholent*, a substantial casserole of meat and potatoes, beans and barley, in the oven of our family bakery. It was a large commercial oven, built of red bricks, and my grandmother knew to a fraction of a degree when the temperature was right for her *cholent*. She would put it in, covered with a kitchen towel, just after the last Sabbath *challah* loaf was taken out early on Friday morning and let it cook until the next morning. She tended her *cholent* all through the night as if it were a child. Every hour, on the hour, she would wake up, march briskly to the bakery, pull the pot out of the deep oven, remove the towel carefully so as not to wake the *cholent*, and measure the amount of liquid left in the pot. Her nightmare was that her *cholent* would dry up. Having raised three children against terrific odds, she had no intention of this happening.

Nothing that I have ever eaten compares with the *cholent* that

came out of that old blackened pot. Aided by plain water, smartly added, the potatoes turned golden and soft, the beans tied up with the barley, and the meat blended with the bone marrow until it was impossible to tell them apart. It took dedication and stamina, and

my grandmother had both. Even her hand-made eggplant salad remains, to my mind, more typically Israeli than anything we eat today. She charred the eggplants over an open fire, peeled them, mashed them with a fork, then added garlic, lemon juice, mayonnaise and hot peppers. Her pickles were excellent. Even her simple breakfast omelets were memorable.

My Polish grandmother, who came from Cracow, had standards every bit as tough and rigid as those of my Russian grandmother. She did not fry, and she never used glowing charcoals, let alone grilled over them. She

◆ *Early morning in Safed, an ancient hilltop town famous for its clear air, occasional snow and its devout residents.*

used to cook meat with sour cream and capers - strictly non-kosher. Her carp, very sweet and totally inedible to the modern Israeli palate, used to quiver in a molded prison of jelly. Her cucumber salad with fresh dill and cream was very good, though. She also in-  troduced me to my first artichoke, which was almost as erotic and exciting as my first girlfriend. She showed me how to remove the outer leaves and nibble the flesh from the stem end, and how to pluck away the thistle- down, and how to slice the heart and dip each tasty morsel in white sauce. I am no expert on sauces, but I can improvise a sauce for artichokes based on what I remember of my grandmother's. She also bought us our first whole goose liver, a round and massive ball wrapped in foil, and taught us how to eat it. That was in the early sixties, when *foie gras* was as foreign as lobster and pheasant, both by the way still unavailable. Unlike my Russian grandmother, who was an extrovert, my Polish grandmother never ate at the table. She never really served either, in the sense of dispensing food to others. She shoved food in front of us and commanded us to eat. She would not relax until everything was finished and was furious if something was left untouched. I always hoped, for her sake, that she sneaked something in the kitchen, but people who knew her better told me not to count on it.

The world's great cuisines were formed during lengthy periods of peace and fun. One might almost say that stability and parties are prerequisites for true gastronomy. Such prerequisites have seldom been the lot of Jews or Israelis. We have scarcely had time for leisure, no time to play enjoyable games, and the dietary laws of *kashrut* have discouraged us from mixing meat with milk and eating seafood. So, all things considered, it is a wonder that so many tasty things have emerged from the Israeli kitchen. In the early years we had to make do with very little. Now we have found our culinary voice. It is high time that it was heard.

◆ *At the end of a day of harvest, bales of hay await collection in the Jezreel Valley.*

Taste of
ISRAEL
A MEDITERRANEAN FEAST

APPETIZERS &

HOT STUFF

◆ Hummus, *an aerial*
view. One of Israel's
national foods, hummus
is filling, nutrititious
and cheap. No knives or
forks are needed, just
pita *bread and an*
expert wrist. In view:
whole chick peas, olive oil,
paprika, parsley, pickled
turnips and raw onion
for added pungency.

ezze can be translated
as appetizers, nibbles,
hors d'oeuvres, snacks. But none of
these words conveys the range of
delicacies, cooked and uncooked,
that constitute the start of a meal in

◆ *A eucalyptus tree in sand dunes near Nitzana, on the desert borders of the northern Negev.*

Israel and throughout the Middle East.

Although going to restaurants is not always the best way to learn about or judge the food of a country, in the case of *mezze* I thoroughly recommend it. You will encounter, in one sitting, an enormous variety of dishes, far more than any single household can muster. Even a modest restaurant runs to at least twenty different items.

The portions are small, but they are an ideal introduction to the exotic and unfamiliar. There are crudités, served with various dips, *hummus*, *tahini*, lemony *labaneh* cheese, cheese in cubes, grilled chicken livers, eggplants prepared in a variety of ways, salads laced with turmeric and cumin, pickled vegetables, fried *kibbeh* or meat patties, stuffed grape leaves, small pastries filled with meat or cheese or spinach, and fiery relishes such as *harissa* and *zhoug*. In fact any dish can be considered part of the *mezze* table if it has a strong individual taste and comes in small portions.

This diversity reveals something else about Israeli food. We shy away from eating our meals as set courses served in sequence, with each course calculated to feed a given number of people. We like to spread our food out on the table so that we can help ourselves. Although variety is the spice of life, an indiscriminate jumble of *mezze* piled on the same plate is frowned upon. One is supposed to pick and choose rather than eat everything in sight, simultaneously.

The fiery concoctions served with *mezze* are as invigorating as they look. *Zhoug*, *shatta*, *hreimeh*, *harissa* and *madbuha* are all based in varying degrees on green and red chili peppers, all locally grown. Fresh horseradish is tame by comparison. Chili-based relishes are a staple of Israeli food. No meal is complete without them. At most restaurants you do not have to ask for them. They are always on the table. They perk up any and every *mezze*, can be blended with *hummus* and *tahini*, squirted over *falafel*, and added to casseroles and grilled meats. They cross ethnic barriers with the same ease as the aroma of baking bread, and even if they were once the prerogative of Yemenite and Moroccan immigrants, they are now consumed by all and considered common property. To the novice diner, they are dangerous and part of a game Israelis love to play on the unwary. Beware of Israelis bearing hot peppers.

◆ *Sunset over the Judean desert.*

Yemenite Jews claim that *zhoug* and *shatta*, two of the most explosive of these condiments, have the power to ward off all sorts of diseases, from the common cold to blocked coronary arteries. There have even been scientific studies that tried to establish cause and effect between hot food and rude health, but they were inconclusive. The ability of various communities to eat *harissa* and its relatives without flinching is an indication of health in itself.

On the face of it, the appeal of the red hot chili pepper is hard to reconcile with the agony it causes. The taste is difficult to describe, for it is not so much a taste as a sensation of great heat applied to a small area. It is wise to have *pita* or some other bread within reach, bread being the only food that seems to soothe chili burns.

The truth is that chili paste is a macho game even deadlier than poker. You never let on when you're down. You never admit that your

◆ *Traditional preparation of Yemenite* zhoug. *Hot chili peppers and garlic are crushed and ground by hand, then mixed with coriander and spices.*

mucous membranes hurt like hell. A man's suffering can only be judged by the sweat on his brow. He never makes a dash for the restroom to stick his head in a sink of cold water. He keeps scooping until the last fragment of *pita* is finished.

Commercially grown chili peppers are regarded, by purists, as lacking in virtue. They lose some of their potency during transport and handling, they say. They would rather pluck the peppers that grow in their grandmother's garden than spend money on store-bought peppers.

Chili peppers are shrouded in folklore. Small jars of home-made chili paste are sold in local markets and those which have an old, old woman standing behind them are thought to have extra potency and

authenticity. In the old Yemenite quarter of Tel Aviv, *zhoug* and *shatta* are still prepared by hand. The preparation is quite simple, but one has to wear gloves and protect the eyes and other sensitive areas. Fresh, crisp chili peppers are ground by hand on a large flat stone, or chopped up and pounded on a stone mortar, then mixed with spices and herbs. Stored in jars with tightly fitting lids, the mixture keeps for months.

◆ *A typical Israeli chili pepper. There are only a few kinds and this is the most common.*

Other Jewish communities have their own hot and not so hot stuffs. Moroccans use *harissa* and *hermulla*, also based on chili peppers and mixed with salt and garlic. Rumanians like to use freshly minced garlic, mixed with vinegar and other liquids, on their meat, serving it like any other condiment.

Chili peppers are second nature to many Israelis, and eaten with all meals, even with breakfast. Bitter comments are made if they are not hot and fiery enough. Regretfully, there are seasons when they are less potent.

Appetizers & Hot Stuff

◆ *A selection of* mezze, *the traditonal Israeli and Middle Eastern appetizers.*

Recipes

STUFFED GRAPE LEAVES

8 oz fresh or preserved grape leaves
1 1/4 cups long-grain rice
2 or 3 tomatoes, skinned and chopped
1 large onion, finely chopped
2 tablespoons finely chopped fresh parsley
1 tablespoon dried crushed mint
1/4 teaspoon ground cinnamon
1/2 teaspoon ground allspice
salt and freshly ground black pepper
2 tomatoes, sliced (optional)
1/2 cup olive oil
1/4 teaspoon powdered saffron (optional)
1 teaspoon sugar
juice of 1 lemon
lemon wedges, to garnish

◆ *Stuffed grape leaves*

are eaten in most

Eastern Mediterra-

nean countries,

including Greece,

Turkey, Lebanon

and Cyprus.

The filling can be

rice or meat or

both.

If you are using grape leaves preserved in brine, the excess salt must be removed. Put them into a large bowl and pour boiling water over them, making sure the water penetrates between the layers. Let the leaves soak for 20 minutes, then drain them and soak them in fresh cold water. Drain and repeat the process.

If you are using fresh grape leaves, soften them by plunging them into boiling water for a few minutes, then shave off the harder part of the stem.

Wash the rice, soak it for 10 minutes, then drain it. Add boiling water, stir the rice around, then drain it and rinse under cold running water.

Mix the rice with the chopped tomatoes, onion, parsley, mint, spices, salt and pepper. Place a generous spoonful of this mixture near the stem end of each grape leaf. Fold the stem end over the stuffing, fold both sides toward the middle, then roll up the package like a small cigar. Squeeze lightly in the palm of your hand. The process gets easier once you have rolled a few!

Pack the stuffed leaves tightly in a large, shallow pan lined with sliced tomatoes and any torn or imperfect grape leaves. Add a clove of garlic here and there if you like.

Mix the olive oil with the water, saffron (if used), sugar and lemon juice, and pour it over the stuffed leaves. Put a plate on top of the leaves to prevent them unwinding, cover the pan, and simmer very, very gently for at least 2 hours, adding water from time to time as the liquid in the pan is absorbed. Leave the stuffed leaves in the pan to cool. Serve cold with lots of lemon wedges.

Serves 5 or 6

TABBOULEH
A salad of cracked wheat, vegetables & herbs

1 cup bulgur wheat
4 tablespoons chopped fresh flat-leaved parsley
2 tablespoons chopped mint
1 cucumber, diced
1 bell pepper, diced
6 scallions, diced
1 large tomato, diced
grated peel of 1 lemon
juice of 2 lemons
1/3 cup olive oil
salt and pepper
pinch ground allspice

Soak the bulgur wheat in cold water for 30 minutes, then drain in a fine sieve, squeezing out the excess moisture. In a salad bowl, combine all ingredients.

Serve as a tangy appetizer, but not before refrigerating for 1 hour.

TAHINI SAUCE
A savory sauce based on sesame seeds

1/2 cup sesame paste
1/4 cup water
1/4 cup fresh lemon juice
1/4 teaspoon salt
1 teaspoon finely minced garlic

Using a fork, blend together the sesame paste and water, then add the lemon juice, parsley and garlic, mixing well after each addition. Alternatively, mix all the ingredients together in a blender. The mixture will thicken later in the refrigerator.

A *mezze* version of *tahini* sauce calls for lots of fresh, finely chopped coriander or parsley as well. Keeps in the refrigerator for up to 10 days.

CUCUMBER AND FENNEL SALAD

1 large cucumber, peeled and finely chopped
1/4 bulb fennel, finely chopped
pinch of salt
1/4 teaspoon freshly ground black pepper
3 tablespoons sour cream
1 tablespoon olive oil
2 tablespoons fresh lemon juice
2 scallions, finely chopped

Thoroughly combine all the ingredients, and chill well before serving. Serves 4.

EGGPLANT SALAD
Three versions out of many

1 lb eggplants

5 tablespoons fresh lemon juice
scant teaspoon minced garlic
1 teaspoon salt
or
1/2 cup tahini sauce
(see recipe left)
coarsely chopped parsley, to garnish
or
1/2 cup mayonnaise
2 tablespoons chopped onion
1 tablespoon diced red pepper
2 tablespoons olive oil
1 tablespoon chopped dill

Prick the eggplants a few times with a fork, then bake over charcoal until the skins are blistered and black. This is usually done after grilling meat, while the barbecue is still hot. Otherwise it can be done under the broiler, or in the oven, but the smoky aroma will be missing. Allow the eggplants to cool, then remove the skins. Mash the flesh in a food processor (connoisseurs never use anything but a fork!), then stir in one of the three flavorings listed above. Serve cold, with hot *pita* bread.

JELLIED CALF'S FOOT

3 - 4 lbs calf's feet
8 3/4 cups water
6 cloves garlic
1 carrot
2 medium-size onions
1 celery
fresh thyme
4 bay leaves
salt and black pepper to taste
2 hard-boiled eggs, sliced
lemon wedges, to garnish

Blanch the calf's feet (plunge them into boiling water, bring the water to a boil again, then remove the feet and wash them). Cut each one into 3 or 4 pieces, put the pieces into a saucepan with the 8 3/4 cups of water, then bring to a boil and skim. Add all the other ingredients, except for the eggs, and simmer until the slices of calf's foot are tender - this takes about 4 hours.

Strain the broth, taste it, and add salt and pepper to taste. At this stage some cooks clarify the broth as for consommé, using egg whites and egg shells. Pick the celery, bay leaves, thyme and bones out of the strainer - this should be done by hand, even though the contents of the strainer are very sticky. Grind whatever is left in the strainer and return it to the broth.

To see whether the broth will gel or not, put a spoonful on a plate and put the plate in the freezer for 10 minutes. If necessary, add 1/2 oz unflavored gelatin to the broth.

Arrange the slices of hard-boiled egg in a shallow dish, ladle the broth over them, and put the dish in the refrigerator for several hours.

When you are ready to serve it, transfer the jelly to a serving plate and garnish with a lime or lemon wedges.

◆ *Jellied calf's foot is a traditional Jewish dish from Eastern Europe. It is eaten with generous helpings of lemon juice.*

◆ *Moroccan*

cigars are rolled

sheets of filo

dough, deep-

fried, with

different

fillings. They

are a favorite on

festive

occasions.

MOROCCAN CIGARS

In Israel *filo* dough is often made into filled "cigars." Several variations on the theme are given below. The fillings are spread on half-leaves of *filo*, then the edges of the *filo* are folded over and the dough is rolled up into a cigar shape. The edges are sealed with egg white or with a mixture of flour and water. The cigars are then fried in deep oil for 2 minutes until they turn golden. Plan on 6-8 cigars per person as an appetizer.

FILLING FOR MEAT CIGARS
1 onion, chopped
1 tablespoon oil
6 oz ground meat
1 teaspoon chopped parsley
1/4 teaspoon ground cumin
pinch of cinnamon
salt and pepper to taste

Fry the onion in the oil, then add the meat, parsley, spices and seasoning. For a real treat, add a little finely chopped goose liver too.

FILLING FOR POTATO CIGARS
1 onion, chopped
1 tablespoon vegetable oil
2/3 cup boiled potatoes, mashed
salt, white pepper and nutmeg to taste

Fry the onions in the oil, then mix well with the mashed potato and seasoning.

FILLING FOR CHEESE CIGARS
1 cup cheese, grated
fresh mint leaves

Put two leaves of mint into each cigar on top of the cheese before you roll it up.

CHOPPED LIVER

1 cup oil
2 large onions, sliced
1 lb chicken livers
5 or 6 hard-boiled eggs
salt and pepper
radishes and tomato slices, to garnish

Heat the oil and fry the onions until they are golden brown, then drain them on paper towels. Set aside 1/4 cup of the oil and fry the chicken livers in the rest. Drain the livers on paper towels and allow them to cool. Discard the oil in which they were cooked.

Grind the chicken livers, the fried onions and the hard-boiled eggs, then mix them all together, adding pepper and salt to taste. Slowly blend in the reserved oil until the mixture is the consistency of a smooth spread. Serve garnished with radishes and slices of tomato. Chopped liver is traditionally eaten with a fork or spread onto a slice of *challah* (see recipe p. 90).

◆ *Chopped liver, pickles, and beer at a Levinsky Street diner in Tel Aviv.*

◆ *One of the wonders of Jewish cuisine - chopped liver, on toasted challah.*

MOROCCAN CARROT SALAD

1 1/2 lbs carrots
1 bulb garlic, finely chopped
1/2 cup vegetable oil
1 tablespoon finely chopped chili peppers
1 teaspoon sweet paprika
3/4 cup water
salt
ground turmeric
1/3 cup vinegar
1 tablespoon lemon juice
1 tablespoon chopped parsley

Wash and peel the carrots, and boil or steam them until they are tender but still firm. Drain them and allow to cool. Gently fry the garlic in the oil until it is soft and transparent - this takes about 12 minutes. Now add the chili peppers and paprika to the pan and fry for 1 minute. Pour in the water, then add the cooked carrots, salt, turmeric, vinegar and lemon juice. Simmer for 5 minutes, then remove from the heat, allow to cool, cover, and refrigerate for 24 hours. Stir well before serving, sprinkled with parsley. Serve as cold appetizer or to accompany *couscous* (see photograph p. 108).

◆ *Chicken livers, egg, onion, and a meat grinder spell...chopped liver.*

ONIONS WITH VINEGAR

2 large mild onions
salt
2 or 3 tablespoons white wine vinegar
1 tablespoon dried mint or
chopped fresh parsley

Peel and slice the onions into half rings and sprinkle them with a little salt. Combine them with the vinegar and mint, and allow to stand for at least 1 hour before serving. They will become soft, lose much of their pungency, and absorb the other flavors. Serve them as an appetizer or as a relish with a main dish.

PICKLED TURNIPS

2 lbs turnips
1 raw beet
juice of 1/2 lemon
1 1/2 heaped tablespoons salt
6 cups water

Wash the turnips and the beet, but do not peel them. Cut both into slices 1/4 inch thick. Sprinkle the slices of beet with the lemon juice and lay them in the bottom of a squat glass jar (they will give the turnips a reddish tinge). Now pack the turnip slices on top and add salted water to cover. Seal and keep in a cool place for 7 days. Serve with other *mezze* dishes.

◆ *Some people*

pickle everything

- turnips,

carrots,

cucumbers, red

peppers, whole

lemons, olives,

garlic...

HOT OLIVE SALAD

1 lb green olives, pitted
2 large ripe tomatoes, skinned and grated
1/3 cup vegetable oil
6 cloves garlic, crushed
1 tablespoon tomato paste
3 slices unpeeled lemon
1 teaspoon chili powder
1 teaspoon red pepper
salt and freshly ground black pepper

Put the olives into a saucepan, cover them with water, and bring to a boil. Drain, cover with water again, and repeat the process. In another saucepan, mix the tomatoes with the oil, garlic and tomato paste and simmer together for a few minutes. Now add the olives, lemon slices, spices, salt and pepper, and mix well together. Add a little water and simmer over a low heat until the water is absorbed. Remove the lemon and set aside to cool. Serve cold as a *mezze* dish.

◆ *A feast of olives: cracked olives, and hot red chili peppers.*

ZHOUG
Chili paste with parsley and coriander

*1 heaped cup puréed fresh chili peppers,
green or red
8 tablespoons chopped fresh parsley
8 tablespoons chopped fresh coriander
1 1/2 tablespoons minced garlic
1 teaspoon salt
1 teapoon pepper
1 teaspoon ground cumin
pinch of ground cardamom*

Use a food processor to purée the chili peppers. Then add the parsley and coriander and blend again. Add the garlic, salt, pepper, cumin, and cardamom.

Re-blend, spoon into a glass jar, seal, and refrigerate. *Zhoug* will keep for several months in the refrigerator.

The red version uses *only* red chili peppers and no herbs and, though more common, it lacks the typical Yemenite flavor of the green version.

Zhoug is served with Yemenite dishes such as *chilbe* or *mlawach*, with a small bowl of freshly puréed tomatoes.

HUMMUS
Chick pea dip with garlic and *tahini*

*1 3/4 cups dry chick peas
1 teaspoon baking soda
3 or 4 cloves garlic, minced
1 teaspoon salt
1/2 teaspoon ground cumin
1/2 cup tahini sauce (see p. 30)
juice of 2 lemons
olive oil*

Soak the chick peas in water overnight, with the soda. Cook them until soft, then drain them, reserving a little of the cooking liquid. Reserve a few whole chick peas for garnishing.

Mash all the ingredients together, but not too finely. If the consistency is too dry, add a little of the chick pea cooking liquid. Spoon the mixture onto a plate and make a well in the center. A skilled hummus artist can make a perfect crater with a thin film of paste in the middle in one swift, circular movement. Put a little olive oil, and the reserved chick peas, into the well and serve. Some cooks like to add extra *tahini*.

◆ *The twin towers of Yemenite cuisine: green* zhoug *and red* zhoug, *two fiery condiments which are chiefly responsible for the flavor of Yemenite food.*

◆ *The Dead Sea is the lowest place on earth. It is rich with minerals and phosphates, and nothing ever grows in it.*

HAZERET/HREIN
Horseradish relish

2/3 cup fresh horseradish
10 oz fresh beets
1/2 cup vinegar
1 teaspoon salt
2 tablespoons sugar

Peel the horseradish. Wash the beets, then boil them for 15 minutes. When cool, peel them. Now grate the horseradish and the beets using a fine grater or a food processor - do this near an open window! Mix the grated horseradish and beets with the other ingredients and refrigerate in a glass jar. Use as a condiment with any traditional Eastern European savory dish, and never ever attempt to serve gefilte fish without it.

HARISSA
A North African condiment

18 fresh red chili peppers
2 red bell peppers
4 cloves garlic
1 teaspoon ground cumin
1 teaspoon coriander seeds
1/2 teaspoon hot chili powder
1 teaspoon coarse salt
3 tablespoons white vinegar
2 tablespoons olive oil

Remove the stems and seeds from the chili peppers - make sure you wear gloves to do this. Using a pestle and mortar (or a food processor, which is less fun), grind the peppers up with the garlic and spices. Deseed the bell peppers and deep-fry or broil/grill them; remove the skins. Add the flesh to the chili paste, with the rest of the ingredients, and grind for another minute or two. Keep a week's supply in the refrigerator and freeze the rest.

HREIMEH
Spicy Moroccan fish

3 tablespoons vegetable oil
1 onion, chopped
2 tablespoons chopped parsley
8 cloves garlic, chopped
2 tablespoons tomato paste
1/2 teaspoon salt
2 tablespoons lemon juice
1/4 teaspoon black pepper
ground coriander or cumin, to taste
1/2 teaspoon paprika
1 1/2 cups water
1 lb fresh fish (sea bass, gray mullet
or carp), cleaned

In a saucepan, heat the oil and fry the onion and parsley for 5 minutes. Add the garlic, tomato paste, salt, lemon juice, black pepper, coriander or cumin, and paprika. Add the water, mix well, and cook for 5-10 minutes over a medium heat.

Lay the fish in the saucepan, cover, and poach in the spicy broth for 25 minutes.

◆ Horseradish sauce, flavored with beets, is the sole hot contribution to Israeli cuisine by Eastern European Jews. A customary condiment of Passover, it is eaten as a reminder of a harsh and bitter past.

DAIRY &

CHEESE

◆ *Shultza, the*

shepherd, tends

his flock of

goats in the

northern region

of the country.

The milk is

used to make

rich, fatty

cheese.

In Byniamina, along a narrow passageway called Cypress Road, in the back room of Shomron Dairy, a shop as fragrant as its name is musical, Moshe Bachar cuts into a burnished-brown wheel of Turkish *kachkaval* with

a small knife shaped like a spade. Using the knife as a wedge, he cracks open the huge, damp, moldy cheese into two craggy halves, then bends down and squints at its texture.

"Horef" he says. "Winter."

Abu-Mussa, an Arab who makes his living tapping the sides of thousands of wheels of *kachkavel* each year, nods in agreement. He taps the cheeses with a tiny steel hammer, listening carefully for evidence of unwanted holes in their moist interior. "Too white, not yellow straw," he comments, referring to the color the cheese should have been if the goats that provided the milk for it had eaten the deep green grass and alfalfa of summer.

Moshe Bachar is a third-generation cheese-maker and a native-born Israeli. The huge 45-lb wheel of 1988 vintage cheese has been made from the milk of goats fed on winter fodder. It is a winter cheese, too white, too young, a bit too acid to eat as a dessert with red wine. But it will be a wonderful cheese for cooking with vegetables, perfect for grating over pasta.

A 1987 vintage wheel, a rare cheese to have since demand is such that Bachar cannot allow his cheeses to age properly and gracefully, is described as "a little elder sister." It is tinged with yellow inside, and its texture is more moist, a sign that it possesses more style and breeding. It was made from the milk of spring. Bachar forgets his dismay over the young and restless *kachkavel* and takes a bite of its elder sister. It deserves its appellation. Just look at its golden color and the ragged veins running through it like a mother lode! "Like silk," Bachar breathes.

◆ *Shultza tending his flock near a water hole.*

◆ *For a fixed price, the Ein Kamonim roadside inn, in the Upper Galilee offers a tray of assorted cheeses, country-style bread, vegetables, homemade wine, pickles, vinegar, and olive oil. Fire crackles in the fireplace in winter.*

◆ Fresh ricotta

cheese in cheese-

cloth, still

dripping whey,

at the Shomron

Dairy,

Byniamina.

Kachkavel, also known as kasseri, is an aristocratic cheese, the people of Byniamina say, the king of cheeses, made by hand and with love, just as it has been for a hundred years. It is also produced in a few villages on the

Golan Heights, Druze villages that have never stopped making it. Their kachkavel is stronger and sharper than Bachar's. Byniamina's citizens boast of the strawberries, oranges and zucchini that grow in the rich fields around their city, but most of all they revel in their cheese. Goats are imported and bred specially for the richness and quantity of their milk, the milk that will become kachkavel. Cheese-making in Byniamina is considered a high calling, an art not taught in any other way than by father to son, mother to daughter. The whey that is the by-product of the cheese-making process becomes food for Byniamina's cows and Byniamina swears that its beef is wonderful only because the milk of its goats is so rich.

Before the cheese-making process begins, two collections of milk are needed, and these must be blended carefully. Cheese-making begins at about five o'clock each morning and ends at about noon, "and it must be done three hundred and sixty-five days a year", Bachar explains "because goats do not know about holy days".

The evening's milk is brought in, poured into shallow stainless steel tanks, and left overnight. It separates into two components, heavy cream that sinks to the bottom and lighter skim milk. The next morning the skim milk,

◆ Dairy produce being delivered in the early morning hours from the back of a truck, Tel Aviv.

containing virtually no fat, is drained from the tanks and mixed in copper cooking kettles with that morning's collection of fresh, whole milk. Combining the two milks is an arduous business. The copper kettles hold 240 gallons each

and although the milks can be and are mixed by giant beaters, the cheese-makers insist on mixing them partly by hand. They like to feel and touch the milk. "It is our way of making the cheese ours," says Bachar.

A portion of the whey from the previous day is added to the milk mixture and the heat is turned on under the kettles. The whey, Bachar explains, is rich in lactic acid, the perfect ingredient for beginning the ripening process. As the milk is heated to 95°F, Abu-Mussa keeps reaching for and reading the temperature on a special thermometer immersed in the milk. When the correct temperature is reached, he turns off the heat and adds a bit of rennet to each kettle. Rennet, from the stomachs of calves, will curdle the milk.

And so the process goes on, fresh milk at one end and ripened cheese at the other. But not so long ago, when Bachar's cheese had a chance to age gracefully, most Israelis subsisted on fresh white cheese. It was the only kind made. It was never aged and had no taste or aroma to speak of. It was spread on bread or used in cakes and cooking. It contained five to nine percent fat and freshness was all. The only milk product with a hint of maturity to it was *labaneh,* made from curdled yogurt, and that was an Arab

◆ *Cows grazing in lush winter pasture, Byniamina.*

invention. *Labaneh*, a thick lemony paste traditionally stored in glass jars filled with olive oil, keeps for a long time without refrigeration. No one grated cheese - there was no cheese worth grating - and no one served cheese as a separate course.

As with other aspects of Israeli food and cooking, it was foreign travel that brought about a change of taste. New demand created new products. Matured cheese has been with us for ten years or so now, but blue-veined cheese, of which we have only one variety, is still viewed with suspicion unless it is disguised in a dip. We are past wine-and-cheese get-togethers as a means of introducing new cheeses, but only just. We have still not assimilated the culinary possibilities of cheese. Of course the Jewish dietary laws forbid the

◆ *Stacks of* kachkavel *wheels drying in Shomron Dairy. The hard yellow cheese is also known as* kasseri.

mixing of milk products and meat, so cooking meat with butter or cream is out of the question. This is one of the reasons why Israeli cuisine makes such limited use of dairy products in cooking. Margarine is substituted for butter and *ersatz* cream for the real thing.

Even in this age of refrigerators and well-stocked supermarkets, a disappointing number of "new" offerings are really old products under new names. Many varieties of cream cheese are sold which are not really cheese at all, but dips which start off as white cheese which is then mixed with various flavorings and colorings. Fortunately, however, not everyone is content with pseudo cheese. There are farms with small dairy herds and flocks which choose to produce the real thing, and we now have a reasonable, although limited, range of bries, chèvres and cheddars, and even a little ricotta and mozarella. These are still a far cry from the great originals, but they hold their own. If you sample them in their own right, and do not make too many comparisons, they are acceptable.

D AIRY
& CHEESE

◆ *If it's* labaneh,
it must be
breakfast.
Labaneh *in*
olive oil with
za'atar *and*
scallions, is
morning fare.

Recipes

BROILED PEPPERS WITH YOGURT

3 red bell peppers, halved lengthwise and cored
vegetable oil
1 3/4 cups pecans, shelled and halved
2 teaspoons salt
2 1/2 cups thick plain yogurt

Lightly brush the peppers with vegetable oil and cook them under a preheated broiler/grill until soft. Fry the pecans in a little oil until golden, then drain on paper towels. Stir the salt into the yogurt.

For a hearty Sephardic breakfast, lay the peppers on top of the yogurt and top with nuts and a sprinkling of mint. Serves 4.

CHILLED CUCUMBER & YOGURT SOUP

1 large cucumber
salt
2 1/2 cups plain yogurt
1/2 cup fresh tomato paste/purée
1 clove garlic, chopped very fine
pinch ground coriander
chopped fresh mint and paprika, to garnish

Wash the cucumber, but do not peel it. Chop it coarsely, sprinkle it with salt, and set aside for 30 minutes - this removes some of the bitter taste. Rinse and drain the cucumber, put it in the food processor with the rest of the ingredients, and blend until smooth and creamy.

Serve well chilled, sprinkled with mint and paprika. Serves 4.

◆ *Red peppers roasted on a charcoal grill, with yogurt, chopped mint and pecan nuts.*

CHEESE BLINTZES
Cheese-filled crêpes

BATTER
1 cup all-purpose flour
1 tablespoon sugar
1/4 teaspoon salt
1 cup milk
4 large eggs, lightly beaten
1 teaspoon unsalted butter, softened or melted
2 tablespoons extra butter for frying

CHEESE FILLING
1 1/2 cups cottage cheese
2 cups cream cheese, softened
2 large egg yolks
heaped 3/4 cup sugar
1/2 teaspoon salt
1/2 teaspoon vanilla extract
1 teaspoon grated lemon peel
1/4 cup unsalted butter
2 cups sour cream
3 cups strawberries

In a blender, mix all the batter ingredients to a smooth consistency and chill for 10 minutes.

Lightly butter a small nonstick skillet and heat it thoroughly. Pour 2 tablespoons of batter into it, tilting the pan so that the batter forms a thin, even layer.

As soon as the batter has solidified, remove the skillet from the heat, flip the blintz over using a spatula and slide it onto a warm dish. Repeat until all the batter is used up.

Beat together the filling ingredients. Fill each blintz with 2 tablespoons of filling, fold the sides over the filling and roll up. To serve, fry 2 blintzes per person for 2 minutes on each side, seam-side down first. Serve with sour cream and strawberries. To be polite, offer sifted confectioners' sugar, too.

LABANEH CHEESE BALLS

2 teaspoons salt
4 1/2 cups plain sheep's milk yogurt
olive oil
1 sprig fresh rosemary
1 - 2 diced chili peppers
coarsely ground black pepper
crushed dried mint or paprika

Mix the salt and yogurt together, then tie it in fine cheesecloth, and leave it to drain over a bowl or sink for 48 hours. This gets rid of the excess moisture. (In this form it can be eaten spread on bread, with a little chopped fresh mint or wild thyme, or used to make the salad below.)

Chill the cheese in the refrigerator, then roll it into balls about the size of plums and store in olive oil with a sprig of rosemary and 1-2 dried chili peppers. When you want to eat them, remove them from the oil, drain, and roll in pepper and mint/paprika.

LABANEH & CUCUMBER SALAD

8 oz labaneh cheese
(see recipe above)
2 tablespoons milk
4 baby cucumbers, unpeeled and finely diced
2 cloves garlic, crushed
1 teaspooon dried mint
salt
1 tablespoon olive oil

Mash the cheese to a smooth paste with the milk, then add the cucumber, garlic, mint and salt, and mix well. Add the olive oil. Serve as a *mezze* dish, with warm *pita* bread.

◆ *A household staple:* labaneh cheese balls in olive oil, with rosemary and chili peppers.

SAMBUSAK
Cheese-filled pastry crescents

DOUGH
1/4 cup butter, melted
1/4 cup olive or vegetable oil
1/4 cup water
1 teaspoon salt
2 cups all-purpose flour
1 egg yolk, or milk, to glaze
1 teaspoon sesame seeds

CHEESE FILLING
8 oz white cheese (feta is ideal)
pepper
1 hard-boiled egg, diced

Mix the butter, oil, water and salt together in a bowl. Add the flour a tablespoon at a time, mixing thoroughly. Any lumps will gradually disappear. The consistency is right when pieces of dough flake away from the sides of the bowl and it can be shaped into a smooth ball. Preheat the oven to 375°F.

To make the filling, simply mix the cheese and other ingredients together.

To make the *sambusak*, break off walnut-size pieces of dough and roll them into circles about 3 inches across. Put 1 teaspoon of filling onto each circle, fold the dough over the filling, and crimp the edges together with finger and thumb. Take care not to overfill - the cheese mixture tends to expand during baking.

Lay the *sambusak* side by side on an oiled baking sheet, brush with egg yolk or milk, and bake for 30 minutes or until golden brown. Makes about 20.

CARROT & SOUR CREAM COLD SOUP

3 tablespoons butter
1 onion, coarsely chopped
1 clove garlic
2 lbs carrots, sliced
1/2 tablespoon each of ground turmeric,
coriander, ginger and chili
2 cups vegetable stock
2 cups sour cream
1 cup plain yogurt
scant 1/2 teaspoon salt
fresh chives, to garnish

Put the butter, onion, garlic, carrots and spices into a pressure cooker and simmer for 10 minutes. Add the stock, put the lid on and pressure cook for 15 minutes. Allow to cool, then liquidize and strain through a fine strainer. Add the sour cream, yogurt and salt, and chill well. Serve with a sprinkling of snipped chives.

◆ Sambusak *can make a hearty meal. Feta cheese gives* sambusak *a tangy taste and each bite is dipped in* za'atar, *a mixture of hyssop and spices.*

◆ *Freshly baked* sambusak *in one of many small, busy bakeries in Jaffa.*

FRIED GOAT'S CHEESE WITH MINT SALAD

12 oz goat's cheese in a log, well chilled
all-purpose flour
1 egg, lightly beaten and seasoned with thyme
and nutmeg
vegetable oil
garlic
1 small onion, finely chopped
1 tablespoon olive oil
1 tablespoon wine vinegar
dash Tabasco sauce
6 heaped tablespoons chopped fresh mint

Slice the cheese and dip the slices first in flour, then in beaten egg, then in flour again. Heat the oil in a skillet until it just begins to smoke, then slide the cheese slices into the pan and cook on both sides until golden brown.

Rub the inside of a bowl with garlic, and mix together the chopped onion, olive oil, vinegar, Tabasco and mint. Spoon the mixture onto individual plates and place the cheese slices on top. Makes 4 portions.

◆ *Goats*

grazing by

an olive tree

near Harduf,

in northern

Israel.

AVOCADO ORANGE CHEESECAKE
Unusual but delicious

7 oz graham crackers
1/4 cup melted butter
3 oranges
1 large avocado
juice of 1/2 lemon
3 oz cream cheese
2 eggs, separated
2/3 cup sour cream
1/2 oz gelatin
2 tablespoons sugar

Crush the crackers, stir in the melted butter and press the mixture into the bottom of a 7-inch cake pan. Grate the peel of 1 orange, squeeze the juice from 2, and prepare a few peeled orange segments from the third. Remove several slices from the avocado and put them in water to which a little lemon juice has been added - this prevents them blackening.

In a food precessor, blend together the rest of the avocado and lemon juice, the cream cheese, egg yolks, sour cream, orange peel and orange juice. Dissolve the gelatin in a little water and add it to the mixture, beating well. Beat the egg whites with the sugar until stiff, then fold them into the creamy orange/avocado mixture. Spoon the mixture into the cake pan, garnish with the orange segments and drained avocado slices, and refrigerate. Makes 12 generous servings.

◆ *Fried goat's*

cheese with

mint salad.

GREEK SALAD

As with watermelon and feta, this salad has become a "native" of Israel.

1 romaine or crisphead lettuce
1 onion, peeled
4 cucumbers
4 large, juicy tomatoes
1 bell pepper, red or green
salt and pepper to taste
wine vinegar
olive oil
11 oz feta cheese
1 teaspoon dried thyme
black olives, to garnish

Wash all the vegetables. Cut the lettuce into 1-inch pieces. Slice the onions into rings. Cut all the other vegetables into cubes or chunks the same size as the lettuce (leave the cucumbers unpeeled). Divide the lettuce among 4 big soup bowls, then arrange the other vegetables, except the onion rings, on top. Season with salt, pepper, vinegar and oil to taste. Cut the cheese into cubes and put it on top. Add the onion rings and a sprinkling of dried thyme. Decorate each bowl with 4 or 5 black olives.

◆ *Feta cheese salad, an Israeli version of a Greek recipe.*

◆ *Waiting for a breeze. A slice of sweet, juicy watermelon is complemented by feta cheese and black olives.*

FISH

◆ *Yuki, a trout farmer, raises trout in the choppy waters of the Banias River. The cold clear waters originate in the melted snow of Mount Hermon.*

N o one ever forgets, even if he or she has enjoyed it only once, the aroma and flavor of freshly caught Mediterranean fish grilled over charcoal. The fish are not more exciting or flavorful than those caught in Boston or Le Havre or Hydra - in all honesty Israel's territorial waters offer a poor catch compared with other Mediterranean countries - but the direct and intense heat of the open fire, the nutty perfume of the smoke and the crispiness of the fish's skin seem to make all the difference. Charcoal-grilled fish can be sampled in any of thousands of restaurants from Alexandria to Athens, from Algiers to Istanbul, but the taste of fish at Jaffa is unique. Here fish need only a hint of garlic, lemon juice and red pepper to be perfect.

◆ *Fisherman's wharf in the port of Acre, one of Israel's biblical towns.*

As you drive south along Tel Aviv's renovated Riviera, the ramparts of the old city of Jaffa rise from the tranquil sea. Jaffa is untouched by time. The city planners keep their distance. There is a quality of age and grace about the place that is better left untouched.

A few years ago a fisherman called Benny Raba came ashore and opened a fish restaurant. He is short and stocky and not at all the slim, trim fellow he was in his fishing days, but in the few years he has been in dry dock

he has become a walking status symbol. He drives a brand-new Mercedes with a car phone and wears gold bracelets and chains. He sits at his table facing the sea and holds court.

Benny's favorite pastime is recalling his seafaring days, when the sea was fierce and the fish were feisty. He cuts the air with chubby, leathery hands to illustrate his points, and as he sails down memory lane an attentive waiter covers the table with *mezze*, small colorful plates of appetizers such as *hummus*, *tahini*, *labaneh*, *tabbouleh*, eggplant purée, pickles, red-hot chili peppers and other delights. Benny pushes a plate of fat, shiny olives toward his guests, urging them to try one, waiting anxiously for the verdict. The olives are meaty and tasty, and they blend well with the moist chunks of feta cheese.

Benny's religion is fresh fish. He will show you the eyes and say, "You can tell a fresh fish by its eyes." His fish are firm of body and bright of color, and do not flake and fall apart when they are deep-fried. No, Benny is not ashamed to deep-fry his fresh fish, although it seems that Israel is, in general, past its deep-frying days. Why fry a fish to a crisp if you can flirt with it? With a charcoal grill going full blast at every street corner, is it not a shame and a sin to fish & chip your fish?

◆ *A fisherman mends a net torn by rocks off Jaffa harbor.*

When he is in the mood or when the restaurant is quiet, Benny dons an apron and goes into his kitchen. Taking an ax to a huge gray mullet, he reduces it to bite-size pieces and grills them on skewers over an open fire. Before he serves them, he flambés them in arak, the local version of ouzo or Pernod.

Authentic, ethnic fish restaurants are a relatively new phenomenon in Israel. Until quite recently, Israelis were anything but adventurous when it came to fish. For generations, Jewish holidays called for fish, but it was fish ground and molded into gefilte fish - the smell was there, there was a even a soupçon of taste, but mainly it was just another patty covered with sauce. The Jews of Poland used to cover their fish with a jellied sauce made of sugar and almonds. And when it was not ground and sauced out of

existence, fish was baked in the oven with vegetables and spices. When it finally arrived on the table, overcooked and falling off the bones, wives insisted that their husbands eat the heads. Since the most widely used fish in Jewish cooking was the impossible and dangerous carp, choking and coughing up bones was a customary part of all festival meals. Now we have discovered that carp is not the only fish worth eating, the excitement of the discovery is everywhere

◆ *Back from an early morning excursion, Benny proudly displays a huge* palamida. *The large fish is cut into generous steaks.*

evident. Diners are learning the names of local fish and pronouncing them with increasing confidence. They can tell a fresh fish from a tired one, a juicy one from an assemblage of skin and bones disguised as fish.

Trout are a new discovery. In northern Israel, in the Galilee region, there are numerous trout farms. The Dan and the Banias, which flow down from Mount Hermon into the Kinneret (Sea of Galilee), are two of the rivers whose cold, choppy waters are used by trout farms. In spring, when the snow on Mount Hermon melts, the rivers are fierce. Now, in small pools and tanks strictly and scientifically supervised, Israeli trout grow to prize-winning proportions. They are sold locally or delivered weekly to the major cities.

Trout have caught on nicely. They are, in many ways, a fish for beginners - not too fishy, not too many bones, and easy to clean and cook. They are elegant, upscale, easy to promote, and make a pleasant change from local gray mullet, red mullet and bream.

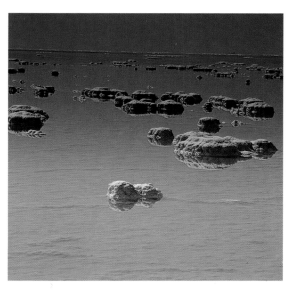

It is a geographical wonder that a country as small as Israel possesses four potentially fishy realms: the Eastern Mediterranean, the Red Sea, the Kinneret, and the Dead Sea. But ecological abuse and neglect have made the last two barren; the Dead Sea is culinarily useless, except for salt, and the Kinneret holds little or no fish, not even the famous St. Peter's fish, now transplanted to fish farms. At one time most fishing in the Red Sea was done along the shores of Sinai, but since this stretch of sea was returned to Egypt it

◆ *The Dead Sea.*

◆ *Eilat on the Red*
Sea is Israel's
southernmost
region. Since the
return of the
Sinai Desert to
Egypt, Eilat has
enjoyed an influx
of tourists.

◆ *Known for its unique therapeutic qualities, the Dead Sea attracts people from all over the world. A day covered in mud does wonders for the skin.*

◆ *Eli Avivi is self-appointed head of state of Achziv. A stretch of white sandy beach along the Mediterranean, Achziv is also the site of a Club Med village.*

◆ *Hammat Gader,*
a kibbutz on the
Golan, raises
crocodiles
primarily for
export. A
restaurant
specializing in
croc meat is
planned.

◆ *Deep-sea fishing*
is forbidden in the
Red Sea so divers
use nets instead of
air guns.

has been out of bounds to Israeli fishermen. So Israel's need for fish is now supplied by fish farms and deep-sea fishing in the Mediterranean.

The Mediterranean contains an extraordinary variety of fish waiting to be tasted by those tired of the ubiquitous frozen mullet. Around the coast of Israel there is a passion - which becomes an obsession in the summer - for catching and eating all forms of seafood. Benny Raba gets very cross about "all the silly fuss in summer." In summer, he says, the sea is too warm. The fish are already parboiled when you take them out. To get good fish in summer a fisherman must sail deep and far and only a few fishermen do that. Why on earth, he asks bitterly, do Israelis associate fish with summer?

To befriend a fisherman or the owner of a fish restaurant means accepting some strange delicacies, all with that unmistakable sea taste of iodine. For stronger stomachs, there are fan mussels and sinewy squid. For the conservative, there are bright red mullet, needing no scaling or gutting, grilled with fragrant herbs. The grouper, which can grow to a great size in the safety of deep rock holes, has a delicate flavor, and the *palamida*, or lesser tuna, has a more subtle taste than its larger relative, as well as being one of the most beautiful fish in the Mediterranean.

The factor that unites all the countries of the Mediterranean is a similarity of recipes for cooking seafood. The Greeks claim that *bouillabaisse* was originally a hearty fisherman's soup or stew. And so it is, and alive and cooking in Jaffa. In Israel fish are also eaten baked, with or without vegetables, or fried whole or in slices, or charcoal-grilled, with many different sauces. They are also braised in the style known as *hreimeh*, or minced and made into loaves and patties cooked in tasty court-bouillons. All of these cooking methods can be applied to most locally caught fish.

F I S H

◆ Mousht,
St. Peter's
fish, is
Israel's
leading
fish.

Recipes

RED MULLET WITH ORANGE BUTTER

2 lbs very fresh red mullet
peel and juice of 2 lbs oranges
salt and pepper to taste
pinch of hot chili powder
1 clove garlic, minced
1 teaspoon sugar
2 tablespoons white wine
mixture of butter and oil for frying
1 cup unsalted butter, melted

If the red mullet are small, simply wash them. If they weigh more than 3 oz, scale and clean them. Cut the orange peel into very thin strips, blanch it in boiling water for 2 minutes, then drain. Put the orange juice into a saucepan and add the salt, chili powder, garlic, sugar, wine and the blanched peel, and simmer until half the liquid has evaporated.

In the meantime, pat dry the fish, sprinkle them with salt and pepper, and dip them in flour, shaking off any excess. Heat the butter/oil in a skillet until it begins to smoke, then slide the fish into the pan. For a crispy result, do not try to fry too many fish at once. Fry for 5 minutes on each side, depending on size, then drain quickly on paper towels. Transfer the fish to 4 preheated main course/8 preheated appetizer plates.

Remove the orange juice/spice mixture from the heat and stir in the melted butter, or simply transfer both to a glass jar, screw the top on, and shake vigorously to a smooth, semitransparent consistency. Pour the sauce over the fish and serve.

BAKED GRAY MULLET

3 or 4 cloves garlic
1 large green pepper, sliced very thin
4 tablespoons chopped fresh parsley
juice of 1 lemon
salt and freshly ground black pepper
3 tablespoons olive oil
1 onion, thinly sliced
1 gray mullet, about 3 lbs, scaled and cleaned
lemon wedges, to garnish

Chop most of the garlic very fine and mix it with the green pepper, parsley, lemon juice, salt, pepper and oil. Pour this mixture over the sliced onion, reserving a little to flavor the inside of the fish.

Cut one or two shallow slits in each side of the fish and insert the rest of the garlic, cut into slivers. Spoon the reserved onion-herb-garlic mixture inside the fish. Lay the fish in a baking dish, surrounded by the rest of the onion-herb-garlic marinade, and leave in a cool place for at least 30 minutes. Turn once so that both sides of the fish have a chance to absorb the marinade.

Preheat the oven to 375°F and bake the fish for about 30 minutes, basting it once or twice and turning it once. When the flesh flakes easily, it is cooked. Serve garnished with lemon wedges, with the cooked marinade as a sauce. Serves 4 or 5.

◆ *Red mullet*

with

orange

butter.

TWO SAUCES FOR GRILLED FISH

Grilling is by far the most popular method of cooking fish in Israel.

LEMON-GARLIC SAUCE

3 tablespoons olive oil
2 tablespoons lemon juice
3 cloves garlic, minced
1/2 teaspoon salt
1/4 cup water

Heat the oil in a small saucepan. Add the lemon juice, garlic and salt. Sauté for a few seconds, then add the water and simmer for 3 minutes. Allow to cool. Serve cold.

SPRING ONION SAUCE FOR FISH

4 tablespoons olive oil
2 scallions, shredded very fine
1/2 teaspoon salt
1 tablespoon vinegar
1 1/2 teaspoons harissa (see recipe p. 41)
1/2 cup water

Lightly sauté the scallions in the oil. Add salt, vinegar and *harissa*, and mix well. Add the water and simmer for 3 minutes. Allow to cool. Serve cold.

WHOLE FISH ON THE SPIT

1/2 teaspoon paprika
4 tablespoons coriander seeds
6 cardamom pods
1 tablespoon anise or dill seeds
2 onions, chopped
2 cloves garlic, crushed
2 tablespoons chopped fresh mint
4 tablespoons chopped fresh parsley
1 green bell pepper, cored and thinly sliced
2/3 cup plain yogurt, whipped
juice of 1 lemon or lime
3 lbs fish (sea bass, gray mullet),
cleaned, with heads and tails removed
salt and pepper
1/4 cup clarified butter

Toast the paprika and coriander in a skillet, then grind them up with the other spices. Add them to the onions, garlic, herbs and green pepper, and mix to a smooth paste with the yogurt and lemon/lime juice.

Prick the fish all over and rub in the spice and herb mixture. Season with salt and pepper and allow to marinate for 1 hour.

Thread the fish onto a barbecue spit, with a pan underneath to catch the juices. Grill for 15 minutes or until the herb paste is dry. Baste with the pan juices, then raise the spit and cook for a further 25 minutes over a gentle heat, turning once.

The fish are cooked when they flake easily. Lower the spit to raise the intensity of the heat, baste the fish with the clarified butter and continue cooking until the skins are crisp. Serve at once, with salad and potatoes. Serves 6.

PALAMIDA
Marinated bonito/lesser tuna

Scale and clean the fish, slice them into 3/4-inch pieces, and marinate overnight in the following mixture: 4 1/2 cups water, 1/3 cup salt, 1 teaspoon vinegar, 1 crushed clove garlic.

For an authentic Bulgarian Jewish breakfast, eat with onions, olives and thin slices of gray mullet roe, washed down with vodka.

◆ *Marinated palamida, stage two. The marinated fish is served with scallions, black olives and Turkish caviar (gray mullet roe sliced very thin).*

◆ *Victor's is a delicatessen deep in the heart of the Levinsky market in Tel Aviv. It is a typical deli specializing in smoked fish and herrings.*

◆ *Marinated palamida, stage one. The fish is cut into chunks and covered with sea salt.*

TROUT BARBECUED IN GRAPE LEAVES

8 trout, 8-10 oz each
1 cup olive oil
1/4 cup fresh lemon juice
scant tablespoon minced capers
2 tablespoons minced fresh parsley
1 tablespoon fresh chives, snipped small
1 teaspoon minced fresh basil
1/2 teaspoon minced fresh rosemary
8 sprigs fresh thyme
40 large grape/vine leaves, fresh or preserved
1 lemon, cut into wedges, to garnish
sprigs of fresh herbs, to garnish

Top, tail and bone the trout, leaving them otherwise whole. Then score them on both sides at 2 1/2-inch intervals, holding the knife at an angle of 30° and cutting a quarter of the way through the flesh.

Mix together the olive oil, lemon juice, capers and herbs and rub this mixture generously over the fish, inside and out. Put a sprig of thyme in each fish, then wrap each one in 5 grape leaves, overlapping them so that they entirely envelop the fish. Secure with string at 1-inch intervals.

Prepare the barbecue. When the coals are ready, scatter soaked mesquite or fruit-wood chips on top. When they begin to smolder, place the fish on the grill and cover with foil. If the fish are about 1-inch thick, they will take about 10 minutes to cook; if thicker, proportionately longer. Turn once during cooking.

To serve, remove the string but leave the grape leaves on, and garnish with lemon wedges and fresh herbs. Serves 8.

TROUT WITH POMEGRANATE

1 large pomegranate
4 fresh trout
2 tablespoons vinegar
1 onion, chopped
1/2 cup butter
salt and pepper to taste
pinch ground cardamom
2 cloves garlic, minced
1 scant cup pecans or walnuts,
coarsely chopped
extra butter

Cut the pomegranate in half and tap rather than scoop out the seeds so that they remain intact. Wash and clean the fish. With trout, it is possible to break the backbone near the head and pull it out whole, leaving the fish intact but deboned. Rub the fish inside and out with vinegar.

Lightly fry the onions in a little of the butter. Season the inside of the fish with salt, pepper and cardamom to taste, then stuff them with the pomegranate seeds, fried onion, garlic, chopped pecans, and put a knob of butter in each. If necessary, close the openings with toothpicks.

Butter an ovenproof dish and lay the fish in it. Bake in an oven preheated to 400°F for 12 minutes. Serve on a bed of mustard and cress or watercress, garnished with the rest of the pomegranate seeds.

◆ *Trout with pomegranate on a bed of cress.*

GEFILTE FISH
Traditional poached fishballs

2 lbs fresh carp
salt
1 slice stale challah *or 1/2 cup matzo flour*
1 hard-boiled egg
1 large onion
2 eggs
2 tablespoons oil
black pepper and sugar to taste

BROTH
4 carrots, sliced
2 onions, sliced
4 1/2 cups water
salt, pepper and sugar to taste

Wash the fish and cut it into slices, reserving the roe for future use. Sprinkle the slices with salt and refrigerate for 1 hour. Soak the *challah* in water, and then drain.

Using a sharp knife, skin the fish, saving any unbroken rings of skin. Discard only the main bones. Ignoring all the other bones, grind the fish twice with the hard-boiled egg, the onion and the *challah* to achieve a smooth consistency. At this stage some cooks would add 8 oz of pike fillet, a few almonds or a raw carrot, but these are optional.

Now blend in the 2 eggs, oil, salt and pepper, and sugar to taste - knowing the powerful emotions aroused by the subject of how much sugar gefilte fish should contain, we do not dare specify the amount of sugar to be added here - and refrigerate.

Put all the broth ingredients into a large saucepan, bring to a boil and cook for 30 minutes. Add the fish's head and continue to simmer. Meanwhile, form the chilled fish mixture into balls, wetting your hands to prevent the mixture sticking to them. If you managed to save any rings of skin, stuff them with the mixture too. Smooth them with your wet hands and slide them one by one, with the other balls, into the simmering broth. Cover the saucepan, leaving a small gap between the lid and the saucepan, and simmer for 2 hours. When cool, put in the refrigerator.

To serve, put 2 or 3 balls on each plate with a slice of carrot on top and some of the jellied broth. Serve the fish head to the head of the family. *Challah* and horseradish relish (see recipes p. 90 and 41) are an absolute must with gefilte fish. Makes enough for 8 appetizer portions.

HERRINGS IN SOUR CREAM

10 fat herrings
2 tablespoons sugar
1 cup heavy cream
2 tablespoons white wine vinegar
1 medium red onion, sliced very thin

Fillet the herrings and remove the skin, then cut each fillet into 5 or 6 pieces. Beat the sugar into the cream and stir in the vinegar. Put the fish into a glass jar, with layers of onion in between, and pour in the cream. Cover and refrigerate. Use within 10 days. Makes 20 servings.

◆ *Sunset over the Kinneret, Israel's only freshwater lake.*

POACHED SEA BASS MARINATED IN LEMON & BASIL

peel of 1 lemon, pared off in strips
6 fillets sea bass, about 8 oz each
1/2 cup fresh lemon juice
1/3 cup white wine vinegar
1 1/2 teaspoons salt
1/2 teaspoon sugar
1 1/2 cups extra-virgin olive oil
3 tablespoons finely choppped basil, plus sprigs
of basil to garnish
2 large cloves garlic, chopped
2 teaspoons dried hot red-pepper flakes
1 cup dry white wine
2 bay leaves
2 sprigs parsley
4 1/2 cups water
red bell pepper, finely chopped, to garnish

Put the lemon peel in the bottom of a shallow dish large enough to hold all the bass fillets flat. Skin the fillets and cut them crosswise into strips about 1 1/4 inches wide.

Beat together the lemon juice, vinegar, 1/2 teaspoon salt, sugar and oil until the mixture emulsifies (thickens and goes cloudy), then beat in half the chopped basil, the garlic and the red-pepper flakes.

In a large saucepan, combine the wine, bay leaves, parsley and the rest of the salt with the water, and bring to a boil. Turn down the heat so that the liquid is just simmering, then slide half a dozen strips of bass into the liquid and poach them for 1–1 1/2 minutes or until the flesh is just firm. Remove with a slotted spoon and transfer to the dish with the lemon peel. Poach the rest of the fish in the same way.

◆ Mousht

with tahini:

St. Peter's fish

with sesame

sauce.

Pour the marinade over the fish, cover, and allow to marinate overnight in the refrigerator.

Let the fish stand at room temperature for 1 hour before serving. Transfer the fish slices to individual plates, strain the marinade through a fine strainer, beat it well to emulsify it, and drizzle it over the fish. Sprinkle with the red bell pepper and the rest of the basil, and garnish with basil sprigs. Serves 8 to 10.

MOUSHT WITH TAHINI
St. Peter's fish with sesame sauce

St. Peter's fish (*mousht* in Arabic) is a Sea of Galilee fish. It is a bony, tasty fish not unlike sea bream.

2 onions, sliced
1/4 cup vegetable oil
4 small mousht (or trout), cleaned
1/2 cup tahini/sesame seed paste
(see p. 30)
2 tablespoons lemon juice
1 clove garlic, crushed
salt and pepper
blanched vegetables and sesame seeds,
to garnish

Preheat the oven to 325°F. Using a large skillet, sauté the onion in the oil until it is soft, then add the fish and cook them for 1 minute on each side so that they absorb some of the onion flavour.

Blend together the *tahini*, lemon juice and garlic. Transfer the fish and the onions to an ovenproof dish, sprinkle them with salt and pepper, and coat them with the *tahini* mixture. Bake, uncovered, for 30 minutes or until the fish flake easily. Garnish with blanched vegetables and sesame seeds. Serves 4.

$\mathscr{B}$ R E A D

◆ *Large, flat Iraqi pita are baked in the traditional taboon, a clay oven, in Ashtanur bakery, Jerusalem. The dough is flattened against the interior of the taboon and falls off when ready.*

I f *falafel* were not such an integral part of Israeli folklore, bread - any bread - would be the king of Israeli food. But dethroning *falafel* would be a political move requiring great boldness and courage. Opposition would be

vocal and nasty. Yet we eat more bread than *falafel*, and how would *falafel* survive without *pita* bread? What other vehicle is there for those tasty little patties and handfuls of salad?

I am biased when it comes to bread. Bread is in my blood. I am a baker's son, and would have been a third-generation baker if I had not betrayed my heritage. My father sold the family's 50-year-old bakery when he became certain that I was a lost cause. He was as much to blame as I was, because this is what he told me about bread. People eat it all the time. It's so ordinary that they stop noticing it. It's invisible. When you bake an invisible staple, you too become invisible. People only notice you when your oven breaks down and your bread is ruined. Then they hate you. People who have never appreciated you resent you the first chance they get. Also, it's a hard, back-breaking job being a baker. Creativity does not come into it. Bread is not about creativity. It is about flour and water and yeast and the way they rise in the steam room and then brown in the oven.

We have always eaten bread in this country. When Jerusalem was under siege in the '48 war, everything stopped. No one came or went. The only convoys that got through were trucks bearing water and bread. When they didn't get through, people baked their own bread, if they had the flour and the yeast. Bread is what you eat when you have no other food.

Even in these affluent times, few Israelis dine without bread. Bread even enjoys a government subsidy - that is how important it is. Israelis have never

◆ *In Israel, the term "black bread" refers to the most common bread. This is subsidized by the government, so anyone can afford it.*

paid the full price of a loaf of bread. By subsidizing bread, the government shows a proper regard for one of the last tenets of socialism. Whatever happens, the government implies, we will always have bread. We will never starve.

If bread is the uncrowned king of Israel, then *challah* is the queen. *Challah* is the traditional Jewish egg-rich braided bread which is ritually blessed and served every Friday night when the members of observant families get together to re-establish the kinship and continuity of family life. On Friday nights one does not talk shop. Business matters are forbidden as a subject of conversation. The name *challah* actually means "the priest's share" and derives from the fact that a little piece of dough is symbolically removed from the main body of dough before it is shaped into loaves and put in the oven. The "priests's share" must rise on its own and be baked separately from the rest, and when it is baked it must be charred or burned beyond redemption - it is a sacrifice and not meant to be eaten. *Challah* is the bread we eat on festive occasions such as holidays and weddings. A special blessing involving a *challah*, usually quite a large one baked specially for the occasion, is part of Jewish weddings. Bread and salt are traditional gifts at a Jewish house-warming.

The heir-apparent is the *pita*, such an essential part of Israeli eating that it is hard to imagine life without it. Most appetizers or *mezze* dishes rely heavily on *pita*. Why use a fork to eat your *hummus* or *tahini* when you can use a hand-torn, edible scoop? *Hummus*-scooping is an art honed over many years. We expect *pita* to be there. We reach for it without even looking up from our newspapers.

◆ *Simcha Haddad of Netanya still uses the* taboon *to bake bread in her backyard.*

◆ *General view of the flat, fertile Jezreel Valley.*

A cultural war is now in progress between the followers of *pita* and the followers of bread. The two staples represent two cultures, Ashkenazi and Sephardic, in the process of become one nation. Jews who came to Israel from Arab countries, Sephardim, have always eaten *pita*. Ashkenazim, from Russia, Poland and Germany, are addicted to bread and have tried hard to preserve their heritage, but their efforts at baking the traditional breads of the old countries have seldom been successful. Over the years they have given up. Bread needs so much attention, with all the rising and kneading and rising again. Now they have to make do with local bread.

In other words, the bread versus *pita* war is not going bread's way at the moment, although the Tunisian open sandwich - a whole loaf of bread

◆ *An old*

flour mill

in the

village of

Shefar'am.

cut in half, hollowed out and filled with salad, tuna, salami, and saturated with virgin olive oil - seems to be standing its ground, principally for heroic reasons. Gone are the days when traditional bakers scoffed at the quickly-made, non-rising Arab *pita*. Now there are specialized *pita* bakeries that do booming business day and night - long lines form in front of them in the dark hours - and the *pitas* they produce are not plain or ordinary. Adapting the principle of the pizza, Israeli *pita* makers have started to add different toppings. *Pita* with the salty herb mixture known as *za'atar* is a big hit. Then there are *pita*-pizza topped with egg, mushrooms, basil and tomato, and a dozen other flavors... This is the age of the *pita* and most Israelis eat *pita* in great quantities, whatever their country of origin.

B R E A D

◆ *The popular Abulafia bakery in Jaffa specializes in doughy* pitas *with assorted toppings. Abulafia also bakes bagels.*

Recipes

CHALLAH
Sweet braided bread eaten on the
Sabbath

1 1/2 tablespoons dried yeast
1/2 cup lukewarm water, to activate
yeast
1 teaspoon sugar
3 eggs
1/2 cup sugar
1 1/2 cups lukewarm water, to
mix with dough
1/2 cup vegetable oil
1 1/2 teaspoons salt
9 cups all-purpose flour
2 eggs, beaten with 2 tablespoons water
sesame or poppy seeds, to garnish

Combine the yeast, the 1/2 cup lukewarm water and the sugar, and set aside. In a large mixing bowl, beat together the eggs and sugar, then add the 1 1/2 cups of lukewarm water, oil and salt. Stir in the frothing yeast mixture and beat well. Using a wooden spoon, beat in half the flour, adding a heaped tablespoonful at a time and beating well after each addition. At this stage, the dough will be sticky. Add half the remaining flour, beating in a tablespoonful at a time as before. The dough should now leave the sides of the bowl.

Dredge the rest of the flour onto a work surface, remove the dough from the bowl and knead it for 10 minutes until all the flour has been absorbed. Return the dough to the bowl, cover it with a damp towel, and let it rise in an unheated oven with the door closed for 1 hour or until it has more or less doubled in size.

Punch down the dough and divide it into three equal portions. Cut each portion into three and shape the thirds into long sau-sages. Braid the sausages together to make three loaves.

Place the loaves on a greased and floured baking sheet, cover, and leave them to rise for about 1 1/2-2 hours, or until they have nearly doubled in volume. Preheat the oven to 400°F.

Brush each loaf with the egg and water mixture, sprinkle with poppy or sesame seeds, and bake for 15 minutes until golden. Tap the loaves on the bottom to see if they sound hollow - if they don't, give them another few minutes. When they do sound hollow, leave them in the oven for another 5 minutes. Cool on a wire rack. Makes 3 loaves.

◆ Challah *comes*
in many shapes
and forms.
Round challah
with poppy seeds
is hard to slice
with a knife.
Kids love to tear
them to pieces.

◆ *A slice of*
sweet
challah *with*
raisins.

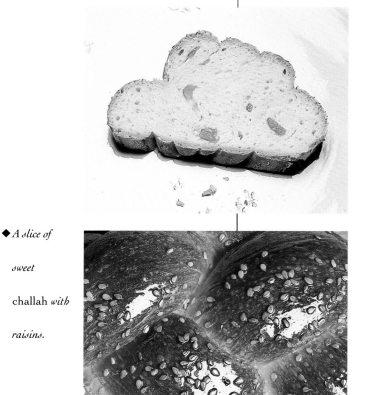

◆ *Abulafia's best, a tray of pita, bagels, ka'ahks (bagels with sesame seeds), pita with egg, za'atar, onion and olives, and Iraqi pita.*

PITA
Middle Eastern flat bread/pocket bread

1 tablespoon dried yeast
2 tablespoons honey
2 1/3-3 cups lukewarm water
6-7 cups all-purpose flour
1 tablespoon salt

Mix together the yeast, honey and 1/2 cup lukewarm water in a small bowl and allow to stand for 10 minutes in a warm place. Put 4 cups of the flour into a large mixing bowl, add the frothing yeast mixture and 2 cups lukewarm water, and beat vigorously for a minute or two. Now add the salt and half the remaining flour and beat again.

On a lightly floured board, knead the dough for 10 minutes, adding more flour if necessary to make a medium-stiff dough. Place the dough in a lightly greased bowl, cover, and leave in a warm, draft-free place to double in volume - this should take about 1 hour. Preheat the oven to 450°F.

Punch down the dough, knead it again, then divide it into 12 equal portions, rolling each one into a ball with your hands. Roll the balls of dough into flat circles about 5 inches across and 1/4 inch thick, place the circles on an ungreased baking sheet, cover and allow to rise for 10 minutes. Cook on the bottom rack of the oven for 8 minutes, or until the bottoms are pale brown. If no pocket appears, raise the oven temperature; if too brown, spray with water. Allow to cool, then put into plastic bags and refrigerate or freeze.

Pita bread should be served warm. Three minutes in a preheated 350°F oven should be enough to warm them through. Any longer, and they become rock hard! Makes 12.

SESAME PITA TOASTS

*2 rounds pita bread about
6 inches across
1/2 cup sesame seeds, lightly toasted
3 tablespoons unsalted butter, softened
salt*

Preheat the oven to 375°F. Cut each *pita* into quarters, then separate the quarters so that you have 8 more or less triangular pieces of bread. Dredge the sesame seeds onto a flat surface, spread the rough sides of each *pita* triangle with butter and press them, butter side down, onto the sesame seeds.

Arrange the triangles, sesame side up, on a baking sheet and bake in the oven for 8 - 10 minutes or until the toasts are crisp. Transfer the toasts to a cooling rack, sprinkle them with salt to taste, and serve warm or at room temperature.

CHILDREN'S PIZZA

*1 pita
1/2 cup tomato sauce
1/2 cup pitted olives
1 bell pepper, sliced
5 oz canned tuna or sweetcorn, optional
7 oz Gruyère cheese*

Made by children, this can be a creative experience. First separate the *pita* into perfect round halves. Spread each half with tomato sauce, arrange the olives, pepper and canned tuna or sweetcorn on top, and cover with cheese, grated or thinly sliced. Put under the broiler until the cheese is nicely melted. Chill and serve.

PITA WITH ONION & POPPY SEEDS

*2 oz fresh yeast
1 teaspoon sugar
salt
1/2 cup lukewarm water
8 1/4 cups all-purpose flour
3 tablespoons oil
3 eggs, lightly beaten
3 onions, finely chopped
1/2 cup poppy seeds*

Dissolve the yeast, sugar and a pinch of salt in the lukewarm water. Cover and leave in a warm place for 10 minutes until the mixture becomes frothy.

Put the flour into a large mixing bowl, make a well in the middle and pour in the yeast mixture, oil and 2 of the beaten eggs. Knead well. Cover with a towel, and put in a warm place for 30 minutes to allow the dough to rise.

Rub a little oil on your hands and roll the dough into about two dozen walnut-sized balls. Place the balls on a floured surface and roll them out into circles about 2 1/2 inches across. Sprinkle each circle with onion, poppy seeds and a little salt, lightly pressing them into the dough with the rolling pin. Brush with the rest of the beaten egg. Cover and allow to rise for 30 minutes. Bake in a hot oven - 400°F - until golden brown.

Makes about 24.

BAGEL/KA'AHK
Pastry rings with cumin and coriander

1/2 oz fresh yeast, or half this amount of
dried yeast
1 1/4 cups lukewarm water
pinch sugar
1 teaspoon salt
1/2 teaspoon ground cumin
1/2 teaspoon ground coriander
4 cups all-purpose flour
1/2 cup unsalted butter or margarine, melted
1 egg, lightly beaten
sesame seeds

Dissolve the yeast in 2 tablespoons luke-warm water, add the sugar, and leave for 10-15 minutes.

Sift the salt, cumin and coriander into the flour, make a well in the middle and pour in the melted butter and frothing yeast mixture. Knead to a dough, adding the water a tablespoon at a time. Knead for 10 -15 minutes until the dough is smooth and comes away from the sides of the bowl. Cover the bowl with a damp cloth and leave in a warm place for 2 hours or until the dough has doubled in volume. Preheat the oven to 350°F.

Working on a floured surface, roll wal-nut-sized pieces of dough into thin 4 x 6 inch rectangles. Roll each rectangle into a cigar shape and bring the ends together to form a circle - press the ends firmly together with a little water. Arrange on a greased baking sheet, leaving 1 inch or so between each *ka'ahk*. Brush with the beaten egg and sprinkle with sesame seeds. Bake for 25-30 minutes until crisp and golden brown. Makes 20.

PRETZELS

1 oz active dried yeast
1 tablespoon sugar
1 cup lukewarm water
3 cups sifted all-purpose flour
2 tablespoons butter, softened
1/2 teaspoon salt
4 teaspoons baking soda
4 1/2 cups water
coarse salt or sesame seeds, to garnish

Dissolve the yeast and a little of the sugar in the lukewarm water. When the mixture is frothing nicely, add it to the flour, butter and salt, and knead, knead, knead. Cover the dough with a cloth and allow it to rise to nearly double the volume. Punch it down, divide it into 12 equal portions and roll each one out into a ribbon 1/2 inch thick. Loop each ribbon into a figure of eight and leave in a warm place, covered with a cloth, to rise again. Preheat the oven to 450°F.

Dissolve the baking soda in the 4 1/2 cups water and bring to a boil. Slide each pretzel into the boiling water and boil until it floats - about 1 minute. Remove with a pancake turner and place on a baking sheet for 12 minutes. Before baking, sprinkle with coarse salt or sesame seeds. Bake until golden brown.

Although pretzels are delicious fresh, they will keep for up to 1 week. They are best eaten with butter.

◆ *A "hero"*
sandwich,
a favorite of
Israeli con-
struction
workers.
It has
everything in
it, on a 1 1/2 lbs
loaf of
bread.

MLAWAH
Flaky bread

1/4 teaspoon baking powder
3 cups all-purpose flour
1 cup water
1 cup butter, melted and clarified
1/2 teaspoon salt
1 teaspoon sugar
1 teaspoon vinegar, optional

Sift the baking powder into the flour, make a well in the center and add water, 1 tablespoon of the butter, salt, sugar and vinegar (if desired). Knead to a smooth elastic consistency. Cut into 6 equal portions, and allow to "rest" in a cool place for 20 minutes.

Flatten each piece to a round the size of a *pita* - patience is a virtue here since the dough is springy and resists stretching and flattening! Liberally brush each round with the melted butter, then roll it into a tight sausage shape. Allow the rolls to rest for 20 minutes. Repeat the flattening, rolling and brushing procedure twice more, waiting 20 minutes between rolling and re-flattening. The final results should be flat and round like *pita*.

Using a non-stick skillet, fry the *mlawah* on both sides until golden brown, flipping them over at half time. Serve with freshly puréed tomatoes and *zhoug*.

Mlawah freeze well. Just put waxed paper between them and seal them in a freezer bag.

◆ Lahuhua,

spongy

Yemenite

pancakes,

with zhoug

and soup.

LAHUHUA
Yemenite sponge bread

1 oz fresh yeast
3 cups lukewarm water
1 tablespoon sugar
4 cups all-purpose flour, sifted
1/2 teaspoon salt
5 tablespoons melted butter or shortening

Dissolve the yeast in a little of the water. When it is frothing, combine it with the rest of the ingredients. Mix well, cover with a cloth and leave to rise in a warm place for 1 hour. Mix again, re-cover and leave for another hour.

Use a small nonstick skillet to cook *lahuhua*. Start each pancake in a cold skillet, then cook for 2 minutes over a medium heat, then move the skillet to a very low heat and continue cooking for another 4 minutes. Cook on one side only.

Lahuhua are traditionally served with soups and stews. They are spongy and savory, and not difficult to make.

◆ *Wheat*

harvest in

the Jezreel

Valley.

◆ *Fresh* pita
being baked
in the ancient
village of
Pequi'in.
The thin
rounds of
dough are
placed on hot
metal, flipped
over and
quickly
removed.

MEDITERRANEAN OLIVE ROLLS

1/2 oz dried yeast
1 teaspoon sugar
1/2-1 teaspoon freshly ground black pepper
1 cup lukewarm water
1 cup buckwheat flour
3 cups all-purpose flour
2 tablespoons extra-virgin olive oil
3 cups brine-cured black olives, pitted and
coarsely chopped

Mix the yeast, sugar and pepper with the water and allow to stand for 10 minutes.

Put the buckwheat flour and the all-purpose flour into a mixing bowl, make a well in the middle and add the frothing yeast mixture, the oil and the chopped olives. Mix to a soft, sticky dough. Transfer the dough to a floured surface and knead gently for 2 minutes. Dust with flour, return to the mixing bowl, cover with plastic wrap and leave in a warm place for at least 45 minutes or until the dough has nearly doubled in size.

Turn the dough out onto a floured surface, cut it into quarters, roll each quarter into a ball, and cut each ball into four - you should now have 16 pieces of dough of equal size. With floured hands, shape the pieces into balls and arrange on an oiled baking sheet. Put in a warm place for 30-40 minutes to nearly double in volume. Preheat the oven to 400°F.

Before you put the rolls in the oven, make a shallow slash in the top of each. Bake in the lower third of the oven for 20-25 minutes or until the bottoms sound hollow when you tap them. Cool on a rack.
Makes 16.

FATTOUSH
Vegetable and herb salad with toasted pieces of bread

1 large cucumber, chopped
5 tomatoes, chopped
10 scallions, chopped
1 small green bell pepper, chopped
1 tablespoon chopped parsley
1 tablespoon chopped coriander leaves, optional
1/2 tablespoon chopped fresh mint
1 clove garlic, crushed
6 tablespoons olive oil
juice of 2 lemons
1/2 teaspoon salt
1/4 teaspoon black pepper
2 pitas, toasted and broken
into small pieces

Prepare all the vegetables and make sure the herbs are chopped very fine. Put them into a large salad bowl, add the oil, lemon juice, salt and pepper, and toss well. Chill until ready to serve, and at the last minute stir in the toasted pieces of bread.

Serves 5 or 6.

◆ Fattoush,

vegetable

and herb

salad with

pieces of

toasted

pita.

$\mathcal{T}$ R A D I T I O N A L

D I S H E S

◆ *Go east young man*
and bring back a
warm, fragrant pot
of cholent.
Weekends are made
for take-aways and
if you bring your
own pot, there are
many restaurants
that will fill it for
you.

$\mathcal{I}$ srael's two most dominant culinary traditions, European and Sephardic/Arab, meet and blend in the casserole. The Jewish observance of the Sabbath, when cooking is forbidden, and the Arab penchant for

◆ *A view of Mea She'arim, Jerusalem's orthodox Jewish quarter.*

slow cooking have led to a comfortable convergence. Casseroles are one of the pillars of Israeli cuisine. By casseroles I mean dishes that require a whole night of cooking in a very low oven, dishes of lamb and chicken which are the staples of North African cuisine, and Arab meat dishes brought to table in large bowls.

From nightfall on Friday, Jews are not allowed to use electricity or to light a fire, which means that all the Sabbath food has to be prepared in advance or put in a warm oven overnight. Food is the main attraction of the Sabbath. Israelis never work on Saturdays and, since orthodox Jews are forbidden to drive, most of the day is spent at home. Special Sabbath dishes have been devised over the centuries, dishes that do not compromise taste and appeal for the sake of observance, but by the very nature of the slow cooking process most of them are heavy and substantial.

Meat and potatoes in a special stew called *cholent* are the trademark of Eastern European Jews. Spicy chicken and lamb *tagines* are typical of Moroccan Jews. *Jihnoon* and *kubbaneh*, which are dough-based, are part of Yemenite Jewish cuisine. All of them go into the oven on Friday night, to be consumed during the Sabbath. The Yemenites start earlier than others; *kubbaneh*, a spongy, spicy bread, is eaten for breakfast, to be joined later by *jihnoon*.

As a rule of thumb, slow-cooked food is usually eaten slowly. There is nothing fresh or crisp or sparkling about it, and there is no point in eating it quickly. Strong Turkish coffee and tea with mint are served with it.

Arab and Jewish traditional cooking are alike in their refusal to allow any change in the role of women as cooks and servants. The Israeli who returns from temple expecting his food to be on the table has much in

◆ *Entrance to a public bath house in Mea She'arim.*

common with the Arab who never enters the kitchen and never offers to help. While orthodox Jews demand their food and do nothing except pray over it and eat it, Arab men are in charge once the food actually reaches the table. An Arab woman never leaves the kitchen during a meal, whether her husband is dining alone or with guests. Women and children invariably eat in the kitchen. Out front, in the dining room, the Arab man hovers around his guests. He fills their glasses. He fills their plates. He refills their plates at the

slightest sign of a dent in the small mountains of rice and meat he has set before them. He urges them to eat whenever their attention wanders....

◆ *Bible class in Mea She'arim.*

Most of the recipes given in this chapter are made in pots of one kind or another. All of them are braised or stewed or baked very slowly, usually covered. They are, by their nature, food for winter. *Cholent* is a typical Eastern European dish, but it also has North African and Iraqi variants. The slow-cooking casserole has evolved wherever Jews have lived. The Moroccans eat *∂feena* and the Iraqis have *tabyeet* - both are versions of *cholent*.

Cholent and its relatives are served in large pots cozily placed in the center of the table so that the whole family can help themselves and come back for more. They are the focus of social occasions. A clear soup, vegetables, condiments and pickles are usually served with them.

A place of honor is reserved for *couscous*, the national dish of Morocco. *Couscous* is also popular in Algeria and Tunisia, and in Paris, where *couscous* joints have long provided bargain meals for students and tourists. *Couscous* and its accompanying condiments and salads were brought to Israel by North African Jews in the 1950s, and the genre continues to flourish.

◆ *A heder or classroom for little boys in Mea She'arim.*

The word *couscous*, as used above, describes a combination of steamed grain, stewed meat (usually lamb), poultry or fish, and vegetables, or sometimes only steamed grain and vegetables. The grain itself is also called *couscous*, and the hourglass-shaped vessel in which the dish is traditionally cooked is called a *couscousier*. When the *couscous* grain is taken from the steamer part of the *couscousier*, fluffed up, heaped on a platter and decorated with fragrant stew, the result is wonderfully satisfying, addictive even. Craig Claiborne has called *couscous* "one of the dozen greatest dishes in the world."

◆ *A couscousier, the authentic vessel in which to cook couscous.*

Couscous is usually served in a flat bowl or deep plate so that you can pour the stew broth over it. Flat *pita* bread is torn into pieces and used to scoop up the grain and stew, and then to mop up the juices in the bottom of the bowl. The condiment most frequently eaten with *couscous* is a paste based on red chili peppers called *harissa*. Moroccan cooks will diligently wash, drain and rake *couscous* with their bare hands for 20 to 30 minutes to add moisture and also get rid of any lumps. Then they steam it in a *couscousier*, toss it in cold salted water, and steam it again. There is a purpose to all this: the grains become remarkably fluffy and absorb the flavors from the vapors that rise from the stew bubbling beneath. But *couscous* does not have to be a career. You can buy quick-cooking *couscous* from most specialty food stores and delicatessens.

Although most of the recipes in this chapter are not uniquely Israeli, they symbolize the way in which Jews from different cultures have assimilated here. It seems that food is the great glue that keeps us together.

TRADITIONAL DISHES

◆ *A crock of gold. Cholent is a meal in itself.*

Recipes

COUSCOUS WITH LAMB

3 lbs lamb, cut into chunks
1 tablespoon salt
1 teaspoon freshly ground black pepper
4 whole cloves, or 1/4 teaspoon ground cloves
1 teaspoon turmeric
2 bay leaves
4 large carrots (2 diced and 2 sliced)
4 onions (2 diced and 2 sliced)
2 sticks celery, chopped
6 quarts water
1 small cabbage, sliced
2 zucchini, cut into bite-size pieces
2 turnips, cubed
10 oz pumpkin, cut into large cubes
1/2 cup raisins
2 lbs quick-cooking couscous
1 lb cooked chick peas, drained

Put the lamb, salt, pepper, cloves, turmeric, bay leaves, diced carrots, diced onions and chopped celery into a *couscousier* or pan wide and deep enough to support a steamer or colander, and cover with the water. Bring to a boil, lower the heat, and simmer for nearly 1 hour, or until the lamb is tender.

Pour the broth through a strainer and reserve. Remove the meat from the strainer and reserve. Discard the vegetables.

Clean the *couscousier* or pan and return the reserved broth to it. Now add the sliced carrots, sliced onions, cabbage, zucchini, turnips, pumpkin and raisins. Partially cover the pan, and simmer for 5 minutes, or until the vegetables are tender.

Meanwhile, cook the *couscous* according to the directions on the package. Add the reserved lamb and the drained chick peas to the broth, then place the *couscous* container over the broth and turn up the heat so that the steam from the broth rises through the *couscous*. Steam for 20 minutes or according to directions, then heap the *couscous* onto a serving platter or onto individual plates and arrange the meat and vegetables on top. Spoon over a small amount of broth, and serve the rest in a jug. Serve with Moroccan carrot salad (see recipe p. 34).

Serves 10 to 12.

◆ *Moroccan carrot salad is a traditional complement to couscous. See recipe page 34.*

◆ *Moroccan couscous with lamb. The golden semolina grains can be topped with all manner of broths and stews - lamb, chicken, fish, and vegetables.*

ASHKENAZI CHOLENT
A layered hotpot of beans, chicken, marrow bones, dumpling and potatoes

12 medium potatoes
2 tablespoons salt
1 1/2 cups dry lima beans
1 1/2 cups red kidney or adzuki beans
salt and pepper
5 beef marrow bones
2 lbs beef shoulder, cut into large cubes
4 large onions, sliced
2 tablespoons vegetable oil
1 cup barley, washed
2 tablespoons sugar
2 tablespoons water

CHOLENT KUGEL
1 onion, sliced
mixture of vegetable oil, margarine
& chicken fat
1 1/2 cups all-purpose flour
slice of challah *bread (see recipe p. 90), soaked*
in water, then squeezed dry
1 chicken bouillion cube
salt and pepper
1 egg, beaten
water

Peel the potatoes and soak them in water, with the 2 tablespoons salt, for 2 hours. Soak the beans in unsalted water for 2 hours, then drain them and season with salt and pepper. Season the marrow bones and beef with salt and pepper.

To make the kugel, sauté the onion in the oil/margarine/chicken fat, stir into the flour, add the *challah*, bouillion cube, salt and pepper, and knead to an elastic dough with the egg and water, adding more water if necessary. Roll the dough into a log shape, put it into a roasting bag, and prick a few holes in the bag.

In a large deep pan, sauté the 4 large onions in the oil. Remove from the heat and add, layered in the following order, the beans, the marrow bones and beef, the barley, the kugel in its roasting bag, and the potatoes.

Melt the sugar in a little water, turn up the heat and cook until the sugar turns dark brown. Stir in 2 tablespoons water, and immediately pour over the *cholent*. Add just enough water to cover all the ingredients, bring to a boil, and simmer briskly for 30 minutes. Cover the pan and transfer to a very low oven to cook overnight.

The *cholent* kugel is usually served separately from the *cholent*, cut into slices like a cake. The cholent kugel mixture can also be used to stuff calf's intestines, to create the famous *kishke*, or chicken necks.

Serves 6 to 8.

◆ *All the*

ingredients

for a fine

cholent.

SEPHARDIC CHOLENT
A layered hotpot of beans, meat, potatoes and eggs

12 medium potatoes
2 tablespoons salt
3 cups dry lima beans
salt and pepper
4 large onions, finely chopped
3 tablespoons vegetable oil
1 - 2 lbs beef, cut into slices
2 lbs calf's foot, cut into slices
3 small onions, unpeeled
10 hard-boiled eggs in their shells

Peel the potatoes and soak them in water, with the 2 tablespoons salt, for 2 hours. Soak the beans in unsalted water for 2 hours, then drain them and season with salt and pepper.

In a large deep pan, sauté the onion in the oil. Remove from the heat and add, in layers, first the beans, then the sliced beef and calf's foot, then the unpeeled onions, then the whole, soaked potatoes, and lastly the hard-boiled eggs. Add just enough water to cover all the ingredients. Bring to a boil and simmer briskly, uncovered, for 30 minutes. Then cover the pan and transfer to a very low oven to cook overnight.
Serves 6 to 8.

DFEENA
Beef stew with calf's foot, hard-boiled eggs, potatoes and pulses. A Moroccan-Jewish version of *cholent*, eaten on festive occasions

1 calf's foot
2 large onions, finely chopped
vegetable oil
2 lbs stewing beef, cubed
6 small potatoes
6 eggs in their shells, well scrubbed
1 2/3-2 1/4 cups chick peas or
navy beans, soaked overnight
2 cloves garlic, crushed
1 teaspoon ground allspice
salt and freshly ground black pepper

Blanch the calf's foot in boiling water and drain. Fry the onions in oil until they are soft and golden.

Put these and the rest of the ingredients into a large ovenproof pot or casserole with a tight-fitting lid. Cover with water, put the lid on, and cook for 1 hour at 375°F. Then lower the oven temperature to the lowest setting and continue to cook for several hours, or overnight. Serves 6 to 8.

Note: If you are using beans rather than the more traditional chick peas, do not add salt until the beans are tender - adding it before seems to prevent them softening.

CHICKEN SOUP WITH KNEIDLACH
Traditional Jewish chicken soup with dumplings

3 lbs chicken, whole or in pieces, with feet
6 1/2 cups water
2 medium onions, peeled
1 small head celery, chopped
4 carrots, scraped and chopped into thick pieces
pinch paprika
salt and pepper
bunch parsley

KNEIDLACH
1 1/2 cups matzo flour
1 cup cold water
3 eggs
1 tablespoon oil
salt, black pepper

Immerse the chicken feet in boiling water for a few seconds and remove the outer skin. Then put the chicken or chicken pieces into a large saucepan, with the feet, and add the water and onions. Bring to a boil, then turn down the heat, cover, and simmer gently for 1 hour. Now add the celery, carrots and other ingredients. Continue to simmer, with the lid on, for another 45 minutes or until the chicken is tender. Pour the broth through a strainer, skim off the fat, adjust the seasoning and return the vegetables to the soup. The chicken can be used for salad or served separately, cut up, with the soup.

To make the *kneidlach*, knead all the ingredients to a smooth dough, cover, and refrigerate overnight. Boil 3 1/4 quarts water to which 2 tablespoons salt have been added. Roll the dough into balls the size of ping pong balls and cook in the boiling water for 30 minutes - use a slotted spoon to slide them in. Leave the *kneidlach* in the water, keeping hot, until you are ready to serve.

A bowl of grandma's chicken soup is always welcome, but instead of *kneidlach* you could add boiled rice, vermicelli, blanched vegetables or homemade soup checks (see recipe below).

SOUP CHECKS

pinch salt
1 tablespoon oil
4 eggs, well beaten
all-purpose flour
oil for deep frying

Beat the salt and oil into the eggs, then add flour a tablespoon at a time until you have a soft, smooth dough - don't add too much flour or the dough will be too dry. Roll out the dough on a floured surface until it is pasta-thin. Cut into strips, then into squares of uniform size. Heat the oil. Fry a few squares at a time until they are crisp and golden. Drain on paper towels. Allow to cool, then store in an air-tight container until the grandchildren pay a visit.

◆ *Chicken soup with soup checks, a marriage between Jewish tradition and Israeli invention.*

KUBBANEH
Steamed sweet rolls

1 oz fresh yeast
2 tablespoons sugar
1/4 cup lukewarm water
4 cups and 2 tablespoons all-purpose flour
3/4 tablespoon salt
1 cup water
2 tablespoons margarine

Combine the yeast, sugar, and water in a small bowl, cover with a clean towel and leave in a warm place for about 10 minutes for the yeast to work.

Sift the flour and the salt into a large mixing bowl, make a well in the middle and pour in the yeast mixture. Knead, gradually adding water, until the dough loses its stickiness. Cover with a towel, put in a warm place and allow to rise for about 15 minutes. Knead again.

Dissolve the margarine in a medium large saucepan which has a tightly fitting lid. Make sure the sides of the saucepan are coated with margarine.

Divide the dough into five portions. Wet your hands and roll each portion into a ball. Put the balls into the saucepan - the margarine will prevent them sticking together. Cover and cook over a very low heat until the balls of dough expand. Now slide an asbestos sheet under the saucepan and continue cooking over a medium low heat until they turn golden yellow and their tops are baked and not sticky. Turn off the heat.

Serve hot, turned upside down. Slice like cake. Serves 5. Serve on Sabbath mornings with *hilbeh* and *haminados* (see recipes pp. 119 and 154).

SENIYEH
A traditional Arab dish of ground meat and *tahini*

8 oz ground beef, lamb or veal
2 tablespoons chopped parsley
2 tablespoons finely chopped onion
1 tablespoon flour
1 tablespoon vegetable oil
1/2 teaspoon zhoug (see recipe p. 39)
1/2 teaspoon salt
1/2 teaspoon pepper
2 tablepoons tahini paste
1 tablespoon lemon juice
2 tablespoons water
pine nuts, to garnish

Preheat the oven to 350°F. Combine the meat with the parsley, onion, flour, oil, *zhoug*, salt and pepper, and press into a small, round ovenproof dish.

With a fork, beat together the *tahini* paste, lemon juice and water, pour over the meat mixture and sprinkle with pine nuts. Bake for 30 minutes. Serve with salad and pickles. Serves 4.

◆ *Yemenite kubbaneh with brown eggs (haminados) and hilbeh. Kubbaneh are eaten for breakfast. Hilbeh is a relish made from fenugreek seeds.*

MEJADARRA
Galilean Arab lentil and rice pilaf

1 lb large brown lentils, soaked if
necessary
1 onion, finely chopped
3 tablespoons vegetable oil
salt and freshly ground black pepper
1 heaped cup long-grain rice, washed
1 cup water
2 onions, sliced into half-moon shapes

Generously cover the lentils with cold water and simmer until tender, removing any scum that rises and adding more water as necessary. Fry the chopped onion in half the oil until soft and golden, then add to the cooked lentils. Season with salt and pepper.

Add the rice and the extra cup of water to the lentils, cover, and simmer gently for about 20 minutes or until the rice is soft. If the rice absorbs the water too quickly, add a little more.

Fry the sliced onions in the rest of the oil until they are dark brown. Heap the rice and lentils onto a warm serving dish and garnish with the caramelized onions.

Mejadarra can be served hot or cold, with fresh yogurt. Serves 5 or 6.

◆ Mejadarra,

a classic

vegetarian

combination

of legumes

and rice,

served with

fresh yogurt.

NEW WAVE CHICKEN
Chef I. Nicolai was the father of professional cooking in Israel. This recipe, created in 1950, is typical of his work and of the style he founded.

1 chicken, weighing 3 lbs, cut into joints
1 cup all-purpose flour
5 tablespoons vegetable oil
2/3 cup olives, pitted
12 cloves garlic, peeled
1 small head celery, diced
1/2 teaspoon black peppercorns
1 teaspoon dried tarragon
4 tomatoes, cut into quarters
salt
pinch ground ginger
peel of 3 oranges
3 tablespoons brandy
1/2 cup white wine

Dip the chicken joints in the flour and shake off the excess. In a large skillet heat the oil and fry the joints, turning them occasionally so that they lightly brown on all sides.

Boil 2 cups water in a small saucepan and add the olives; bring to a boil, then drain and reserve the olives. Blanch 11 of the cloves of garlic in the same way, allowing them to boil for 3 minutes before draining them. Crush the other clove of garlic.

Add all the garlic, olives, celery, peppercorns, tarragon, tomatoes, salt and ginger to the skillet and continue frying for 30 minutes. Now add the orange peel. Heat the wine and brandy in a small saucepan, pour over the chicken and set a match to it. Serve immediately with fresh salad, brown bread and fruity white wine. Serves 4.

◆ *A version*

of chicken

with olives,

tarragon and

cognac.

KUGEL
Savory noodle pudding traditional among Eastern European Jews

8 oz thin vermicelli
salt
1/2 cup vegetable oil
1/2 cup sugar
1 1/2 teaspoons freshly ground black pepper
3 eggs, lightly beaten

Preheat the oven to 350°F. Cook the vermicelli in salted water until it is tender, then drain well and set aside.

In a medium saucepan, heat the oil and add the sugar. Cook over a very low heat, stirring constantly, for about 10 minutes or until the mixture turns very dark, almost black. Immediately stir in the vermicelli, salt, pepper and beaten eggs. Taste to see if the mixture is peppery enough. If not, add more pepper. Place in a greased pan and bake, uncovered, for at least 1 1/2 hours, or until golden brown on top.

Remove the kugel from the oven and unmold it by turning it upside down on a plate. Serve slices with meat, salad or pickles. Other versions with raisins, onions or both are also popular, traditionally served after *cholent*.

◆ *Kugel*

in a pot,

waiting

its turn

after the

cholent.

HILBEH
Fenugreek relish, an exotic addition to soups, excellent for health and stamina

2 tablespoons ground fenugreek seeds
1 fresh tomato, cut into quarters
1/2 teaspoon freshly ground black pepper
2 teaspoons zhoug (see recipe p. 39)

Soak the fenugreek seeds in cold water for 2 hours, then pour off excess water. Using a blender, mix all the other ingredients together, then beat/whisk until fluffy.

◆ *Kugel*

served with

pickles.

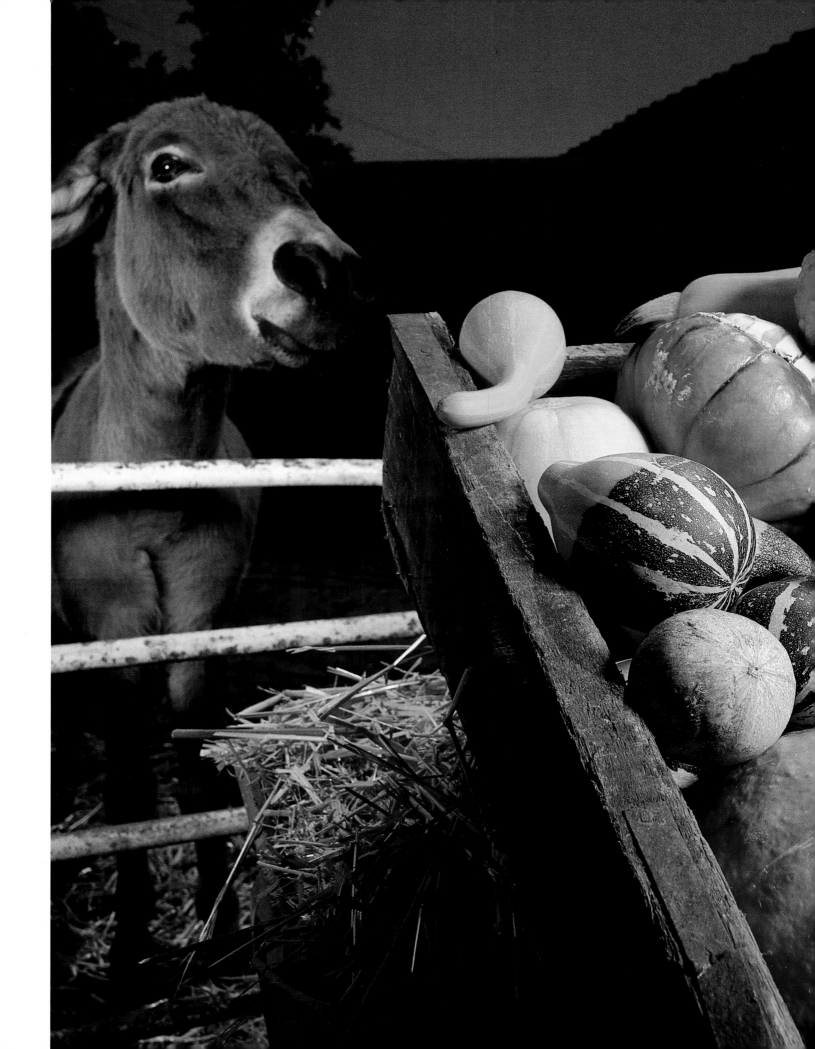

VEGETABLES

To city-dwelling Israelis, in Jerusalem, Tel Aviv and Haifa, working the land is a romantic, even noble occupation. They like to refer to Israel not as plain Israel but as "the land of Israel" as if annexing to

◆ *A colorful display of summer and winter squash.*

themselves the romance and nobility of the agricultural way of life. In truth, a very small proportion of Israelis lead this life today. Their lot is the city, an overwhelming density of traffic, and nowhere to park.

To Israel's early settlers agriculture was a necessity. Dreamers were not welcome; they were unproductive. And yet it was the dreamers who saw in an apple not a fruit but a laboratory, not the status quo but a point of departure for bigger, juicier, firmer apples, and trees that yielded bigger crops at more convenient times. Advancing the cause of apples for the good of Israel was a long, tedious process, and the same can be said of many other fruits and vegetables. But the result has been that Israel is, and always has been, a driving force in advancing the principles of modern agriculture. Necessity has taught us to achieve better crops from given plots of land.

Many regional fruit and vegetable specialties have endured down to the present time, although few of our regions now enjoy the isolation which made them regions in the first place. Grapes and apples are grown on the Golan, cereals in the Jezreel Valley and the northern Negev, oranges in the Vale of Capernaum, winter vegetables and subtropical fruits in the Jordan Valley, tomatoes and other salad vegetables in the Judean desert. Today Israel is self-sufficient in vegetables and supplies planeloads of them, out of season, to Western Europe. Many of them are grown in miles and miles of plastic tunnels.

◆ *Most of the*
country's
wheat is
grown in the
sandy soil of
the northern
Negev.

◆ *Jacob Lichansky*

has played a part

in creating the

new Israeli cuisine.

He has an

unfailing sense

of humor and a

deep understanding

of vegetables and

fish.

◆ *At the experi-*

mental farm of

Neve Yaar, where

new vegetables

and fruits are

coaxed from the

soil - dwarf sweet

corn of various

colors and mini-

watermelons

without seeds.

◆ *Kaspi is a*

local grower who

supplies the hotel

and restaurant

trade. He delivers

everything from

fresh quail eggs

to ripe

pineapples.

◆ *Shimon Shalvi of*

Nahalal holds the

record for the

largest radish ever

grown in Israel.

He refuses to

reveal his secret.

His pickles are as

incredible as his

radishes.

Thrown in among local Arab communities, with few if any utensils brought from their countries of origin, the early settlers had no choice but to adapt to local conditions. They dug clay ovens in the ground, as the Arabs did. They churned their own butter, and drank the buttermilk. They discovered which vegetables grew and which did not. They made wine out of peaches, apricots and plums. It was a vast learning experience, but its aim was survival, not self-education. They ate what they raised, and they raised what they ate. If they discovered that you get a stronger, more durable orange tree by crossing it with a lemon, they went ahead and crossed it. Their victories were hard-fought and hard-won, and they resented citification and the different morality that it represented.

Longevity is one of the attributes of those who have devoted their lives to inventive farm work. We, or rather the kibbutzim or moshavim in which they live, do not generally allow such people to ease off until they reach their seventies or eighties. Our long-lived, patient, persevering agriculturalists have adapted papayas to regions they were not meant to grow in; perfected new shapes and sizes and flavors of different apples (and often named them after their

◆ *Freshly pressed olive oil is checked for color, aroma and consistency. The right blend of green and black olives yields the desired quality.*

◆ *During the olive harvest the entire village of Mrar is busy with olive oil production.*

$\mathcal{V}$EGETABLES

◆ *Israeli salad is an adaptation of an earlier Arab dish.*

$\mathcal{R}$ecipes

AVOCADO WITH TAHINI YOGURT

1 cup plain yogurt
1/3 cup tahini *paste*
1/2 teaspoon ground cumin
pinch ground coriander
1/4 teaspoon finely chopped garlic
1 tablespoon lemon juice
1/4 teaspoon salt
1/4 teaspoon pepper
pinch cayenne pepper
3 ripe avocados
1/2 cup slivered almonds, toasted

Beat the yogurt into the *tahini*, then add the spices, herbs, and seasonings. Blend well, cover and refrigerate. Peel the avocados a few minutes before serving, halving them lengthwise and removing the pits. Thinly slice each half lengthwise and fan out the slices on individual plates. Spoon the yogurt dressing over them and sprinkle with toasted almonds. Serves 6.

Note: When preparing avocados, squeeze a little lemon juice into a bowl of water and dip the avocados into it as you peel or slice them. This will prevent the flesh turning an unappetizing gray-black.

AVOCADO & POMEGRANATE SALAD

2 ripe avocados
1 pomegranate
4 oz black grapes
lemon juice
water

DRESSING
1 teaspoon sugar
4 tablespoons white wine vinegar
2 tablespoons corn oil
1 tablespoon groundnut oil
4 tablespoons chopped mint
salt and pepper

Peel the avocados, remove the pits, and slice into thick half rings. Drop the rings into a bowl containing water and lemon juice - this will prevent them turning black.

Cut the pomegranate in half and crush it over a bowl to remove and collect the seeds. Wash the grapes and mix them with the pomegranate seeds. Drain the avocado pieces and add them to the fruit.

To make the dressing, put all the ingredients into a glass jar, screw the lid on firmly and shake vigorously for 2 minutes. Pour over the avocado and fruit. Toss well before serving. Serves 4 to 6.

◆ *Avocado and pomegranate salad. Israel and the avocado are almost synonymous. In fact avocados have now outstripped oranges as our top export .*

FRIED EGGPLANT SALAD

2 lbs eggplants
2 tablespoons coarse salt
1 cup all-purpose flour
oil for deep frying
1/2 cup white vinegar
4 oz chili peppers, assorted colors, seeded
and finely sliced
6 cloves garlic, finely chopped
2 or 3 tablespoons water

Cut the eggplants, unpeeled, into slices 1/2 inch thick. Put them in a colander and sprinkle them with salt. Leave for 30 minutes to drain, then squeeze out excess moisture. Dust the pieces sparingly with flour and deep-fry in hot oil.

In a large bowl, mix the vinegar with the chili peppers and garlic, and add 2 or 3 tablespoons of water. Add the hot slices of eggplant and mix gently. Allow to cool, then pack into glass jars, seal and refrigerate. This salad can be eaten freshly made, but it improves with keeping.

◆ *Spaghetti*

squash with

eggplant &

sesame

seeds.

SPAGETTI SQUASH WITH EGGPLANT & SESAME

1 large eggplant
3 tablespoons olive oil
3 lbs spaghetti squash
1/2 cup sesame seeds
1 cup grated Parmesan cheese
2 tablespoons butter
3 cloves garlic, minced
salt and pepper to taste

Preheat the oven to 450°F. Top and tail the eggplant, cut it into 8 slices lengthwise and sprinkle with salt. Allow to drain for 20 minutes, then squeeze out excess moisture and pat dry. Brush with olive oil and place, in a single layer, on a baking sheet. Bake for 15-20 minutes or until the slices begin to soften.

To prepare the spaghetti squash, cut the squash in half, discard the seeds, and boil for about 20 minutes. Rinse under cold water to loosen the "spaghetti" and drain well. Lightly toast the sesame seeds, taking care not to let them singe. Dip the eggplant slices in the seeds, then roll them up with a spoonful of Parmesan inside.

Heat the butter in a large skillet and fry the garlic for 2 minutes. Carefully stir in the spaghetti squash, season with salt and pepper, and add the rest of the Parmesan.

Transfer to a warm serving dish, arrange the rolled eggplant slices on top and serve immediately.

◆ *Spaghetti*

squash

undergoing

further

development

at Neve Yaar.

MEDITERRANEAN SALAD

6 tablespoons olive oil
1 large clove garlic, minced
1 teaspoon cumin seeds, crushed
1/4 cup fresh lemon juice
4 large tomatoes, cut into wedges, then halved
2 medium zucchini, sliced into
thin rounds
2 medium green bell peppers, cut into
bite-size squares
2 small onions, chopped
2/3 cup black olives, pitted
4 tablespoons chopped parsley
salt and freshly ground black pepper

Heat the oil in a large, heavy skillet, but do not allow it to smoke. Add the garlic and cumin and fry for 2 minutes until the cumin releases its fragrance. Remove from the heat and cool to room temperature. Stir in the lemon juice.

Combine the tomatoes, zucchini, peppers, onions, olives and parsley in a large bowl. Add the dressing and toss well. Season with salt and pepper. Cover and refrigerate. Serve chilled. Serves 12.

◆ *An old*

olive press

in the

Druze

village of

Mrar.

ISRAELI SALAD

For this you need good vegetables, good olive oil and the ability to enjoy the simple things in life.

2 large tomatoes
2 cucumbers
1 large onion
4 tablespoons finely chopped parsley
1/2 lemon
1/4 cup superb olive oil
salt and black pepper to taste
chopped fresh mint, optional

Dice the vegetables with a very sharp knife - they should be cut very small and evenly. Red cabbage, green bell pepper or garlic can be added to the standard recipe given above, but only one deviation is allowed at a time! Squeeze and strain the lemon juice over the vegetables, then add the other ingredients. Toss well before serving.

PICKLED CUCUMBERS

fresh dill
10 cloves garlic
2-4 lbs baby cucumbers
water
sea salt

Put a sprig or two of dill and 4 or 5 cloves of garlic in the bottom of a large glass jar, then pack the cucumbers on top. Cover with water, measuring it into the jar. For each cup of water added, add 1 tablespoon sea salt. Add more dill and cloves of garlic, then seal. Put the jar in the sun so that the cucumbers change color.

EGGPLANT STUFFED WITH MUSHROOMS & OLIVES

2 eggplants
1 tablespoon salt
1 tablespoon vegetable oil
1 cup olives, pitted
2 onions, sliced
1 bell pepper, cut into strips
12 oz baby mushrooms
3 tablespoons fresh lemon juice
3 tablespoons olive oil
2 cloves garlic, crushed
2 tablespoons wine vinegar
2 tablespoons chopped dill

Preheat the oven to 375°F. Cut the eggplants in half lengthwise, sprinkle with salt, and leave to drain for 20 minutes. Squeeze out the excess moisture, then place on an oiled baking sheet. Bake until they are fairly soft, then scoop out some of the flesh and reserve.

Meanwhile, boil up a little water and blanch the olives in it - do this twice to remove their saltiness. Lightly fry the onions in the vegetable oil, remove the skillet from the heat and add the pepper strips, mushrooms, lemon juice, olive oil, garlic and vinegar. Mix well together. Mash the scooped out eggplant and add to the mixture. Divide the mixture between the four eggplant halves and put them back in the oven for 10 minutes.

Serve sprinkled with dill, accompanied by a yogurt-based sauce.

PICKLED BELL PEPPERS

1 1/2 lbs green bell peppers
1 1/2 lbs red bell peppers
8 cloves garlic
4 teaspoons vegetable oil
4 sprigs dill
2 teaspoons salt
2 1/2 cups distilled white vinegar
scant 1 1/2 cups sugar
2 1/2 cups water

Remove the stems and seeds from the peppers and cut into 2-inch wide strips. Put the strips into a large bowl, cover with boiling water and allow to stand for 5 minutes. Drain well, then pack the strips into 4 pint-sized sterilized jars, adding 2 cloves of garlic, a teaspoon of oil, a sprig of dill and 1/2 teaspoon of salt to each jar.

In a stainless steel or enamel saucepan, combine the vinegar, sugar and water, and bring to a boil. Ladle this mixture into the jars, filling them to within 1/4 inch of the top. Wipe the tops of the jars with a damp cloth and put the lids on.

Place the jars in a deep saucepan with a rack in the bottom and add enough water to cover the jars by 2 inches. Bring the water to a boil and boil for 5 minutes. Remove the jars from the saucepan with tongs and allow them to cool. Store in a cool, dark place.

◆ *Eggplant*
and garlic
could be the
cure to many
of the great
problems of
our time.

STUFFED VEGETABLES

Stuffed vegetables, as an appetizer or a main course, are the pride of everyone who serves them. They are very Mediterranean, whether baked, poached or gently stewed in a tomato sauce. The stuffing in the next recipe is a typical one, but it can be varied by adding liver or pine nuts, or by using lamb instead of beef. If you are stuffing eggplants, remember to salt and drain them first.

◆ *Assorted stuffed vegetables - onion, zucchini, eggplant, and red and green bell peppers.*

◆ *Eggplant stuffed with mushrooms, olives, red pepper and onion.*

STUFFED ONIONS

2 large onions
1/4 cup butter
water
2 tablespoons lemon or lime juice

STUFFING
8 oz lean beef, ground
3 oz rice, washed thoroughly and drained
2 tablespoons finely chopped parsley
1 teaspoon salt
1/2 teaspoon black pepper
1/2 teaspoon ground allspice

Peel the onions. With a sharp knife, make a cut in each one from top to bottom on one side, cutting toward the center. Cook the onions in boiling water for about 45 minutes or until the layers detach easily. Drain and leave until cool enough to handle.

Meanwhile, knead together all the stuffing ingredients to a smooth, well blended consistency.

Carefully separate the layers of onion. Into the hollow of each layer put 1 tablespoon of stuffing, more for the outer layers, less for the inner. Roll up each layer into a little parcel and tie with a piece of thread. Preheat the oven to 350°F.

Melt the butter in a skillet and sauté the onion parcels, a few at a time, turning occasionally, until they are a light golden color. When all the parcels have been sautéed, pack them tightly into a shallow oiled ovenproof dish and pour in just enough boiling water to cover them by 1/2 inch or so. Sprinkle with the lemon or lime juice and cover.

Bake in the oven for about 1 hour or until the meat is cooked. Serve with fresh salad or boiled potatoes. Serves 4 to 6.

 TREET

FOOD

◆ Falafel

fried in the

traditional

manner.

The patties

are shaped

with a special

implement

which is also

used to slip

them into the

hot oil .

A lot of eating out in Israel is done standing up. The sit-down restaurant-type meal has only recently evolved, for in many ways we are still an eat-it-while-you-can society. We are obsessive, short-tempered, driven, on the move. We have a need to consume quickly, to eat and run. Leisure is not part of the Israeli lifestyle.

Nothing more clearly reveals this fact than the roaring trade done by restaurants and snack stands at gas stations. Most countries provide food and refreshment at gas stations, usually of the franchised, fast-food variety, but in Israel roadside culinary attractions are more ambitious. While the tank is being filled and the oil is being checked, you are invited to consume - quickly

◆ Mezze *are calculated to make gourmands of the most dedicated gourmets!*

of course - a sample of *mezze*, grilled meat or fish, or something in the dessert line. The quality is comparable to that of most average restaurants serving similar food. Do not expect gourmet. Do not expect fancy. When you stop in the middle of the desert on your way to Eilat, do not think *haute cuisine*. Think adequate. And you will be pleasantly surprised.

Gas station dining is now such an institution that we eat in gas stations even when we are not in the car. We walk there, treading gingerly around the oil slicks and gas puddles. We sit down. We order off a paper napkin or off the wall. And the food arrives at a furious pace, whole trayfuls of it. Could we survive without *pita* bread? Probably not. Here it is, any way you want it - warmed over, grilled to a crispy cracker, cut open and toasted. Here comes the *mezze* selection - a dozen small plates of dips and salads and pickles. As the pumps ring, we scoop up their colorful contents with our *pita* bread. Knives and forks only slow you down. Sweet Turkish coffee to finish. With the last gulp, we move off. We do not linger. Traffic continues to pour in.

◆ *Turko is a*
borekas
vendor in
HaCarmel
market.
He fills his
borekas *with*
whatever his
customers
want.

◆ *A sunflower seed vendor on his rounds during a soccer game.*

When leisure is not a part of life, food tends to be consumed rather than enjoyed, and Israel is not noted for its leisure time. So far, the need to eat and run has found many admirable solutions. Perhaps, when we slow down a bit, we will be less rough and ready, but never more colorful.

Pedestrians are exposed to other kinds of street food. The king - by popular consent - is *falafel,* fried patties made from chick peas, herbs and spices crammed into *pita* bread with salads and relishes. Israel has contributed much to the course of *falafel.* It was here, ready and waiting, when we needed a national food. A newly created state, a toddler nation, what were we to eat that we could call our own? *Falafel.* It mattered little that *falafel* was an Arab invention, that it had existed longer than Israel and Israelis. We needed something, and *falafel* was it. Nutritious, tasty, spicy, quick and easy to prepare and plentiful at street corners. Colorful, photogenic *falafel* stands, manned by boisterous, aggressive vendors stuffing half or whole pockets of *pita* bread full to bursting with hot, round, fragrant patties, various salads and deep-fried potatoes dipped in batter - what could be better? The whole package was then handed to the customer, who proceeded to add the condiments of his choice from an array of large containers on a tray. All-round favorites were *harissa* (hot pepper paste) and *tahini* (savory sesame seed paste), watery and diluted so that they trickled and flowed through the contents of the *pita* pocket, down your arm and into your sleeve...You ate leaning forward slightly, so that whatever dropped did not stain your shirt or land on your shoes.

◆ *Still life with sunflower. Sunflower seeds are high on Israeli shopping lists.*

That was then. In those days *falafel* was judged by its texture and taste, by the way the crushed chick peas yielded to the teeth, by whether it was mild and restrained - the tamed Ashkenazi variety - or hot and spicy - the genuine Sephardic kind. The salads had to be fresh, the *pita* warm from the oven, the condiments fiery, aggressive and reeking of cumin.

That has all gone now. If you search hard, in Arab villages and along country roads, you may still stumble on an old-fashioned *falafel* stand. But you have to know where to look, and when you get there it may have disappeared. Today's *falafel* joints are huge hangars in which all the components are laid out like the ammunition of a fighter plane. Today *falafel* is about quantity, not

quality. Competition is fierce. Arab vendors, who prepare better *falafel* than anyone else, are confined to their own trading areas.

For the price of one *falafel*, you are allowed any number of refills, so really the *pita* pocket is all you pay for. We seem to have devised a way of having our *falafel* and eating it. But there is some-thing demeaning about the free *falafel* economy. The sky-high piles of pickled cabbage and salad and assorted pickles, and the precariously balanced heaps of cold patties, are hardly inviting. Street food should be sensual, oily, noisy and satisfying. But by encouraging us to pig out on multiple, self-served refills, the *falafel* industry has set back the cause of street food. I want my *falafel* man to fill my *pita* himself. He knows his patties, his salads and his hot stuffs. As he as-sembles the package, he signs it with a seal of quality. He is a proud craftsman. He would not sell me cold patties or stale potatoes. By removing *falafel* from his supervision, we rob him of his art.

Which brings me to the lynchpin and *sine qua non* of the *falafel,* the *pita*. Whatever you do with a *pita*, it is always a meal. Even when we eat at a table, we Israelis would rather have our food in a *pita* than on a plate. The small *pita* is the most common, but a larger one, commonly called the Iraqi *pita* since

◆ *Jerusalem mixed grill is a whole meal in a pita. Chicken spleens, livers, hearts and spices are some of the ingredients.*

it was introduced by Iraqi Jews, is also popular. It does not have a pocket, so its role is limited to scooping up *hummus* and similar delicacies, and wrapping. There is a suburb of Tel Aviv, well known for its culinary offerings, which is big on Iraqi *pita*. When you order your favorite meal on a skewer, the grill man will place your skewer on a hot Iraqi *pita*, fold it once and pull the skewer expertly

out, leaving the meat in place. He then opens the *pita*, adds *tahini* or *harissa*, a salad or French fries, and re-folds it in such a manner that it will not leak or break as you eat it. Folding an Iraqi *pita* is an art in itself.

The Tunisian answer to *falafel* is the *brik*, a crusty little triangle of *filo* dough filled with cheese or potato. In fact the *brik* is a cousin of the larger *boreka,* which plays a strong second to *falafel.* Today *borekas* are mass produced and franchised by a central bakery, but not so long ago vendors would fill a *boreka* in front of your very eyes and offer vegetables and a brown egg with it.

A lot of our street food moves. Since Israel is a small country and mostly flat, you can cover it quite easily with a pushcart. Fruit and vegetables, especially watermelons, are sold from the back of horse-drawn carts. Step out in your pajamas to meet the roving watermelon man! But gone are the days when small carts pushed by children brought prickly pears to the door. We used to buy them already peeled and almost thornless and eat them then and there.

Warm local bagels are still sold on street corners, but there are few vendors today who will freely and happily give you their home-mixed *za'atar*, a salty mixture of spices, hyssop and other herbs. They hide it and you have to ask for it. But once upon a time little cornets of *za'atar* done up in newspaper were openly displayed and you helped yourself. You dipped your chewy bagel into the *za'atar* between each bite.

A combination of the Israeli sweet tooth and the hot, humid climate is chiefly responsible for two other street food relics: the *tamarindi* seller and the *malabi* cart. *Tamarindi* is a sweet, syrupy beverage derived from the tamarind fruit and it is poured from a jar carried on the vendor's shoulder. *Malabi* is a dessert, a white, caramel-like custard sold in small tin cups. Since the mixture is practically tasteless, it is sold with a choice of syrups. You select a syrup flavor and the vendor splashes a generous amount of it into the little cup and hands it to you with a spoon. His little cart is totally self-contained catering unit. It has a bed of ice for the *malabi* to stand in, and a small water tank and faucet for washing out the empty cups. More than any other form of street food, the *malabi* cart is a magnet for a strange mixture of clients. Hurrying mechanics

and well-groomed businessmen flock around it, happily absorbing the contents of the little cups. *Malabi* is hardly food. It does not nourish or allay hunger. It is a dessert through and through. You only eat it because you are addicted to it.

◆ *A large*

Iraqi pita

used to

wrap a

kabob,

hummus,

mango

chutney

and

cabbage.

STREET FOOD

Recipes

FALAFEL

1 1/2 cups dried chick peas
5 cups water
1 teaspoon baking soda
1 teaspoon salt
1 teaspoon cumin seeds
1 teaspoon coriander
1 onion, quartered
2 tablespoons minced parsley
2 cloves garlic, mashed
freshly ground black pepper
1 tablespoon lemon juice
pinch hot chili powder
vegetable oil for deep frying

Soak the chick peas in the water for 24 hours, then drain them and put them and all the other ingredients, except the oil, through a meat grinder, twice. Mix together lightly with a fork. The mixture should be loose and crumbly.

Pour 2 inches of oil into a wok or other utensil for deep frying and set over a medium low heat; the oil should be 350-375°F when you put the *falafel* in.

While the oil is heating, shape the first batch of patties. Use a generous spoonful of mixture for each patty and don't be too neat about the shaping. Because the mixture is crumbly, it will only just hold together. Each patty should be about 2 1/2 inches across and 3/4 inch thick in the middle. Slide the first batch of patties into the hot oil and fry for about 4 minutes, turning at least once. Remove with a slotted spoon and drain on paper towels. Repeat until all the mixture is used up. Serve as a *mezze* dish, or in *pita* bread with salads, *zhoug*, *tahini* and more.

JERUSALEM MIXED GRILL

4 oz chicken livers
4 oz chicken hearts
2 oz chicken spleens
2 tablespoons oil
1 onion, sliced
3 cloves garlic, chopped
1/2 teaspoon each of salt, ground cumin,
coriander and turmeric
2 pitas, halved and warmed

Jerusalem mixed grill is not broiled, but fried! Cut the livers into small pieces, and halve the hearts and spleens. Using a heavy skillet, heat the oil and sweat the slices of onion. Add the garlic, salt and spices, and fry gently until the meat is tender. Serve in *pitas*, perhaps with a lacing of *hummus* (see recipe p. 39). Real gourmets make their mixed grills with pigeon livers, hearts, etc.

◆ Falafel *stands*

are shrines of

creativity.

You pay for a

pita *and you*

assemble your

own filling.

Pickles, zhoug

and tahini *are a*

CHEESE OR SPINACH BOREKAS

8 oz filo *pastry*
2/3 cup butter, melted
1 egg yolk, beaten with 1 tablespoon water,
to glaze
sesame seeds, to garnish

CHEESE FILLING
1/2 cup soft white cheese
2 cups finely grated Gruyère cheese
2 tablespoons cream cheese
1 large or 2 small eggs, lightly beaten
salt and pepper

SPINACH FILLING
1 lb fresh spinach
1 egg, lightly beaten
2 cups finely grated Gruyère cheese
salt and pepper

Remove the *filo* leaves from the refrigerator 2 hours before you need them.

To make the cheese filling, simply mash all the ingredients together with a fork or combine them in a food processor.

To make the spinach filling, wash the spinach several times, put the wet leaves into a saucepan without any extra water, cover tightly and sweat over a medium heat for 4 or 5 minutes until tender. Drain in a strainer, pressing out any excess moisture. Chop fine and combine with the egg, cheese, salt and pepper.

Preheat the oven to 350°F.

Taking one leaf of *filo* at a time, cut it into a strip about 6 inches wide by 12 inches long and brush with melted butter. Now fold it in half so that it is the same length but half the width. Brush with butter again. Place a heaped tablespoon of cheese or spinach filling at one end, and fold the end over to make a triangle. Butter the top of the triangle, then fold over again. Continue until the entire strip is folded into a triangle, brushing with butter between each folding. Put the completed triangles onto a greased baking sheet and brush the tops with egg yolk and water to glaze. Sprinkle with sesame seeds.

Bake for 25-30 minutes, until golden brown and puffy. Serve warm or cold, but not hot.

Borekas can also be made with puff pastry. Just fold the pastry over the fillings and proceed as above. Although baking is the traditional method of cooking borekas, many street vendors deep-fry them. The shape of a boreka usually tells you what the filling is - triangles for cheese, squares for potatoes, twists for spinach.

◆ *Assorted*

borekas with

brown eggs

(haminados).

The fillings vary

from cheese

through spinach

to potato.

GREEN OMELET

2 eggs per person
2 tablespoons water
1 tablespoon oil, or oil and butter together
2 tablespoons finely chopped parsley
1 tablespoon finely chopped coriander
1 tablespoon finely chopped dill
2 tablespoons finely chopped watercress,
optional
salt and black pepper
pinch cumin

This can be cooked with the greenery beaten into the eggs or spread on top of the finished article.

Beat the eggs and water together first. Heat the oil in a skillet, make sure it is really hot, then swiftly cook two very thin omelets, turning them so that they cook on both sides. Serve in a brown bread roll with lettuce and a few slices of tomato.

HAMINADOS
Brown eggs

12 eggs
skins of 2 lbs onions
1 tablespoon all-purpose flour

Put the eggs in a casserole of cold water, with the onion skins. Bring to a boil and cook for 30 minutes. Mix the flour with a little water, smear the mixture around the rim of the casserole, put the lid on, and put in a very low oven - 120°F - overnight. The flour makes a perfect seal. Serve with *borekas* and *hummus.*

◆ Borekas

served with

drinking

yogurt and

a brown

egg.

FRIED KIBBEH
Lamb and bulgur wheat patties

2 cups fine bulgur wheat
8 oz lean lamb, ground three times
1 onion, minced
3/4 teaspoon curry powder
1/4 teaspoon ground allspice
1/4 teaspoon ground cinnamon
1/4 teaspoon paprika or cayenne
salt and pepper
1/4 cup olive oil

FILLING
8 oz ground meat
3 tablespoons water
1 onion, chopped
2 tablespoons oil
1 teaspoon pine nuts, optional
black pepper and salt to taste
pinch allspice and cinnamon

Soak the bulgur in cold water for 10 minutes, then drain in a fine strainer and squeeze out the excess moisture.

Now combine the lamb, onion, curry powder, allspice, cinnamon, paprika or cayenne, salt and pepper with the soaked bulgur and knead to a smooth, even consistency (if you moisten your hands occasionally, the mixture will not stick to them).

To make the filling, knead the meat and water together, fry the onions in the oil until golden brown, then add the meat and the rest of the ingredients. Fry until fairly dry and crumbly. Chill.

Now form the bulgur mixture into sausages 4 inches long, and make a hollow in the middle with your finger - wet your finger so that the mixture does not stick. Fill the hollows with the crumbly meat mixture, and pinch the ends together.

Heat the oil in a large, heavy skillet until it is hot but not smoking, and fry the *kibbeh* for 3 or 4 minutes on each side or until they begin to color. Transfer them to a warm serving dish with a slotted spoon. Serves 6.

TUNISIAN SANDWICH

4 lemons
1 tablespoon coarse salt
1/2 teaspoon turmeric
2 potatoes
4 long brown loaves or 2 small baguettes
harissa *(see recipe p. 41)*
1 tomato, diced
1 cucumber, diced
1 onion, finely chopped
2 tablespoons capers
8 oz canned tuna
2/3 cup black olives, pitted

At the sandwich stand, they always seem to work very slowly, considering deeply such matters as proportion, tactics and the order of things. This is what sandwich selling is all about.

First you prepare 3 of the lemons, by slicing them, soaking them in cold water for 5 hours, boiling them, draining them, covering them with water again, adding salt and turmeric, and boiling again. Then you cut each slice into 4 triangles and add the juice of the fourth lemon. Then you boil the potatoes until they are soft, after which you drain and peel them, and cut them into 1/2-inch cubes. Now you cut the loaves in half lengthwise, leaving a hinge of crust on one side, spread each half with *harissa* and pile in the lemons, potatoes, vegetables, capers, tuna, olives and lemons again.

◆ *Tunisian*

sandwich, a

"hero sandwich"

with an

amazing

filling.

$\mathscr{B}$ ARBECUES

I sraelis are prepared for two emergencies: army reserve duty and barbecues. The two are not necessarily separate. They may even be complementary. The gear in both cases is very basic. For the first one

◆ *A leg of lamb roasting over an open fire.*

needs a pair of army boots, a backpack containing the bare necessities, and a licensed gun or pistol. The second requires a miniature hibachi forged from the cheapest tin, a pair of rusty tongs, and a bag of charcoal. Some reservists are more ready than others; some do not even bother to remove their equipment from the trunk of the car. Since emergencies always occur in the middle of the night, it is wiser to keep everything in the car rather than clang down the stairs at dawn.

Simple equipment has a lot to recommend it. It is the stripped down, modest approach which is chiefly responsible for the quality of grilled meat. Who needs fancy charcoal - mesquite, cherry wood, walnut wood, and so on? Honest charcoal has been made and used in Israel for ages - the largest Arab town, Um-el-Fahem, is named after the stuff. Most Israelis spend their lives within meat-turning distance of an open charcoal grill, but I do not remember a single conversation in which the nature of the charcoal was discussed. Nor do I remember any fancy fire starters. How do we start a grill? The most prevalent method involves heavy use of gasoline. You go into the woods, set up the hibachi, empty a bag of charcoal into it, then douse it liberally with gasoline from the car. You warn the children to stay away, then you throw in a match. The hibachi catches fire with a whoosh that endangers the whole forest, but the conflagration soon dies down and the coals reach the desired state of white glowing ashes. Generations of Israelis have grown up confusing the odor of gasoline with the taste and smell of grilled meat.

On calm windless days we resort to that indispensable tool of the dedicated griller, the fan. Any fan... the back of a broken chair, a piece of card, a magazine. Fanning is an art in itself. You hold your fan and wave, and the frequent gusts of air bring the coals to life. It is not a task to be taken lightly. It requires full attention, a flick of the wrist, a sense of rhythm and timing. Self-igniting charcoal, mostly French, was introduced here recently, but it takes

◆ *Our favorite pastime: cooking in the woods. Note the cardboard being used as a fan.*

forever to get going, and flickers and hisses gloomily when it does. There is no substitute for a good breeze or a talented fanner.

In Israel, barbecuing is part of the collective memory. It is a national pastime that spares no one, except members of the orthodox community. Twenty years ago, a barbecue was the highlight of a country outing.

Families drove into the hills, children picked wild flowers, mothers spread blankets and fathers got the fire started. Today it is customary to forego the beauty of the scenery and the fresh country air and make do with any grassy knoll. Some Israelis even grill their chops at the grassy intersections of busy streets.

The quality of Israeli meat is steadily improving. One can now ask for and get specific cuts of meat. There are butchers who really know their meat and hang it properly and recommend what cuts to buy. But even though the quality of our meat is better and we have learned to appreciate a good lamb chop, the grills we use allow minimal distance between the rack and the coals.

More than any other facet of Israeli cuisine, grilling meat over an open fire represents an assimilation of Arab tradition with that of Western and Eastern Europe. Most restaurants serving meat offer grilled skewers of meat. Arabs lean more heavily toward lamb, while Jews still prefer lean beef and ground meat. There are exceptions of course. South American Jews know a lot about *carne asado* and *chorizos*, and keep their meat away from open fire, and Jews from North Africa and the Yemen have a cuisine

◆ *Israelis*

raise geese

for their

livers.

◆ *Free-range*

chickens are

catching on.

which is all their own. But most of the grilled meat consumed in Israel is skewered in cubes on metal spits and quickly cooked over intense heat. Only fancy restaurants comply with requests for rare or medium rare. In most places you are not asked what degree of doneness you require. You get it well done.

"We stole this idea, like so much else, from the Indians," wrote one American food critic, referring to the barbecue. Late in the sixteenth century John White, who was with the settlement on Roanoke Island, Virginia, wrote about the Indians he saw "broyling their fishe over the flame," adding "they took great heed that they bee not burnt." In 1705 Robert Beverly, in *The History and Present State of Virginia*, described the "Indian thing" in a little more detail: "The meat was laid... upon sticks raised upon forks at some distance above the live coals, which heats more gently and dries up the gravy." Two centuries later the United States Department of Agriculture pronounced: "Barbecue is meat that shall be cooked by the direct action of heat resulting from the burning of hard wood or the hot coals therefrom for a sufficient period to assume the usual characteristics...which include the formation of a brown crust." All of these educated essays ignore the Middle East and its humble but considerable contribution to the history of the barbecue. It is difficult to say,

faced with so many conflicting stories, how or where the barbecue came into existence, but my opinion is that it did so 27,000 years ago, within hours of the discovery of fire. The first barbecue writer has to be Homer: "Automedon held the meats and brilliant Achilles carved them, and cut them well into pieces and spitted them."

◆ *Much of the beef raised in Israel ends up sizzling over a grill.*

◆ *Although*

they are no

longer

nomads,

Bedouins

still herd

sheep in the

Negev.

In 1960 James Beard, discussing the changing art of the American barbecue, wrote: "What a phenomenal change! Just twenty years ago when I first wrote about outdoor cooking, backyard chefs were few. And their usual fare was steak or hamburger, blackened in an inferno of smoke and flame." Without wishing to defame a whole nation, it is my sad duty to state that he must have had Israel in mind in that sentence. Unlike cooks in large parts of the rest of the world, Israeli cooks started with the barbecue and advanced backward to sauces and soufflés.

I grew up knowing more about barbecuing than about any other method of cooking. For many years, going out meant eating grilled meat. Other people went out for hamburgers and pizzas, but we went out for kabobs. They were cheap and satisfying. A kabob is still the cheapest form of cooked meat one can buy. To the suspicious mind, the fact that it cost so little suggests meat of dubious origin. Once upon a time, when you asked for lamb, you got turkey laced with lamb fat, and when you asked for veal, you got chicken. If meat carved from a spit was mysterious, the ground meats used for skewered patties were even more so. But all this is changing. Steaks are usually beef, cut thin. When we come across genuine ground lamb, or cubes of lamb, we know what we are eating. Lamb is the king of kabobs - fragrant, spicy, sometimes spiked with cinnamon, and loaded with chopped parsley and pine nuts.

Considering the years of hostile criticism leveled at grilled meat, it took an amazingly long time for fish to make its way onto the barbecue rack. Mediterranean fish responds well to intense heat and a touch of smoke. Try it once, and you will be converted. The grill leaves gentle marks on the crisp skin and the sea taste is sealed inside. A good, lemony sauce is all the accompaniment it needs. We also have gentler methods of barbecuing fish, in wrappings of grape leaves for instance.

As all food and restaurant guides recommend on those rare occasions when they include Israel: when in Israel, barbecue.

BARBECUES

Recipes

◆ *Spitting*

images:

shish kabob,

skewered

backbone

marrow,

and lamb

shashlik.

SHASHLIK
Lamb on skewers

MARINADE
1/2 cup fresh lemon juice
1/2 cup dry red wine
3 tablespoons chopped fresh rosemary, or
1 tablespoon dried, and
rosemary sprigs to garnish
1 tablespoon finely chopped garlic
1 teaspoon dried hot red-pepper flakes
1 1/2 teaspoons salt
3/4 teaspoon freshly ground black pepper
3/4 cup olive oil

MEAT AND VEGETABLES
leg of lamb weighing 4 lbs, boned and cut
into 2-inch cubes
4 medium zucchini
4 small onions
4 yellow bell peppers
1 lb cherry tomatoes

Mix together the marinade ingredients, beating in the oil in a steady stream so that the mixture emulsifies. Add the cubes of lamb and stir them around to coat them in the marinade. Cover, and put in the refrigerator for at least 6 hours or overnight.

If using wooden skewers, soak them in water for 1 hour before threading the meat and vegetables onto them; if using metal skewers, brush them with oil. Light the barbecue.

Cut the zucchini into quarters lengthwise, and then into 1 1/2-inch pieces; cook them in boiling, salted water until just tender. The onions should be cut into 8 pieces, secured with toothpicks, and also blanched in boiling, salted water. Cut the bell peppers into bite-size pieces.

Thread the meat, onions, zucchini, peppers and tomatoes onto the skewers (remove the toothpicks from the chunks of onion), and brush with a little of the marinade.

Grill on an oiled rack set 5-6 inches above glowing coals, basting frequently with the marinade and turning occasionally. The lamb will take 15-18 minutes to cook, or less if you like your meat medium rare. Alternatively, put the skewers under a preheated broiler; medium well done will take 12-15 minutes.

Discard the marinade when you have finished basting - it should not be served with the *shashlik*. Makes 16 skewers.

♦ *Romanian Jews*

like their kabobs

large and

liberally flavored

with garlic.

LEG OF LAMB MARINATED IN HERBS

MARINADE
1/2 cup white wine vinegar
1 cup olive oil
2 tablespoons fresh thyme
2 tablespoons fresh rosemary, or
2 teaspoons dried
1 tablespoon fresh oregano, or 1 teaspoon dried
3 tablespoons fresh mint, or 1 tablespoon dried
2 large cloves garlic
1 teaspoon freshly ground black pepper

leg of lamb weighing 3-4 lbs
12 cloves garlic, halved

Using a food processor, blend together all the marinade ingredients. Place the lamb in a large dish and pour the marinade over it; using a small knife, stab the leg randomly, and insert half a clove of garlic with each stab. Cover and refrigerate for 24 hours, turning occasionally so that the meat thoroughly absorbs the marinade flavors.

Remove from the refrigerator and allow to stand for 1 hour. Transfer the meat to the rack of a broiling pan and sprinkle with salt. Preheat the broiler and cook for 14 minutes on each side if you like your meat medium well done. Alternatively, cook the meat on a rack set 6 inches above glowing coals, allowing 12 minutes each side for medium rare.

Transfer the meat to a carving board and allow to stand for 10 minutes before carving. Holding the carving knife at an angle of 45°, slice the lamb thinly across the grain. Serve immediately with grilled vegetables.

Serves 8 to 10.

GRILLED LAMB CHOPS

1/4 teaspoon each of ground allspice,
black pepper, cardamom,
cinnamon and salt
8 lamb chops

Mix the spices and seasonings together and sprinkle over the chops. Put the chops on the barbecue or under a preheated broiler and cook on both sides until brown and sizzling. Serve with rice.

◆ *Rosemary*

growing wild

in the grounds

of a monastery

near

Jerusalem.

RED CHICKEN À LA TOURAN
Many chefs and restaurateurs come from
this little village in the Upper Galilee

4 poussins, weighing 1 lb each
3 tablespoons coarse salt
3 onions, sliced
3 cloves garlic, crushed
1/2 teaspoon black pepper
1/2 teaspoon saffron
1/4 teaspoon ground cardamom
1/4 teaspooon ground cloves
2 tablespoons somek ✳
1/2 cup olive oil
4 large pitas

Clean the chickens, rub them with salt
inside and out, and refrigerate for 1 hour.
Put the onions and garlic into a shallow
casserole dish just big enough to hold all
four chickens. Mix all the spices together.
Take the chickens out of the refrigerator,
wash them, pat them dry and rub them with
the spice mixture inside and out. Put them
on top of the onions in the casserole dish,
breast up. Refrigerate for several hours.

Transfer the contents of the casserole
dish to a large shallow saucepan, add 2
cups water, bring to a boil, cover and cook
until the birds are very tender. The water
will evaporate, but if this happens too fast,
add a little more. Remove from the heat
and add the olive oil. Transfer to the
casserole dish and broil for 8 minutes.
Spread most of the onions on the 4 *pitas*,
put the chickens on top and top with the
remaining onions.

*✳Somek is a red, salty powder that gives a
pleasant flavor to almost any savory dish. It is
an excellent addition to any spice shelf, but it can
be omitted here if difficult to obtain. Its chief
value in this recipe is its color.*

SHISH KABOBS
Ground meat on skewers

12 oz veal
1 1/4 lbs lamb
small bunch parsley
1 onion
4 cloves garlic
1/2 teaspoon allspice
1/2 teaspoon cinnamon
salt and pepper to taste

Grind together the meat, parsley, onions
and garlic. Add the spices and mix well.
Take generous spoonfuls of the mixture
and shape into thin sausages. Thread onto
flat metal skewers and broil or put on the
barbecue until they sizzle and begin to
brown. Turn and cook the other side.

In Israel, grilled meat is usually served on
a plate by itself, *pita*, bread, *mezze* and Israeli
salad already being on the table. In the
street, grilled meat is put into *pitas* with
salad and *tahini*, or sold wrapped in the kind
of large *pita* shown on p. 148.

◆ *Red*

chicken

served on

pita

bread.

FISH GRILLED OVER CHARCOAL

2 lbs fish (bass, grouper or red snapper),
or one small fish (bream, gray mullet)
per person
chopped parsley and lemon wedges,
to garnish

MARINADE 1
1/3 cup olive oil
1 tablespoon salt
1 teaspoon ground allspice
2 tablespoons fresh lemon juice

MARINADE 2
1 onion, cut into rings
2 tablespoons lemon juice
3 tablespoons olive oil
1 tablespoon salt
1/2 teaspoon black pepper
1 clove garlic, finely chopped
1 teaspoon ground cumin
4 bay leaves

Clean and wash the fish, and pat them dry. If you are using large fish, cut them into steaks. Mix the marinade of your choice and pour it into a shallow dish. Add the fish, turning them so that the marinade coats them all over. Allow to marinate for 2 hours.

Remove the fish from the marinade and put them on a lightly oiled grill or onto skewers. Cook over charcoal, turning every 2 or 3 minutes and basting regularly with the marinade. Average cooking time is 15 - 20 minutes, depending on the size of the fish. The skin should be crisp and the flesh flake easily.

Transfer to a serving platter, garnish with parsley and lemon wedges and serve immediately.

SMOKE-GRILLED GROUPER

1 medium grouper
(or sea bass, red snapper, barracuda or bonito)

If you have the luck to meet and catch a grouper on a scuba fishing day, you can have yourself a real feast, and save yourself the hassle of getting the fish home and putting it into an already full refrigerator. You cook it right there on the beach.

Collect three big stones and arrange them in a triangle, with their tops level. Collect dry wood, put it between the stones and make a fire. Clean and scale the fish, rinsing it in sea water. Collect three sticks (or better still find three metal rods), wet them thoroughly, and place them on the stones so that they form a small triangle - this is your grill rack. When the fire starts to die down, place the fish on the rack. Cook for 20 minutes on each side - a fish weighing 4 lbs takes at least 45 minutes to cook. Now gather fresh herbs such as thyme, rosemary and marjoram (if you are not in Israel you may have to bring them with you!) and smother the fire with them. The aim is to work up a good smoke. Let the fish cure for 1 hour, and be ready to extinguish the herbs with sea water if they catch fire. Eat hot or cold.

◆ *A large*

grouper

absorbing

the flavor of

fresh herbs

over an open

fire.

WINE & SPIRITS

◆ *Without*
quality grapes
there can be no
quality wines.
Wine is now
more widely
appreciated in
Israel.

Israelis are not drinkers. They may order a bottle of white wine with a meal, or nurse a bottle of beer for a whole evening, or even sit around a table covered with empty bottles, but they are not serious drinkers.

175

There are many reasons why Israel has never made it into the league table of drinking nations. History for one. Drinking was never a favorite pastime with Jews. They may have sneaked a schnapps in the long, cold winters of Russia or Poland, but most of their social drinking was done on Friday nights and on holidays. Their wine was blessed, but it was sacrificial and sweet, not the

kind of wine that goes with dinner. Security is another reason. Despite the unaccountable state of readiness of the armies of various nations of heavy drinkers, we prefer to stay sober. Our unique security problems call for sobriety at all times. Weather is another reason. We have long, hot summers when it is just too hot to drink. When we do, we find that a cold beer, *arak* (an anise-based beverage not unlike ouzo or Pernod), or chilled white wine goes down best. Heavy, syrupy liquers are out and so are whiskies and brandies.

The truth is that for many years we had no local wine industry to speak of. Even in ancient times, we were not great wine-makers. Wine culture and wine appreciation in Israel is really a phenomenon of the 1980s.

Most Israeli wineries date from the beginnning of this century. The two largest, in Rishon Lezion and Zichron Yaakov, were founded with the financial support and know-how of Baron de Rothschild. French wine-makers and local farmers planted vines. Two well-equipped wineries were built. But the wine they produced was too sweet to be true table wine. Yet when table wines were finally produced, the makers discovered that it was almost impossible to market them in Israel. The gourmet revolution that hit us in the eighties had not yet arrived. So although we had drinkable wine, we had no food to drink it with. In those days we had Sauvignon Blanc and Cabernet Sauvignon, and the

◆ *The trademark of Israel's largest wine maker shows the two biblical spies sent out by Joshua. They returned carrying grapes as proof that the land ahead was "flowing with milk and honey."*

◆ *Israel's first winery was founded by Baron de Rothschild in Rishon Lezion.*

occasional bottle of Semillion or Colombard. These were distributed to small neighborhood stores where they were propped upright in direct sunlight. Of course they spoiled quickly. When the tentative gourmet tried his first bottle, it was sour, which naturally discouraged him.

So for the time being we stuck to beer. Our founding fathers realised that beer was the most fitting alcoholic beverage for a hot and busy country. Beer is a thirst quencher. It is filling, the liquid equivalent of bread. It is also a natural foil to the hot, peppery foods we are so fond of. We have three local brands of beer, more or less. All of them are adequate, but one of them - a clear and flavorsome European-style pilsner - is superb.

When the great food revolution finally came, Israel's wine producers were quick off the mark. To see how this happened, we must go back a decade or so. The first decent Israeli wine was fermented and bottled on the Golan Heights at the Golan Winery. Wine-growing on the Golan was the bright idea of a moshavnik who was very successful with apples. The soil of the Golan is unique, the result of volcanic eruptions that once shook the whole region. The cool upland climate - cold at night, pleasantly warm during the day, liberally sprinkled with rain, seldom touched by frosts - is also ideal for grape-growing.

In the early 1980s, after a few years of trial runs under the supervision of an American wine-maker from California, Golan produced its first commercial vintage, a very dry and distinctive Sauvignon Blanc. In the

◆ *The original site of the first winery in Rishon Lezion.*

◆ *The winemaster at work.*

◆ *A container of grapes harvested in the early morning is quickly sent to the winery.*

belief that it would be much easier to win honors abroad than sell their carefully perfected product at home, Golan sought and found an appreciative market in Europe and the United States. Their wine was a great success abroad. Not only was it good, it was also from Israel, where wine had been produced for centuries!

With chestfuls of medals and citations from international wine shows, Golan started to tackle the home market. Their timing was perfect. While their wines had been conquering the world, Israel had undergone its long-awaited gastronomic revolution. I do not use the word revolution lightly. The change was dramatic. Hundred of restaurants opened almost overnight, and the emphasis shifted away from Middle Eastern and Arab cuisine to International. For the first time we had an opportunity to find out what we really liked - French, Japanese, Italian, American... Acquiring a taste for good wine was a natural progression. When that happened, Golan was ready with new and exciting wines.

Today, instead of three home-grown wines to choose from, we have twenty-five. The old sweet wines were no longer commercially viable, and with Golan setting the pace, other wineries had no choice but to join the race. Wine began to be promoted and discussed. Wine societies and wine newsletters appeared. There were aggressive advertising campaigns, with each winery claiming supremacy. Consumers were faced with an array of labels and styles of wine. Prices were high to begin with, but increasing demand has brought them down.

We are still not a nation of wine-drinkers as the French or Italians are, but if we do decide to celebrate, we have good local wine to celebrate with.

WINE & SPIRITS

Recipes

GROUPER WITH FENNEL & ARAK

*1 large grouper (or sea bass, or red snapper),
scaled and cleaned
(allow 12 oz per person)
4 bulbs fennel, thinly sliced
salt and freshly ground white pepper
2 onions, thinly sliced
3 cloves garlic, crushed
1/2 cup olive oil
1/2 cup arak (or ouzo, or any other
anise-flavored liqueur)*

Season the inside of the fish and the slices of fennel with salt and pepper. Mix the onions, garlic and olive oil with the fennel, and stuff the fish with half of this mixture. Cover the bottom of an earthenware baking dish with the rest, place the fish on top, cover the dish with foil, and bake in a moderate oven (350°F). A large fish will take about 1 hour to cook, a smaller one less than half that time. Warm the *arak*, pour it over the fish as it comes out of the oven, and set light to it. Serve as soon as the flames have died down.

◆ *Grouper*

with fennel

and arak.

BREAST OF MOULLARD IN WINE SAUCE

The moullard is a cross between a goose and a Berber duck.

2 moullard breasts (or duck, or goose),
weighing 12 oz each
1 onion, finely diced
2 tablespoons dried cherries
1/4 teaspoon black pepper
pinch brown sugar
1 cup dry red wine
3 tablespoons rich brown sauce base
4 tablespoons butter

Prick the breasts a few times with a fork, then lay them in a cold, heavy skillet, fatty side down. Cook over a medium heat until the breasts color a deep brown, then add the onion, cherries, pepper and sugar. Turn the breasts, and add the wine and sauce base. Remove the breasts, slice them, and transfer them to a warm serving dish. Reduce the contents of the skillet to a quarter, then remove from the heat and stir in the butter. Spoon over the slices of breast and serve straight away, with roast potatoes. Moullard should never be over-cooked. Serves 4.

◆ *Breast of*

moullard in

wine sauce.

GOOSE LIVER FLAMBÉ

4 oz goose liver per person, well chilled
salt, white pepper
freshly grated orange peel
rich brown sauce base
Halleluya liqueur (orange-based) or
Grand Marnier

Carefully cut the liver into slices 1/3 inch thick. Season with salt and pepper, and chill in the refrigerator.

Heat a heavy skillet and sauté the slices for about 2 seconds on each side - no oil is needed since goose liver contains a lot of fat. Pour off excess fat for future use.

Add a sprinkling of orange peel, 1 tablespoon of brown sauce base and 2 tablespoons of heated liqueur. Set alight with a match and serve immediately. This superb delicacy should be served by itself, accompanied by nothing but a good white wine.

SAUCE BASE

Most classic cookbooks contain a recipe for a rich brown sauce base made from beef, beef bones and vegetables. In Israel we make something very similar, often cooking it overnight and serving it as a soup.

◆ *Goose liver*

flambéed

in orange

liqueur.

STUFFED PIGEONS

1 heaped cup rice
salt and freshly ground black pepper
6 pigeons, plucked and cleaned, with livers
5 cloves garlic, crushed
1 cup chopped walnuts or pistachios
4 tablespoons chopped parsley
pinch ground cardamom
freshly grated nutmeg, to taste
vegetable oil
3 onions, sliced
1 carrot, sliced
1 teaspoon celery salt
4 1/2 cups black non-alcoholic malt beer
1/2 cup brandy

Boil the rice in salted water for 12 minutes, then drain well. Cut the pigeon livers into cubes, then mix with the rice, 3 of the garlic cloves, the nuts, parsley and spices. Stuff the birds loosely with this mixture and close the openings with skewers. Fry the birds for 5 minutes on each side (a Dutch oven would give better results in this recipe), put them on their backs, then add the rest of the garlic, the onion, carrot and celery salt to the pan. Sauté for 10 minutes, then add the malt beer and brandy and transfer to an ovenproof dish.

Cover and bake for 2 hours in an oven preheated to 300°F. When the birds are cooked, the flesh should come easily off the bones. Uncover and continue cooking for another 15 minutes. Add a little more malt beer if the birds look dry. Put the birds on individual plates to serve. Strain the sauce, spoon a little over the birds and serve the rest in a jug. Serves 4 to 6, accompanied by pickles.

COMPOTE OF DRIED FRUIT IN RED WINE

equal quantities of dried apricots,
prunes, raisins, dates and blanched almonds
2 cloves
2 cardamom pods
1 stick cinnamon
red wine
whipped cream, to serve

Soak the fruit in cold water for 10 minutes, then discard the water. Put all the fruit, the almonds and the spices in a heavy saucepan, and add enough red wine to cover them. Bring to a boil, then simmer for 12 minutes, stirring occasionally. Take out the cloves, cardamom and cinnamon, and allow to cool. Cover and refrigerate. Serve in individual glasses with whipped cream in a separate bowl.

ROSEHIP COCKTAIL

1 lb rosehips, preferably from damask roses
1 heaped cup sugar
1/2 cup lemon juice
2 cups rosé wine
1 cup white rum
juice of 1 pomegranate, optional

Wash the rosehips, cover in water and refrigerate for 4 hours. Boil the rosehips until they are soft, then strain the liquid into another saucepan and discard the rosehips. Add the sugar and boil for 5 minutes, then add the rest of the ingredients and chill. Serve with ice, with rose petals for decoration.

◆ *Stuffed pigeon with baby eggplants.*

◆ *Compote of dried fruit in red wine.*

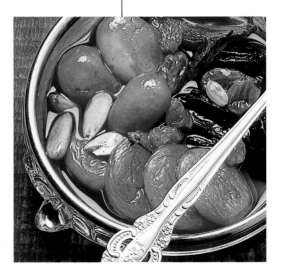

CHAPTER 10

FRUITS & DESSERTS

◆ *A feast of*

ripe figs

and peeled

prickly

pears.

The Hebrew word *sabra* means prickly, thorny, rough. A *sabra* (plural *sabres*) is a prickly pear, a regional and popular fruit, but the word also describes an Israeli stereotype, the Israeli-born Israeli complete with all the traits typical of his or her fruity namesake. The epithet has been in use for so many years now that we have stopped being offended by it, and at times we even take a certain pride in it. How many other nations are named after a fruit?

For a time the name was appropriate. Prickly pears are thorny. They have a thick skin. They have a short season - less than two months in

summer. They are extremely difficult to pick and they used not to be sold commercially, or at least not on a large scale. But when you do pick them, and remove the thorns, and peel them, and cut them open, they are sweet and unique in taste and texture. If a whole nation must be named after a fruit, perhaps *sabra* is not such a bad name.

◆ *When you buy a watermelon the greengrocer willingly cuts out a little piece for you to try.*

We used to buy prickly pears from the back of very small carts, most of them pushed along by kids who would clean the fruit and hand it to you on the street. We ate it straight away. It was rather special, something you could not buy by the kilo like other fruit. Then the plant breeders stepped in.

The prickly pear is now in decline, a victim of commercial sophistication. A new, improved,

◆ *Watermelon*

stands appear

in summer

and vanish

when the

season is over.

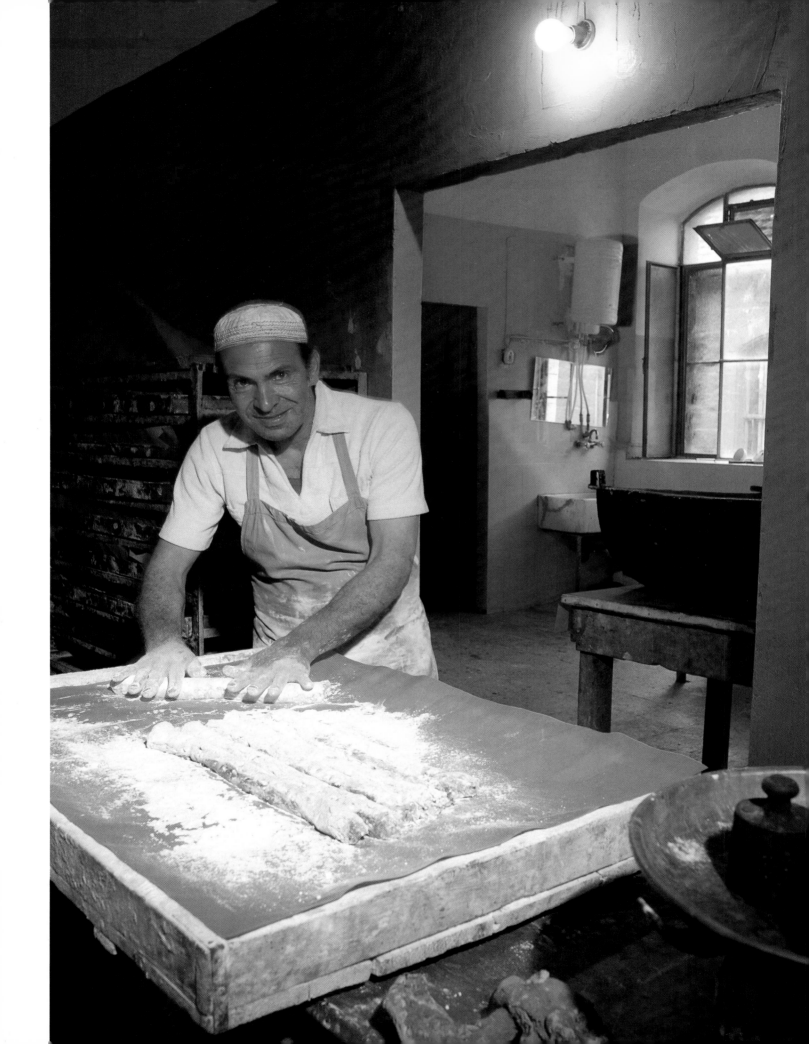

thornless, perennial *sabra* is now available. The moral of this story is that the
sabra may no longer stand for what we are, unless of course we too have become
new, improved, thornless and perennial.

The abundance of fruit in Israel is staggering. The fruit we grow
today knows no season. Grapes start in spring and continue through to
November. Watermelons and melons start in March and go on through Sep-
tember. Citrus fruit is available all year round. It is an amazing sight. The typical
Israeli fruit stall is lush and heavy with fruit in all seasons, all ripe, all sweet, all
ready to eat. And as if indigenous species were not enough, in the last few years
we have also managed to grow tropical and exotic fruit - papaya/pawpaw and
kiwi fruit, Sharon fruit/persimmons and carambolas/star fruit, passionfruit
and pineapples, lychees and kumquats, dates and figs, Chinese apples and
feijoas. Every season brings a new arrival.

It has become almost a tradition that every year some far-seeing
and resourceful moshav or kibbutz will introduce a new fruit that it has secretly
nursed to perfection, forcing it to adapt to local conditions. Young botonists are
busy changing the size and color of watermelons - they want the new genera-
tion of watermelons to be smaller, sweeter and seedless. They are also changing
the shape and size of pickling vegetables. It is easier, they say, to pickle round
cucumbers than long ones, so they are growing cucumbers that look like green
tomatoes. Some of these exciting fruits survive for one season and never return.
If they do not prove commercially attractive, why grow them? But there is
alway as another designer fruit in the
wings.

We put our great va-
riety of fruit to good use. For example,
it is all but compulsory for every

◆ Rahat
lokum,
Turkish
delight,
is still made
by hand in
an old
factory in
Jerusalem.

◆ *Assorted*
candies by
Havillo of
Jerusalem.

◆ *Fruit*

boulevard in

affluent

Ramat Hasharon,

a suburb of

Tel Aviv.

The simultaneous

display of

summer and

winter fruit is

an Israeli

phenomenon.

◆ *Prickly pear*

picking in

the traditional

way helps

to avoid

the thorns.

household to offer a large selection of fresh fruit, dried fruit and nuts to inmates and visitors. Fruit is not something we buy for special occasions. It is a staple. We eat it all the time. In fact it is a wonder that such a fruity nation ever bothers with cakes and pastries. Yet cakes and sweet desserts are an integral part of the culinary cultures of all the ethnic minorities living in Israel, and none of them has yet given up cakes in favor of fruit.

Baklava and *konafa* are the grandest of Arab pastries, although their origin is probably Turkish or Greek. They are made at home and commercially. Proud housewives may scorn store-bought pastries, but most are fresh and tasty and a good bet for those who do not want to bother. *Baklava* and *konafa* should be light, crisp and delicate, and the fillings should consist of pistachios and walnuts, and not peanuts. Although they look elaborate, *baklava* and *konafa* are easy to prepare, and they are dual-purpose, desserts as well pastries to be consumed with coffee or tea. No party or grand occasion is complete without them.

Another essential of Israeli dessert is Turkish coffee. A lot of myth and folklore is attached to the small demitasse cups of strong, fragrant liquid. The Bedouins brew their coffee in narrow-necked, long-handled pots called *finjans* or *tanakas*, which come in various sizes. Their coffee is made from very finely ground coffee beans to which a few cardamom seeds have been added, and it is drunk thick, strong, and usually very sweet. The coffee is boiled in the *finjan* seven times before it is served, the repeated boilings producing a froth which is very tasty and part of the enjoyment.

FRUITS & DESSERTS

◆ Old and new.
Jaffa oranges
have a world-
wide reputation,
but Israeli
strawberries are
less well known.
Every year
they get bigger
and better.

Recipes

BAKLAVA
Layered pastry with nuts and syrup

1 lb filo *pastry (about 24 sheets)*
1 cup unsalted butter, melted
2 1/2 cups pistachio nuts, walnuts or
almonds, coarsely chopped
2 tablespoons sugar

SYRUP
1 1/4 cups sugar
1/2 cup water
1 tablespoon lemon juice
1 tablespoon orange blossom water

To make the syrup, dissolve the sugar in the water and lemon juice, and simmer until it is thick enough to coat the back of a spoon. Add the orange blossom water and simmer for another 2 minutes. Allow to cool, then chill in the refrigerator.

To cook the *filo* pastry you will need a large round or square baking pan. Brush the bottom and sides of the pan with the melted butter, then lay half the *filo* sheets in the pan, brushing each sheet with melted butter as you lay it in and overlapping the sheets or folding the sides over as necessary. Preheat the oven to 350-375°F. Mix the chopped nuts with the sugar and sprinkle evenly over the top sheet of *filo*. Now lay the rest of the sheets of *filo* in the pan, brushing with butter as before. Brush the top sheet with melted butter. Using a very sharp knife, cut the pastry diagonally into diamond shapes.

Bake for 30 minutes at 350-375°F, then raise the oven temperature to 450-475°F and cook for another 15 minutes. The *baklava* should be very puffy and light gold in color. Remove from the oven and immediately pour the chilled syrup over the hot pastry. Leave in the dish to cool.

To serve, cut along the diagonal lines and arrange on a serving dish; alternatively, turn out upside down onto a large plate, put another plate on the bottom, turn the right way up, then cut along the original lines.

FROSTED ROSES
A very luxurious and special garnish for desserts

10 unblemished roses, half open,
with their stems
4 egg whites
4 or 5 tablespoons water
2 1/4 cups superfine sugar

Choose mostly red roses, and roses which have not been sprayed! Shop-bought roses have been sprayed, so pick roses from your own garden. Rose petals are edible and tasty.

Thoroughly stir (do not beat) the water into the egg whites and dip the heads of the roses into it, moving them about so that all the petals become coated with the mixture. Now stand the stems in a bowl and leave for 10 minutes. Using a sugar sifter, dust the flowers heavily with sugar. Do the same with any loose petals. Now hang the roses up by their stems and let them dry for 2 days. Then put them on a tray and let them dry for another 3 days. Store carefully in an airtight container or in the freezer. Use for decorating custards and other desserts. Providing they are well coated with egg white and thoroughly dried, frosted roses should keep for up to six months.

◆ *Layered pastries*

with nuts and

syrup come in

different shapes

and flavors.

◆ *Sesame and peanut bars.*

CONFIT OF FIGS

2 lbs whole fresh figs
4 1/2 cups sugar
1/2 cup water
1/3 cup sesame seeds
1/2 cup blanched almonds
2 tablespoons fresh lemon juice

Wash the figs and prick them a few times with a fork. Dissolve the sugar in the water, add the figs, sesame seeds, almonds and lemon juice, and simmer over a very low heat for 2 hours. At the end of this time the figs should look almost translucent. Cool and serve at room temperature.

SESAME BARS

1/2 cup sesame seeds
1 3/4 cups sugar
3/4 cup water
1 teaspoon cinnamon
pinch ground cloves
1/2 teaspoon lemon juice

Using a nonstick skillet, fry the sesame seeds until they are golden (no fat is required because sesame seeds are rich in oil). Dissolve the sugar in the water, bring to a boil and continue boiling until the sugar begins to turn golden brown. At this point, add the sesame seeds, cinnamon, cloves and lemon juice, and continue to stir for 3 minutes. Remove from the heat, pour onto a wet marble slab and, using a wet rolling pin, roll the mixture to an even thickness of about 1/2 inch. Using a pancake turner or metal spatula, quickly lever the toffee off the marble slab and cut it into bars. Alternatively, leave it to harden and then snap it into chunks. Keep in an airtight container. Bars of almond or pine nut brittle can be made in the same way.

CANDIED ORANGE & GRAPEFRUIT PEELS

2 large oranges
2 thick-skinned grapefruit
5 cups sugar
2 cups water
juice of 1 lemon

◆ *Candied*

orange

and

grapefruit

peels.

Scrub the skins of the fruit with a hard brush, then cut them in half and scoop out the flesh. Put the half shells into a bowl of water, cover with a plate, and soak for 2 days, changing the water once during this time. Drain and cut into strips. Put the strips into a large saucepan, cover with water, bring to a boil and simmer for 15 minutes. Pour off the water. Cover with water again, bring to a boil, simmer for 15 minutes, and drain. Repeat the process once more.

Now add the sugar and 2 cups of water to the peel, bring to a boil and simmer very gently for 2 hours, with the lid of the saucepan off. When all the liquid has evaporated, stir in the lemon juice, making sure that it coats all the pieces of peel. Drain the peel and cut it into bite-size pieces. Roll the pieces in sugar if you like but this is not absolutely necessary. Leave on a plate or on wax paper for several hours to harden. Store in an airtight container.

◆ *Confit*

of figs.

TANGERINE SORBET

1 heaped cup sugar
1 cup water
2 lbs tangerines
1/2 grapefruit
1 teaspoon Cointreau or orange liqueur

Dissolve the sugar in the water and bring to a boil. Cook for 5 minutes, remove from the heat and allow to cool. Pare the zest from 3 of the tangerines and reserve. Remove the segments from half the tangerines and carefully peel them. Squeeze the juice from the rest of the tangerines and from the grapefruit.

Blend together the syrup, zest, juice and liqueur, pour into a bowl and freeze and beat. Repeat the whipping every 20 minutes or so, two or three more times, so that the sorbet stays soft when frozen. Serve decorated with the tangerine segments.

BAKED APPLES

10 cooking apples
1 cup red wine
2 tablespoons sugar
1 teaspoon powdered cinnamon
1 cup raisins
1/4 cup butter, melted
Grand Marnier or orange liqueur, optional

Wash and core the apples, but do not cut right through to the base. Arrange the apples in a greased baking pan and preheat the oven to 350°F.

Mix together the wine, sugar, cinnamon and raisins and spoon a little of the mixture into each apple. Top with melted butter. Bake for about 1 hour. Serve hot or cold, with a teaspoon of Grand Marnier on top, if liked.

BAKED QUINCE OLYMPUS

5 quinces
1 1/4 cups lemon juice
4 1/2 cups water
1 1/2 lbs sugar
3 whole sticks cinnamon

Trim the quinces at both ends and cut them in half lengthwise. Peel them, then soak them in water with a little lemon juice added to it to prevent them from discoloring.

Dissolve two-thirds of the sugar in the water and bring to a boil. Add the lemon juice, cinnamon and quince halves and simmer for 15-25 minutes, or until the quinces are soft (prick them with a fork to see if they are tender). Place the quinces in a baking pan, cut side up, pour the syrup over them and sprinkle with the rest of the sugar. Bake in an oven preheated to 450°F until they are a dark golden color. Turn off the oven. Leave the quinces in the oven to cool. Serve at room temperature. Serves 10.

◆ *Baked quince Olympus.*

◆ *Baked apple stuffed with raisins.*

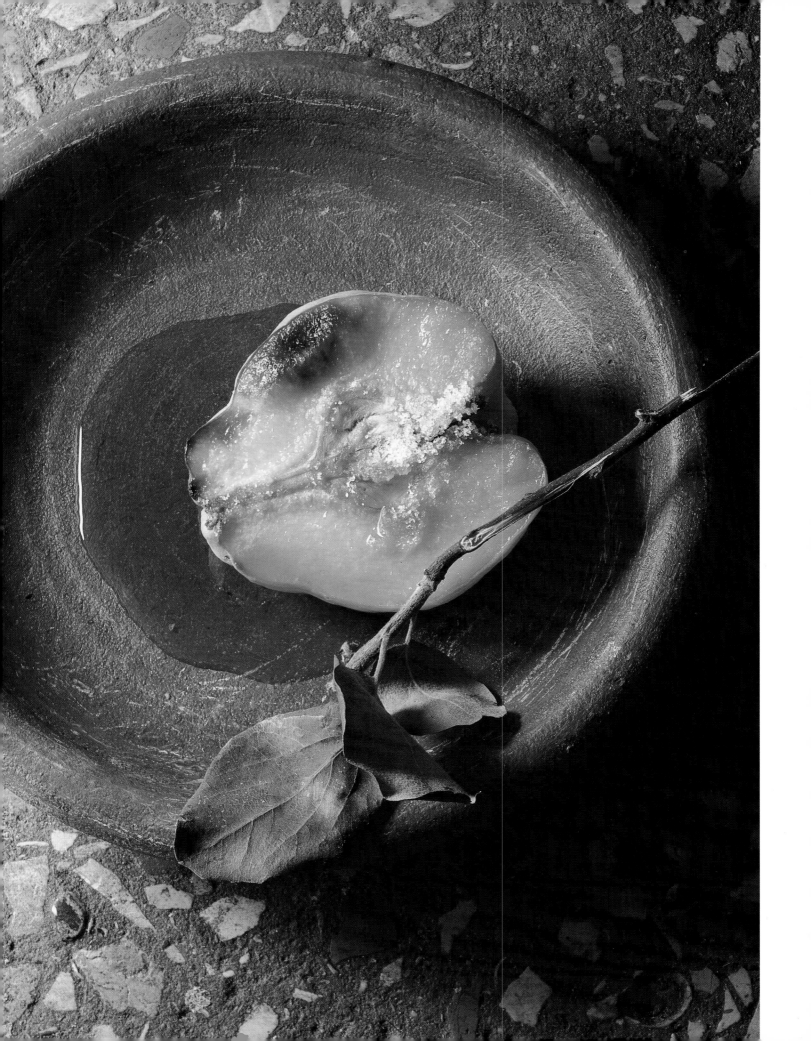

◆ *Prickly*

pear

salad.

PRICKLY PEAR SALAD

juice of 1 orange
juice of 1 lemon
1/2 teaspoon ground cardamom
1 tablespoon nut oil
3 prickly pears
2 dessert apples, cut into small strips
1 red bell pepper, cut into small cubes
2 small cucumbers, cut into strips
pinch hot chili powder

Combine the orange juice, lemon juice, cardamom and nut oil in a salad bowl. Carefully peel the prickly pears under running water, wearing gloves. Slice and add to the bowl, together with the strips of apple, red pepper and cucumber. Sprinkle with a little chili powder, toss well and serve with other salads at the dinner table.

PRICKLY PEAR SAUCE

8 prickly pears
juice of 1/2 lemon
2 1/2 tablespoons Kirsch
2 level teaspoons arrowroot

Carefully peel the prickly pears. Chop them, then rub the flesh through a nylon sieve into a small saucepan. Add the lemon juice and Kirsch and warm through. Mix the arrowroot to a smooth paste with a little cold water, then stir it into the purée and Kirsch mixture. Bring to a boil and simmer gently for 2 or 3 minutes until the mixture turns syrupy. Serve hot or cold with fruit sorbets or brochettes of broiled fruit.

MA'AMOUL
Small pastries filled with dates & nuts

FILLING
4 oz dried dates, pitted
1 cup walnuts, coarsely chopped
3/4 cup almonds or pistachio nuts,
coarsely chopped
2/3 cup water
1/2 cup sugar
1 heaped teaspoon ground cinnamon

DOUGH
4 cups all-purpose flour
1 cup unsalted butter, melted
2 tablespoons rosewater
4 or 5 tablespoons milk
confectioners' sugar

To prepare the filling, chop the dates, put them into a saucepan with the chopped nuts, water, sugar and cinnamon, and cook over a low heat until the dates are soft and the water has been absorbed.

To make the dough, sift the flour into a bowl, add the melted butter and lightly cut it in. Add the rosewater and milk, and knead to a softish consistency. Divide the dough into walnut size pieces. Preheat the oven to 300°F.

Taking a piece of dough at a time, roll it into a ball between your palms, then hollow it out with your thumb, pinching the sides up to make a large thimble shape. Now fill the thimble with a little of the date mixture and press the dough back over the filling to make a ball. Slightly flatten the ball in the palm of your hand and use a fork to make an interesting pattern on top - straight lines are the traditional pattern.

When you have used up all the dough and filling, place the *ma'moul* on a greased baking sheet and bake for about 30 minutes. Do not allow them to brown or they will become hard. When they are cold, roll them in confectioners' sugar and store in an airtight tin.

HALVAH SOUFFLÉ

6 sponge fingers
6 oz halvah
2 level tablespoons cornstarch
2 tablespoons sugar
pinch salt
6 egg yolks and 4 egg whites
2 tablespoons brandy
1 cup milk
2 level tablespoons all-purpose flour

For this you will need a 4 1/2 cup soufflé dish. Butter and flour the inside, and shake out any excess flour. Line the bottom with sponge fingers, trimming them to fit.

Crumble the halvah and mix to a smooth paste with a little water. Add the cornstarch, half the sugar, a pinch of salt, the 6 egg yolks and the brandy, and mix thoroughly. Heat the milk almost to boiling point, then pour it into the halvah mixture, beating non-stop with a fork as you do so. Now sift in the flour, give the mixture a brisk beat, and leave to cool. Preheat the oven to 400°F.

Beat the egg whites to stiff peaks with the rest of the sugar. Stir one-third into the halvah mixture, and carefully fold in the rest. Pour into the prepared soufflé dish, put into the oven and bake for 25 minutes. Do not open the oven door while the soufflé is in - if there is a chance of the top burning, place a sheet of greased foil on top as you put the soufflé into the oven. Serve immediately.

◆ *Ma'amoul*

are small

pastries

filled with

dates and

nuts

◆ *Halvah*

and thick

Turkish

coffee with

cardamom

BISKOTCHOS
Crisp, salty cookies shaped like
bagels

1 oz fresh yeast
1/2 teaspoon sugar
1 cup lukewarm water
3 cups all-purpose flour, sifted
3/4 cup plus 2 tablespoons margarine or
shortening, in small pieces
1 level teaspoon salt
1 tablespoon oil
ground anise, cumin or coriander, optional
sesame seeds

Dissolve the yeast and the sugar in a little of
the water and leave for 10 minutes. Make a
well in the flour and add the margarine or
shortening, the salt, the oil, the yeast mixture and the rest of the water. Add a little
anise, cumin or coriander too, if liked. Knead
to a smooth elastic dough. Cover and leave
in a warm place for 1 hour. Preheat the
oven to 375°F.

Divide the dough into 25-30 walnut-
sized pieces. Sprinkle a board with sesame
seeds and roll each piece
into a pencil shape about
4 inches long, making
sure it is well coated with
sesame seeds. Pinch the
ends together to form
small rings. Arrange on
an oiled baking sheet and
bake for 45 minutes. Store
in an airtight container.

◆ *A Jericho*

fruit and

vegetable.

vendor takes

an afternoon

tea break.

◆ *Mint*

tea and

biskotchos.

NEW ISRAELI CHEFS

Some of my best friends are cooks, and they are a strange lot. They stay up far into the night trying to remember the exact two weeks in spring when white Judean truffles bloom. If cornered, they will admit that the white Judean truffle, collected by Bedouins in the Judean desert, is not worth losing sleep over. It is a dry, powdery object, but it's the only truffle we've got, and we have to be patriotic. If we were not patriots, why on earth would we live in a country that does not have truffles, oysters, clams, lobsters and decent shrimps, which the laws of *kashrut* forbid us to cook in any case.

My friends also sit by their windows at night waiting for rain, for when it rains the fish are fresh and firm and the mushrooms grow. When I point out that the only mushroom that grows here is gooey and fleshy and requires

hours of cleaning, which spoils both the taste and the texture, they get furious.

Our gallant new chefs are first in the produce markets, poking the tomatoes, squeezing the lettuces, listening to the watermelons and angrily turning down fish with dull eyes. The merchants spot them a mile off. For you, they say, we have a catch of red mullet, just off the boat. See how bright and red their skin is. Come on, insist my friends, show us the good stuff. And the good stuff is always there, hidden at the back of large refrigerators, well away from Philistines. They squeeze the fish and purse their lips. It is not in the prime of youth and vigor, but it will have to do. Trout is delivered from the north once a week, and if they do not buy now they will be troutless for a whole week. It does not do to disappoint one's customers too often.

These, then, are the new Israeli chefs, although they have no use for the word "chef." They are cooks. They love good food. They adore new ideas. They attempt the impossible. They have a mission: to create an Israeli cuisine. There are food critics who believe it is a suicide mission. There are no more culinary frontiers, they say, no more gastronomic wildernesses to be discovered or created. Everyone has been everywhere and eaten everything. Israeli food is what it is and will always be, a lively hybrid, a medley of hits - a little Arab spice, a touch of the Orient, a dash of Eastern Europe, and the zest of fresh locally grown produce.

My friends beg to differ. Every once in a while they sit down and write new recipes, describing at length the new factor in the formula. For example, if you take avocados and make a soup out of them, omitting coriander and adding hyssop, the result is no longer Mexican but Israeli. Hyssop, an in-

digenous and biblical herb, has wrought a species change. If you leave out the pigeon in stuffed pigeon and use quail instead, the result is not French but Israeli. Our forefathers ate quail in the desert. Quail are our heritage. In fact it took us a long time to raise quail in captivity, but we managed it, so we must make the most of them. There is more. If you fry goat's cheese in batter and add mango sauce, and if both the cheese and the mangoes are locally produced, the result is 101 percent

Israeli. It cannot be anything else.

Israel's new cooks fortify themselves behind hot stoves, write books, and appear on television, but it is still too early to claim total victory over the critics. Their quest for a specifically Israeli culinary identity is sometimes spurious. Ever since Jordan severed its ties with the West Bank, Arab olive oil producers have been burdened with a glut of oil, of which only a portion can be consumed by Israelis, so now is not the time to be claiming olive oil as an Israeli invention. They also call Israeli an amazing carrot which grows only in Gaza; it is a vivid purple, crisp, tasty, and marvelous for garnishing. Their quest is also frustrated by the here-today, gone-tomorrow phenomenon. This was exactly the case with fresh ginger.

Ginger is widely used in Chinese and Japanese cooking, of course, and was introduced here a few years ago. A few farmers began to grow it and there was a big publicity campaign, heartily endorsed by an Israeli cook who is an expert on Chinese cooking. Everywhere you went, people talked about ginger. A year later, the ginger was gone. The cook who had promoted it so hard called his supplier. Where is my ginger? he asked. Not profitable enough, replied the farmer. It never really caught on. What do you mean profitable? shouted the cook. Everyone's been talking about it. People bought bushels of the stuff. No, said the farmer, it was left to rot in the market. No one bought it.

And that was the end of the Israeli ginger dream. The Chinese-style cook still uses it, but he relies on friends and customers to bring it back - illegally of course - from abroad.

Then there was the saga of the quail eggs. Where there is a female quail, there are eggs, and these eggs are ideal for pickling and cooking. Test kitchens around the country worked hard to come up with an original recipe. They were very close, so close they could almost taste it, but the closer they got the scarcer the tiny eggs became. What has happened to our eggs? they asked, and the hardy moshavnik who had promised them a lifetime's supply mumbled something about the productivity of quails going down in captivity. In captivity, it seemed, the quails were too crowded and too scared to lay eggs. We'll pay for larger cages, said the experimental cooks. We must have the eggs. Forget about the eggs, said the moshavnik. I have a new product: eels. How do you feel about eels?

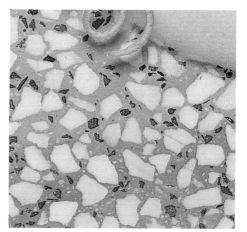

There was indeed something fishy about the farmer's story. Eventually the eggless cooks found out that quail eggs have strange healing properties, including the ability to cure asthma and allergies. The farmer who produced them had opened several fresh quail egg snack bars and was doing terrific business. People were driving in, quaffing the fresh eggs, and driving out feeling a lot better. No shipping, no packing, no mess.

A farmer from the southern part of Israel showed up recently with a sample of Japanese *shiitake* mushrooms. He was sent packing.

New chefs also have to contend with a body of opinion which thinks it improper to promote good food and wine. These Jeremiahs see food as part of a long tradition of atonement and suffering. They like to believe that austerity is still with us, that none of our political problems have been solved, that we perch permanently on the brink of war, that the economy is on the skids. They eat to survive, not to celebrate life. To discuss the merits of beluga caviar or the bouquet of a new wine is decadent and irresponsible. There is nothing admirable or artistic about the preparation of food. They care about Israel, not about what Israelis eat.

Perhaps to escape the debilitating effects of such rhetoric our new cooks travel a lot. They must keep up. They go to food conventions, attend demonstrations and give lectures. Their peers judge them less harshly than their compatriots. They always have the avocado to fall back on, and the whole range of citrus fruits. They win medals, which give them great comfort, but they do not wear them at home. They make contacts, and if they are lucky they get invited to the great kitchens of Europe. Roger Verge might ask them to drop by and spend a few days nosing around the kitchen. Anton Mosimann in London is known to be cooperative; he is a great host, free with advice, outgoing and friendly. Once a year they feel honor-bound to make it to Paris. This is

an expensive but priceless exercise, during which they visit lots of two-star restaurants and lay bets as to which will receive the coveted third star in the next Michelin. They go to Fouchon and spend silly amounts of money on canned truffles (of the Périgord variety), herb vinegars and extra-virgin olive oil. If the oysters at the fish market are fresh, they buy a cooler, fill it with crushed ice and cram it with a few dozen oysters. You can always recognize a new chef on the plane home. He's the one who sits upright for five hours clutching a giant ice box to his chest.

He and his peers belong to a culinary grapevine. He will be the first to know if an Iranian refugee escapes the ayatollahs with a cart of caviar. He is also a guru. Sheep farmers will carry whole sides of lamb up six flights of stairs to get his honest opinion. Deep-sea fishermen will seek him out if a stray lobster gets entangled in their nets.

What has emerged from all this is a young, bold and innovative cuisine. It has been worth waiting for. Cooking is one of those rare professions where the process is as rewarding as the end result.

$\mathcal{N}$EW ISRAELI CHEFS

$\mathcal{R}$ecipes

HAIM COHEN

◆ *Haim Cohen.*

is the young

chef of Keren

à la Carte,

a French

restaurant.

Cohen

frequently

visits France

to study under

a master chef.

LAMB CUTLETS WITH BAKED TOMATOES

MARINADE
1 cup dry red wine
1/4 cup olive oil
3 cloves garlic, unpeeled and crushed
1 bay leaf
fresh thyme and rosemary
1 onion, sliced
1 carrot, sliced
salt and freshly ground black pepper

rack of lamb containing 12 cutlets
4 or 5 large tomatoes

Mix together the marinade ingredients and marinate the lamb for 24 hours. Remove the lamb from the marinade, and trim the flesh and fat from the ends of the bones so that the cutlets are easy to pick up. Preheat the oven to 425°F.

Drain the lamb and thoroughly rub the strained marinade liquid into it before placing in a baking sheet and roasting in the oven for 10 minutes. Turn down the heat to 350°F and cook for another 15 minutes, basting with the cooking juices.

Remove the rack of lamb from the oven, and allow it to rest for 5 minutes before separating the cutlets. Meanwhile add some of the marinade to the cooking juices and reduce over a high heat. Spoon this over the cutlets as you serve them.

The tomatoes, sliced in half, sprinkled with sea salt and fresh thyme and placed on an oiled baking sheet, can be baked with the lamb; in a moderate oven, they take about 15 minutes. Serves 4 or 5.

MINTED MELON WITH DATES AND ARAK

16 dried dates, pitted and finely chopped
12 leaves fresh mint, finely chopped
1/2 cup arak *(or ouzo)*
3 small melons

Marinate the chopped dates and mint in the *arak* for 3 hours. Cut the melons in half, remove the seeds, and fill with the date and mint mixture. Chill before serving.
Serves 6.

ARUGULA WITH PINE NUTS

2 lbs arugula leaves
16 spinach leaves
1 romaine lettuce
3 tomatoes
1 cup pine nuts, toasted
olive oil
salt and pepper

Wash and pat dry all the greens, and remove the stems of the arugula. Cut the tomatoes into thin slices and shred the lettuce.

Spread the arugula and pine nuts on a bed of lettuce and arrange a circle of tomato slices on top. Add another layer of arugula and pine nuts and a layer of spinach, and season with the olive oil, salt and pepper. Serves 6 to 8.

◆ *Lamb cutlets*

with baked

tomatoes.

Avocado Soup

1/2 onion, finely chopped
1/4 cup margarine
3 tablespoons all-purpose flour
4 1/2 cups milk
2 ripe avocados
2 cloves garlic, crushed
3 tablespoons lemon juice
1 tablespoon chopped fresh dill
1/2 cup heavy cream
2 egg yolks
salt and freshly ground black pepper

Fry the onion in the margarine until golden brown. Reduce the heat and sift in the flour. Add the milk, stirring all the time, then bring to the boil and simmer gently until the mixture thickens.

Peel and mash one of the avocados with the garlic and 2 tablespoons of the lemon juice. Peel and cube the other avocado and sprinkle with the remaining lemon juice so that it does not turn black. Over a low heat, stir the mashed avocado into the thickened milk, then add the avocado cubes and dill. Blend the cream and egg yolks together and add them to the soup, with salt and pepper to taste. Serve warm. Serves 6.

Note: Do not allow this soup to boil or the avocado will taste bitter and the soup will curdle.

Mousht in Mango Sauce
St. Peter's fish with puréed mango

juice of 1 lemon
2 tablespoons Worcestershire sauce
salt and freshly ground black pepper
2 tablespoons all-purpose flour
2 fresh mousht (or trout), about 1 1/4 lb
each, cut into fillets
vegetable oil
1/4 cup butter
1/2 cup dry white wine
1 mango

Mix together the lemon juice, Worcestershire sauce, salt and pepper, and pour it over the fish. Allow the fish to marinate for at least 30 minutes. Pour off the marinade and reserve it.

Flour the fish, then pan-fry them in hot oil on both sides. Remove the fish from the pan, discard the oil, and add the butter, white wine, and the reserved marinade juices.

Peel the mango and cut away the flesh. Purée half and thinly slice the rest. Add the slices to the pan. Return the fish to the pan and continue cooking until it flakes easily. Lay the fish on a hot dish. Stir the puréed mango into the pan juices and spoon over the fish. Serves 4.

Uri Guttmann

◆ *Avocado*

soup.

URI GUTTMANN

◆ *Uri Guttmann is a*

well-established

chef who represents

Israel at

congresses and

international

food shows.

He is the owner

of the Panorama

Restaurant in

Tel Aviv.

BANANAS TEL-KATZIR

FILLING
1 cup milk
1 tablespoon sugar
2 tablespoons butter
vanilla extract
1 tablespoon cornstarch
1 egg yolk
salt
1 1/2 cups shelled pecans
8 fresh dates, pitted and whole
4 dried dates, finely chopped
grated peel of 1 orange

4 bananas, peeled and whole
4 crêpes (thin pancakes)

SAUCE
1/4 cup butter
1 heaped cup sugar
1/2 cup fresh orange juice

Boil the milk with the sugar, butter and vanilla. Mix the cornstarch with the egg yolk, add a pinch of salt, and add to the boiling milk, stirring well as the mixture thickens. Allow to cool, then cover and chill.

Grind the pecans in a food processor, then add them, with the fresh dates and the finely chopped dried dates, to the chilled custard. Stir in the grated orange peel. Preheat the oven to 420°F.

Put a spoonful of filling and a banana onto each crêpe and roll up. Place in a lightly oiled baking dish, and cook in the oven for about 20 minutes, or until the bananas are soft. Transfer the filled crêpes to a warm serving dish.

To make the sauce, melt the butter in a small saucepan over a very low heat and add the sugar. When the sugar has dissolved, add the orange juice. When the mixture is thoroughly hot, pour it over the crêpes.

Serves 4.

BREAST OF MOULLARD WITH HYSSOP

1 teaspoon honey
2 cloves garlic, finely chopped
2 teaspoons hyssop
salt and freshly ground black pepper
4 tablespoons brandy
1 cup water
2 moullard (or duck) breasts,
about 12 oz each
2 tablespoons butter
fresh melissa leaves,
to garnish

Mix together the honey, garlic, hyssop, salt and pepper, brandy, and water to make a marinade. Add the moullard breasts and marinate for 2 hours.

Having removed the breasts from the marinade, fry them quickly in butter on both sides, transfer them to a baking dish, add half the marinade, and cook for 5 minutes on each side in a hot oven. Slice the breasts, and serve sprinkled with hyssop, with the marinade as a sauce. Garnish with melissa leaves. Serves 4.

EREZ KOMAROVSKY

LAMB CUTLETS WITH WATERMELON

12 lamb cutlets
1/2 cup red wine
1/4 cup extra-virgin olive oil
1 clove garlic, thinly sliced
4 tablespoons finely chopped fresh coriander
sprig lemon grass (Cymbopogon citratus),
minced very fine
sprig fresh sorrel
sprig arugula
1 lb watermelon, without skin or seeds
8 oz goat's cheese

Marinate the lamb cutlets in the wine, olive oil, garlic, coriander and lemon grass for 1 hour. Wash the sorrel and arugula and pat dry. Cut the watermelon into small regular-sized strips.

Put the cutlets in the broiler pan with a little of the marinade, and cook under a hot broiler for a few minutes. Turn the cutlets and put a slice of goat's cheese on each. Cook for another 5 minutes or so until the cutlets are done, but don't overcook them. Serve the cutlets on a bed of sorrel, arugula and watermelon strips, with some of the grilling juices poured over them.

Serves 6.

FIGS AND PRICKLY PEARS WITH ROSE & VANILLA YOGURT

1/2 cup sugar
1/2 cup water
1/2 vanilla bean
handful of rose petals
1 cup plain fresh yogurt
butter
1 lb ripe figs
1 lb prickly pears

Dissolve the sugar in the water, then add the vanilla bean and most of the rose petals. Bring to a boil and simmer for 5 minutes. Pour the liquid through a nylon sieve and let it cool.

Now stir the yogurt into it and put the mixture in the refrigerator for at least 1 hour. Preheat the oven to 400°F.

Wash and dry the figs. Carefully peel the prickly pears, under running water, preferably with gloves on, and place them on a buttered baking sheet. Bake for 10 minutes. Serve hot with the cold sauce, decorated with the rest of the rose petals.

Serves 6 to 8.

◆ *Erez Komarovsky's catering service offers Japanese delicacies with an Israeli flavor.*

**EREZ
KOMAROVSKY**

RED SNAPPER WITH MYRTLE

*1 extremely fresh red snapper,
weighing 2lbs
6 cups water
1 tablespoon sea salt
fresh myrtle leaves
1/2 cup extra-virgin olive oil
1 chili pepper, very finely chopped
4 cloves garlic, crushed
4 baby eggplants
2 or 3 lemons*

Fillet the fish and make several diagonal incisions in the skin. Bring the water and salt to a boil. Plunge the fillets into the boiling water for 30 seconds, then transfer them immediately to a bowl of ice-cold water. When cold, drain and pat dry with paper towels.

Rub the myrtle leaves between your hands to release their fragrance and put them in a shallow dish with the olive oil, chili (wear gloves while you are chopping it!) and garlic. Lay the fillets in the dish. Steam the eggplants until soft, remove the skins and put them in the dish as well.

Allow the fillets to marinate for at least 3 hours, turning once so that they absorb the other flavors.

When ready to serve, remove the fillets from the marinade, drain them and garnish with one of the eggplants cut into quarters.

Serves 4 as a main course or 8 as an appetizer.

◆ *A*

version

of red

snapper

with

myrtle.

RED MULLET IN GRAPE LEAVES

8 large fresh grape leaves
4 tablespoons olive oil
juice of 1 lemon
1 tablespoon chopped fresh parsley
20 coriander seeds
1 tablespoon fresh chopped basil
salt and freshly ground black pepper
8 red mullet, about 8 oz each,
cleaned and patted dry

Blanch the grape leaves in hot water for 20 seconds, then drain on paper towels (if you are using grape leaves preserved in brine, see instructions given for stuffed grape leaves, p. 28). Mix together the olive oil, lemon juice, parsley, coriander seeds, basil, salt and pepper. Prick the fish all over with a needle, spread the oil and herb mixture over them and leave them to marinate for 1 hour.

Fold a grape leaf around each fish, leaving the head sticking out. Brush the leaves with olive oil. Preheat the broiler or grill and cook for 2 minutes on each side. Serve with other *mezze*. Serves 8.

BOTTLED KUMQUATS

1 lb fresh kumquats
4 1/4 cups sugar
1 1/2 cups water
1 tablespoon rosewater, if liked

Wash the kumquats thoroughly, then slice them lengthwise. In a large saucepan, dissolve the sugar in the water, add the kumquats, bring to a boil, and simmer gently for 1 hour. Remove from the heat, stir in the rosewater, and allow to cool. Store in a jar with a tightly fitting lid.

MEDITERRANEAN TART

PASTRY
2 cups all-purpose flour
1 cup olive oil
1/3 cup water
1 egg
salt and freshly ground black pepper

FILLING
1 small eggplant
4 small zucchini, thinly sliced
2 cloves garlic, finely chopped
2 onions, thinly sliced
1/4 cup olive oil
salt and freshly ground black pepper
1 teaspoon fresh thyme
6 small tomatoes, thinly sliced
1 cup black olives, pitted and halved

Put all the pastry ingredients in a food processor and mix for 2 minutes with a plastic blade. Roll the dough into a ball, wrap it in plastic wrap, and chill in the refrigerator for 1 hour.

Cut the eggplant in half lengthwise and slice each half very thinly. Soak the slices of eggplant and zucchini in salty water for 30 minutes, then drain.

Using a moderate heat, fry the garlic, onions and eggplant in the olive oil for about 15 minutes, or until the eggplant softens. Stir in the salt, pepper and most of the thyme, and set aside. Preheat the oven to 425°F.

Roll out the pastry and line a tart pan (the type with a removable base). Cut off any excess pastry around the edges, and prick the base with a fork. Spread the eggplant and onion mixture over the pastry, and arrange the tomatoes and zucchini decoratively on top. Top with the olives, add a sprinkling of thyme, and brush with olive oil. Bake for 45 minutes. Serve hot or cold.

Serves 5 or 6.

ISRAEL AHARONI

◆ *Israel Aharoni,*

owner and chef

of Israel's

leading Chinese

restaurant

Yin-Yang.

Aharoni's other

passion is

French food.

◆ *Mediterranean*

tart.

ZACHI BUKSHESTER

◆ *Zachi*

Bukshester

is the owner

and chef of

The Pink

Ladle. He

serves Israeli

nouvelle

cuisine with

great

attention to

presentation.

HORN OF PLENTY

4 leaves filo *pastry*
1 tablespoon all-purpose flour
vegetable oil

MARINADE
1 tablespoon olive oil
1/2 tablespoon brown sugar
1 tablespoon white wine vinegar
1 clove garlic

BEAN SAUCE
1 lb fresh fava beans
1/4 cup heavy cream
1 cup chicken stock
dill, nutmeg, salt and pepper to taste

FILLING
8 oz fillet steak, cubed
8 oz fillet of sea bass
1 tablespoon pistachio nuts, shelled
1 small onion, chopped
1/3 cup diced carrots
1/2 cup chopped leeks
1 1/3 cups chopped asparagus
1/3 cup diced turnips
1/2 cup dry red wine

Roll each leaf of *filo* into a cone shape, sticking the pastry to itself with a dab of flour and water. Allow the cones to dry.

Mix the marinade ingredients together, add the beef, fish, pistachios and onion, and allow to marinate for 1 hour.

Boil or steam the beans until just tender, then drain. Purée them with the cream, chicken stock and spices in the food processor, and keep warm.

Simmer or steam the carrots, leeks, asparagus and turnips until they are *al dente.*

Drain the beef, fish, pistachios and onion, sauté them in butter in a hot skillet, and add the cooked vegetables and red wine.

Deep fry the *filo* cones until they are crisp and golden, then fill them with the meat and vegetable mixture. Make sure the bean purée is hot, then spoon it onto individual plates and place a filled *filo* cone on top.

Serves 4.

PRICKLY PEARS FLAMBÉES

1/2 tablespoon butter
1 teaspoon brown sugar
powdered cardamom
2 prickly pears per person, peeled and sliced
2 tablespooons Sabra or Grand Marnier liqueur
whipped cream, to serve

Melt half the butter, add the sugar and cardamom powder, and sauté the prickly pear slices in this mixture for 1/2 minute. Add the liqueur and set light to it. When the flames die down, add the remaining butter and allow it to melt. Serve with whipped cream.

FRIED GOAT'S CHEESE WITH MINT SALAD
See p. 56

◆ *Horn of*

plenty

ITAMAR DAVIDOV

JERUSALEM ARTICHOKE CREAM SOUP

1 lb Jerusalem artichokes, peeled
4 1/2 cups chicken stock
juice of 1 lemon
4 oz chicken breast, skinned and cubed
1/4 cup butter
3 tablespoons all-purpose flour
salt and freshly ground white pepper
4 strands saffron
1 cup heavy cream
freshly ground black pepper

Cook the artichokes in the chicken stock and lemon juice until they begin to soften. Strain off the stock and reserve it, then purée the artichokes, adding just enough stock to make blending easy.

Stir-fry the chicken cubes in half the butter - 2 minutes is enough, or until the pink turns white. Drain on paper towels.

Melt the remaining butter, add the flour and cook for 3 or 4 minutes, stirring constantly. Stir in the reserved chicken stock, artichoke purée, salt, white pepper and saffron. Bring slowly to a boil, stirring all the time, and allow to simmer for 5 minutes.

Add the chicken cubes and adjust the seasoning if necessary. At the last minute, stir in the cream. Serve sprinkled with black pepper. Serves 5 or 6.

DATES & POPPY SEEDS IN HOT TOFFEE

1/2 cup heavy cream
1/2 cup sugar
2 tablespoons water
20 fresh dates, pitted and whole
3 teaspoons fried poppy seeds
1 1/2 cups heavy cream, whipped

Heat the 1/2 cup cream in a bain-marie. In a small saucepan, dissolve the sugar in the water, turn up the heat and boil until the mixture turns golden. Remove from the heat and stir in the hot cream. Bring the mixture to the boil and cook for 5 minutes, stirring all the time. The mixture should now be toffee, thick and smooth. Stir in the dates and poppy seeds and cook for another minute or two. Serve warm, topped with the whipped cream.

Serves 4.

◆ *Itamar Davidov is chef and owner of Pitango. He is reknowned for his astonishing food combinations.*

◆ *Dates and poppy seeds in hot toffee.*

CELIA REGEV &
REVIVA APPEL

◆ *Celia and*

Reviva are

restaurateurs

who have

introduced

new tastes in

pastries and

desserts.

JAFFAS BAVAROISE

6 oranges
fresh mint or citrus leaves, to garnish

BAVARIAN CREAM FILLING
1/2 cup sugar
8 egg yolks
1 cup orange juice
2 level teaspoons gelatin
1 cup heavy cream, whipped

SAUCE
1/2 cup sugar
1 cup orange juice
4 tablespoons lemon juice

Peel the oranges and remove the segments. Grease 6 individual molds with butter and line the bottom of each with a circle of wax paper cut to size. Sprinkle the sides of the molds with sugar and tap out the excess. Line the sides of the molds with orange segments, trimming them to fit snugly.

To make the Bavarian cream filling, beat the egg yolks and sugar together until pale and fluffy, then bring the orange juice to a boil and add it to the egg yolks. Dissolve the gelatin according to the instructions on the package. Cook the egg yolks and orange juice over a low heat until the mixture is thick enough to coat the back of a wooden spoon, then add the dissolved gelatin. Stir well and pass through a strainer. Allow the mixture to cool, then put it in the refrigerator until it is on the point of setting. Remove from the refrigerator and fold in the whipped cream. Pour the cream into the molds and leave to set for 3 or 4 hours.

To make the sauce, dissolve the sugar in the orange and lemon juices, bring to a boil, and simmer for a few minutes to thicken. When cool, spoon onto individual plates and turn out the molds. Decorate with a mint or citrus leaf. Serves 6.

SORBET OGEN

1 1/2 cups sugar
1 1/4 cups water
1 1/4 cups puréed Ogen melon, chilled
juice of 1 lemon

Dissolve the sugar in the water and bring to a boil. As soon as the mixture begins to bubble, remove from the heat, cool, then refrigerate.

Mix the puréed melon with the lemon juice and the chilled syrup, pour into a shallow container and put in the icebox until barely firm. Remove from the freezer and blend to a smooth consistency, then re-freeze. Serve in chilled glasses with sugar-frosted rims. Serves 4.

◆ *Jaffa*

bavaroise.

DALIA PENN-LERNER

SALAD OF FOIE GRAS & POMEGRANATE

8 oz fresh foie gras (or chicken livers)
various salad leaves (romaine, radicchio,
chicory, spinach)
1 tablespoon white wine vinegar
2 or 3 tablespoons pomegranate seeds
salt and freshly ground black pepper

DRESSING
1 tablespoon white wine vinegar
1 tablespoon lemon juice
4 tablespoons olive oil
salt and pepper

Cut the liver into 1/2-inch cubes. Cover and refrigerate until firm. Put the salad leaves in a bowl, beat together the dressing ingredients, pour over the salad and toss well.

Preheat a nonstick skillet (only add oil if you are using chicken livers, which have very little fat compared to goose liver). Quickly stir-fry the liver - the cubes should remain pink inside - and transfer to a warm plate.

Pour off any fat that has accumulated in the skillet, and add the vinegar. Remove from the heat, return the liver cubes to the skillet and season with salt and pepper. Spoon the warm liver and the pomegranate seeds over the salad and serve immediately. Serves 4.

CHEESE PACKAGES

full-fat feta or goat's cheese
fresh savory or thyme, finely chopped
filo pastry
melted butter
fruit (watermelon, ripe figs, grapes)

Mash the cheese with a fork and season with savory or thyme. Cut the sheets of *filo* into 4-inch squares. Place a teaspoon of the cheese mixture in the center of each and draw the sides up to form a little pouch. Press the edges together with water to seal them. Preheat the oven to 375°F.

Brush the pouches with melted butter and bake for 10-15 minutes until crisp and golden. Serve with cubes of watermelon, figs, grapes, etc.

If making pouches sounds too fiddly, you could make triangular or square packages instead. Deep-frying would also be an alternative to baking.

◆ *Dalia Penn-Lerner, a former actress, is a chefs food writer and editor who has traveled widely.*

◆ *Cheese packages.*